LOVE, LOOSHA

LOVE, LOOSHA

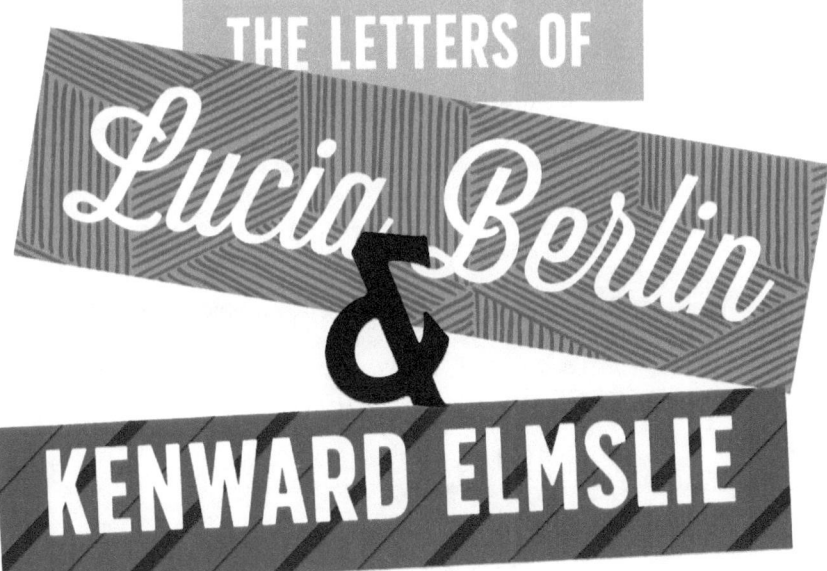

THE LETTERS OF

Lucia Berlin & KENWARD ELMSLIE

EDITED BY CHIP LIVINGSTON

HIGH ROAD BOOKS | ALBUQUERQUE

HIGH
ROAD

High Road Books is an imprint of the University of New Mexico Press

First paperback printing 2024 | ISBN 978-0-8263-6731-0

Library of Congress Cataloging-in-Publication Data
Names: Berlin, Lucia, author. | Livingston, Chip, editor. | Elmslie, Kenward, author.
Title: Love, Loosha : the letters of Lucia Berlin and Kenward Elmslie / edited by Chip Livingston.
Description: Albuquerque : University of New Mexico Press, [2022] |
Includes bibliographical references and index.
Identifiers: LCCN 2022013205 (print) | LCCN 2022013206 (e-book) | ISBN 9780826364166 (cloth) |
ISBN 9780826364173 (e-book)
Subjects: LCSH: Berlin, Lucia—Correspondence. | Elmslie, Kenward—Correspondence. |
Authors, American—Correspondence. | BISAC: LITERARY COLLECTIONS / Letters |
LITERARY COLLECTIONS / American / General
Classification: LCC PS3552.E72485 Z48 2022 (print) | LCC PS3552.E72485 (e-book) |
DDC 816/.54 [B]—dc23/eng/20220420
LC record available at https://lccn.loc.gov/2022013205
LC e-book record available at https://lccn.loc.gov/2022013206

Cover illustration by Kenward Elmslie
Designed by Felicia Cedillos
Composed in Adobe Garamond Pro 10.25/14.25

for Lucia and Kenward

CONTENTS

Acknowledgments

My thanks must begin with Lucia and Kenward. I wouldn't be the teacher, writer, or person I am without the enormous influence of these two friends and mentors.

Thank you to Jeff Berlin and the Berlin family. Thank you to Ron and Pat Padgett.

Thanks to Katherine Fausset at Curtis Brown Ltd. and to Stephen Hull at the University of New Mexico Press.

Thanks to the University of California–San Diego and Harvard University libraries, which house the Kenward Elmslie and Lucia Berlin archives and the original copies of these letters.

Thanks to Lizzie Davis at Coffee House Press for permission to reprint Kenward's lyric "Who'll Prop Me Up in the Rain?"

Thanks to Jenny Dorn, Stephen Emerson, Ivan Suvanjieff, Maxine Chernoff, Paul Hoover, Erik Haagensen, Howard Pollack, Barbara Hogenson, Lori Styler, Bill and Margaret Weir, Sophie Constantinou, Brad Gooch, Allison Hedge Coke, David Groff, Jim Elledge, Kathryn Harrison, and Emily Firetog.

Thank you y gracias, Charles Dearmond and Felicia Zapata.

Thanks to CU friends from Lucia's workshops: Cecilia Johnson, Kelly Moore, Dave Cullen, David Yoo, Mitzi Miles-Kabota, Scott Handy, Ashley Simpson Shires, Jenny Shank, Elizabeth Geoghegan, and Erika Krouse.

Gracias a *La Máquina de Pensar*, Andrés Capelán, Silvia Carrero Parris, Gabriel Insiburo y Lenín Gómez.

Introduction

In 1994, internationally acclaimed fiction writer Lucia Berlin met New York School poet/librettist Kenward Elmslie at Naropa University's Summer Writing Program, where they were both visiting writers. "We just clicked," Lucia said in a 2002 interview. "It was as if we'd known each other forever and just talked and talked under a tree, like we'd been sitting on a stoop for ages." Lucia called it an "instant friendship." "We cut through right away into each other's deep feelings. It was like falling in love, or going back to your childhood best friend in first grade, that kind of really pure friendship."[1]

Lucia Berlin (1936–2004) was born in Alaska but moved frequently throughout her childhood and spent most of her youth in Santiago, Chile. As an adult, she lived in New Mexico, New York City, Mexico, California, and Colorado. Her short stories began to appear in literary magazines in the 1960s and in collections, from *Angel's Laundromat* (Turtle Island, 1981) to *Where I Live Now* (Black Sparrow Press, 1999). During her lifetime, Lucia had a relatively small but devoted following. In 2015, a posthumous collection of her stories, *A Manual for Cleaning Women* (Farrar, Straus and Giroux), debuted on the *New York Times* bestseller list its first week and was named a best book of the year by many international critics. In 2018, *Evening in Paradise*, a second collection of her stories, and *Welcome Home*, a memoir with letters, were also published by Farrar, Straus and Giroux to wide acclaim in the United States and abroad.

Kenward Elmslie (1929–2022) was born in New York City but spent

---

1   Lucia Berlin with Margaret Weir, "Pen Pals," video interview for Kenward's website, April 2002 (Citizen Film production 2016 on Vimeo).

his youth in Colorado Springs, Colorado, and at the St. Mark's Boarding School in Southborough, Massachusetts. After graduating from Harvard in 1950, this grandson of Joseph Pulitzer began his professional career writing librettos and lyrics for operas and Broadway musicals starting in the 1960s (*Miss Julie, Lizzie Borden, The Sweet Bye and Bye*), the same decade his first three poetry collections were published (*Pavilions, The Champ, Album*). These were followed by twenty-five additional books of poems, some of which were collaborations with visual artists, and a novel, *The Orchid Stories* (Doubleday, 1973). Kenward would write the lyrics for at least seven more musicals and operas, including *The Grass Harp* and *The Seagull*, which are still widely produced. He wrote the lyrics for *Love-Wise*, a song recorded by Nat King Cole and others. In 1973, Kenward founded *Z Magazine* and Z Press, which published many of the poets and writers now associated with the New York School.

Lucia and Kenward's correspondence began in 1994, when she was living in Boulder, Colorado, and he was dividing his time between New York City and Calais, Vermont. It quickly grew to a literary exchange of about two letters per week for a decade. Despite the geographical distance between them, and having only been in person together a total of five or six times, Lucia and Kenward depended on their intimate friendship and deeply valued their faithful correspondence.

"We're able to write letters where we feel that we are ourselves with each other," Lucia said. "When he writes about Calais, he writes all the details of the town, the mailman and the grocer. I wrote a long letter about how upset I was when my mailman dyed his mustache. Things like that . . . we loved to tell each other."

They also loved to gossip, to write "bad things about good friends," as Lucia described it, admitting, "We can also be really catty." But mostly Kenward and Lucia wrote with great affection for those writers and artists closest in their memories and their current daily rounds: Joe Brainard, Ed and Jenny Dorn, Ron and Pat Padgett, Bobbie Louise Hawkins, Ivan Suvanjieff, John Latouche, and others.

Lucia and Kenward led theatrical lives of glamour, drama, travel, love, loss, and literature. And because they began writing as new friends, they contextualized their pasts with vivid details. Lucia told Kenward of

Lucia Berlin, 1995, photo by Valari Jack.

her childhood in Chile, her homes and moves around the world, how her beauty opened doors for her and helped her get out of difficult situations. Kenward wrote of his privileged childhood as the grandson of Joseph Pulitzer, his own family's angsts and maneuverings.

The two responded to national events such as the September 11th attacks, weapons of mass destruction, and President Clinton's impeachment trial; Lucia recounted watching the Kennedy inauguration during an editor's meeting at the Harvard Club. They reviewed the new books they were reading, as well as performances and shows by friends, a mix of international artists, opera singers, movie and stage actors, composers, and producers, friends and writers such as Gore Vidal, John Ashbery, George Plimpton, Anne Waldman, James Schuyler, Paul Auster, Frank O'Hara, Grace Paley, Tony Kushner, Ishmael Reed, Robert Creeley, Denise Levertov, Elaine Stritch, Leonard Bernstein, Felicia Montealegre, Sandy Duncan, Stella Adler, Stephen Sondheim, Brenda Lewis, Ned Rorem, John Cameron Mitchell, and Truman Capote. Their same thoughtful attention was given to the favorite authors they return to each summer: Chekhov, Proust, Barbara Pym, Trollope, Henry Green.

Kenward Elmslie, photo by John Sarsgaard.

As attentive as they were to their beloveds and to each other, they responded to reactions and reviews of their own publications and performances. Kenward described the writing, rewriting, rehearsing, and producing involved in staging musicals and operas, his "post standing O" fatigue and depression, as well as his many collaborations with other poets and artists. He recounted conversations overheard as unhappy theatre-goers left one of his productions: "Who could've written a thing like that?" "Well, somebody must of." Lucia lamented losing new friends after they'd disapproved of her stories. She wrote of a poorly attended reading where she decided to read from her worst stories, and audience members shouted out their least favorites: "No, Lucia . . . the Texan Christmas was worse" . . . "Read 'Rainy Day,' I can't stand that one." Kenward and Lucia told each other of their current writing projects, and the dread of not writing.

They wrote of their former loves and lovers, Kenward remembering his thirty years with artist-writer Joe Brainard, and Joe's death from AIDS in 1994. Kenward also told Lucia of his life with author-lyricist John Latouche during Hollywood's Red Scare, of their being escorted out of movie production offices because of Latouche's name being on McCarthy's blacklist. Lucia wrote of leaving her jazz musician husband

Race Newton in New York and "eloping" to Mexico with musician Buddy Berlin, as well as how her actions and publications ended some friendships. She spoke of her mentor, the poet Ed Dorn, his illness and death, and they both shared griefs as other friends succumbed to age and mortality. Lucia and Kenward wrote of their own physical aging, their health and other problems, their loneliness, Lucia recounting her ailments with delicate humor, including a surprising trip to a wheelchair repair shop.

They shared their joy and dependence on each other's letters. "I don't actually say it when I see your handwriting but when there is a letter from you, I feel Kenward loves me and am cheered up before I even open it," Lucia wrote in November 2000. They're also aware of the literary value in the exchange: Kenward wrote, "Your last big letter meant the world to me, had the same voice as your stories [. . .] there you are, much to my surprise, side-by-side with [Chekhov]. Anton, meet Lucia. Lucia, meet Anton." Lucia wrote, "Your letters remind me of Flaubert's . . . they are where your prose, which is poetry, shines and takes off. They would be enjoyable if only because of the exquisite New York and Calais daily life chronicles, but you have written so much about opera and musicals, other lyricists and poets and painters."

I met Lucia Berlin in 1996 at the University of Colorado, where I was her student in the master's program in fiction. The first time I visited her home, she introduced me to Kenward's writings, first via his postcards and recent letters attached to her refrigerator, dramatically reading aloud from those Kenward sent under various pseudonyms he imagined. Then Lucia sent me home with Kenward's recent books *Bare Bones* and *Routine Disruptions*. Their friendship and correspondence inspired her, and she often read excerpts from his letters to her writing classes.

In 2002, four years after I graduated from CU and during a period when Lucia and I had deepened our friendship, she proposed that I become Kenward's live-in assistant, and in January 2003, I moved to New York City and into Kenward's West Village townhouse, where I lived and worked as his helper for nine years. During the remaining two years of Lucia's life, I often delivered her letters from the mail slot to Kenward at his desk or dining room table, and I frequently xeroxed copies for him and mailed Kenward's letters to Lucia from the post offices in New York and Vermont. I counseled Lucia by e-mail or phone if a week went by and she hadn't received a letter from him. Was Kenward okay? Was he mad at her? They both relied on receiving written news from the other.

Lucia often spoke to me and also wrote to Kenward about the descriptions of his theatrical works: "Kenward, these performance letters, or pre-and-post performance letters, are wonderful and should be published as a Something? of their own. They are beautifully written, very visual and filled with the excitement of the Performance . . . so they are in a genre not literary. You're Describing what's going to be LIVE and on stage but more than that is the undercurrent of Stage THRILL. Lovely."

As would be expected with the hundreds and hundreds of letters they exchanged, the volume of their written dialogue is enormous, and many of the earliest letters were lost. As Lucia described in 2004, "I started to tackle the Elmslie Letters. HUGE TASK. There are big envelopes, boxes, files, bags, folders bulging with letters. Many many so far have no legible post office date nor date written by you inside. How could I have such a massive mess? I see how it happened. For weeks and months, I would file the letters as they came in, until the folder in my filing cabinet was simply too full. They would be moved to giant envelopes, then into a box. Finally that box would be filled with envelopes, bags would be filled with more envelopes. Some giant envelopes would end up in early boxes, others in later boxes. More confusion would occur when letters were taken out then replaced in envelopes and boxes without any sort of label. Only way to make sense of things would be to read these letters, but there are so many it might take months and months! It would take days just to count the letters so as to even make an estimate! Right now I have a new folder in my filing cabinet, labeled ELMSLIE and containing only one letter. Anticipating the next one, your loving pen pal, LOOSHA."

In my own compilation of these letters as located and provided by Ron and Pat Padgett and Jeff Berlin, as well as from Kenward's and Lucia's literary archives, I had more than a thousand pages to sequence and then select from for this volume. I tried to choose letters most representative of Kenward's and Lucia's long friendship and their lives at the time. There are some gaps in this selection, due mainly to space restriction, though two periods of time passed in 2003 and 2004 in which Kenward was out of touch with Lucia for a few months; for those periods, I have provided bridging information. I lived in Kenward's home during those times, when I would assure Lucia that Kenward wasn't upset with her, explaining, "He's still in Australia" or "He's in rehearsals at the theatre fifteen hours a day."

I hope readers forgive any errors or lapses in judgment, which are solely mine. I've done my best to honor Lucia's longtime desire that Kenward's letters, if not her and Kenward's combined correspondence ("That would be 2000 pages," she wrote) should be published. I've done my best to respect their relationship, as well as their friendships with the many public and private figures they came in notable contact with. I tried to retain their inventive spellings and punctuations, Lucia's love for and use of the fragment and ellipsis . . .

In other areas I've used bracketed ellipses [. . .] to indicate omissions and [bracketed alterations] for clarity. Some omissions were necessary, given the length of some of the letters—one letter from Kenward was twenty-four pages; Lucia said it should be published as a chapbook itself. More seldom was an omission to ensure the privacy of nonpublic individuals. In a few other cases, the ellipsed content was simply a contextual reply to something written in a previous but unselected letter.

Love, Loosha reveals two great American writers writing to each other, but also writing *for* the other, hoping to cheer and delight their very important pen pal. These letters now become a correspondence for the public, offering dual epistolary memoirs and the authors' intimate perspectives on international literature, opera, and theatre, a sustained conversation of literary history and literary gossip, as well as their own lives, in their own funny and carefully chosen words.

PART I | 1994-2000

Letters from Maxwell Avenue, Boulder, CO
Letters from Calais, VT, and New York, NY

[In their earliest letters, Lucia and Kenward are still getting to know each other, filling in the details of their lives, introducing the other to friends, familiar surroundings, and families. Lucia remembers her ex-husband, musician Buddy Berlin, and writes of visiting her sons in California. Kenward writes of his mother, Constance Pulitzer, and of his sisters. Kenward gives updates of ongoing productions and rewrites of his newest musical, Postcards on Parade, *with composer Steven Taylor. Lucia sends new short stories, as she's finishing her collection,* Where I Live Now, *for Black Sparrow Press in 1999. Kenward shares plans and preparations for a collection of "selected poems and lyrics," which became* Routine Disruptions, *published by Coffee House Press in 1998. They write of the books they're reading and rereading, of Lucia's classes at the University of Colorado, where I was her student in the graduate fiction program. They recount recent visits with good friends, writer/artists Ed and Jenny Dorn, Ron and Pat Padgett, Ivan Suvanjieff, Bobbie Louise Hawkins, and a young helper/companion of Kenward's they refer to as CW.]*

BOULDER, CO

DECEMBER 1994

Dear Kenward,

When I realized that it was actually you singing I was so moved that I truly didn't know what to say—I hope I said Thank you.

When I met you I told you how many many people had raved to me about your work. I don't know what I had expected—the adjectives had all been brilliant, witty, poetic, magic, hilarious, beautiful, unlike anything else. *Postcards*[1] was all that. I had been unprepared for the exquisite tenderness in your work.

This is so rare, & so difficult to show deep feelings of love, with lightness. I always avoid deep feelings, usually with a joke, so I envy your skill & courage.

---

1   Kenward Elmslie and Steven Taylor, *Postcards on Parade* (Bamberger Books, 1993). A musical play with book and lyrics by Kenward. Lucia is responding to a recording made at Naropa University in Boulder, CO, July 30, 1994.

December, 1994

Dear Kenward,

When I realized that it was actually you singing I was so moved that I truly didn't know what to say. I hope I said Thank you.

When I met you I told you how many many people had raved to me about your work, I don't know what I had expected. The adjectives had all been brilliant, witty, poetic, magic, hilarious & beautiful, un-like anything else, & Postcards was all that. I had been unprepared for the exquisite tenderness in your work.

This is so rare, & so difficult to show deep feelings of love, with lightness. I always avoid deep feelings, usually with a joke. So I envy your skill, & courage.

— Damn. I really meant to

Peace On Earth

say I hope this holiday isn't difficult. & that you are with friends. I hope too that next year brings you joy. Dear man— I don't "know" "you" but I care for you very very much.

love, Lucia

Handwritten Christmas card from Lucia, December 1994.

Damn. I really meant to say I hope this holiday isn't difficult & that you are with friends. I hope too that next year brings you joy.

Dear man—I don't "know" "you," but I care for you very very much.

> Love,
> Lucia

CALAIS, VT
LATE SEPTEMBER 1995

Dear Lucia—

Happy Autumn Solstice & End of Summer!

Thanks so much for your hello. My quiet isolation in Vermont is so rarely impinged on, by anything more violent than the reverberating whine of a saw cutting wood—I was horrified by Ivan [Suvanjieff]'s SLORC mugging.[2] I've talked to him—he lost control, sobbed, and

---

2   Ivan Suvanjieff, editor, artist, activist, co-founder of PeaceJam with Dawn

pulled himself together. Two years ago, though it seems further back, I made a collage book for Joe [Brainard],[3] for his first trip to hospital, in Burlington, Vermont. So I made a collage book for Ivan.

When someone you care about gets hurt, make something pretty to look at. Except Ivan, I guess, is in pain, lung that leaks, so it's a strain to deal with a book of visuals, when he has a film to edit the footage of . . . I sent him some Z Press[4] moolah, for *New Censorship*[5] technically, but of course to ease him past this rough patch. The poets on the Z [Press] board said OK, bless them. It's a non-profit "org" that no longer publishes, so it rides to the rescue, occasionally, courtesy its savvy & mysterious poet board. If you go see him, please, pretty please ask to see the book I made for him, OK? A Hurry Job, so it's not refined, but it does show off my new visual stuff.

That's been my summer discovery, that I can branch beyond post-card-size collages into works to hang on the wall. I made them for my St. Johnsbury VT Athenaeum performance, to be paraded down the aisle, like religious icons. Bill Corbett's[6] daughter Marni did the parading. I vowed to get a standing O, rehearsed like a fiend, added pantomime, did the dialogue scenes more fully. My previous outing last spring (Michigan U, Ypsilanti) was one of those recurring academe disasters that scare the shit out of me. The money's great, the kids sit on their hands, robotic and brain-dead. Fortunately, I'm not on any college

---

Engle. Ivan was a close friend of Lucia's. Kenward is referring to an attack Ivan suffered in Burma in 1995. SLORC: State Law And Order Restoration Commission.

3   Joe Brainard, American artist and poet, 1942–1994. Joe was Kenward's partner for more than thirty years. Joe's artworks were displayed throughout Kenward's New York and Vermont homes, with favorite pieces packed and moved back and forth as Kenward relocated, winter and summer. Kenward's book *Bare Bones* and his musical play *Postcards on Parade* both dealt with Joe's death from AIDS-related pneumonia in 1994.

4   Initially a small press and literary magazine Kenward founded, Z Press evolved into a nonprofit foundation to allocate funding for artists.

5   *The New Censorship*, a literary magazine published by Ivan Suvanjieff with coeditors Charles Bukowski, Anselm Hollo, Anne Waldman, and Andrei Codrescu.

6   Bill Corbett, poet, editor, and teacher, 1942–2018. Friend of Kenward's.

academic gig list, and—sob—have no future gigs at all! Must bestir myself, phone strangers, but I'm hopeless at self-promo.

Vermonters' ears are great. Regular "people." Loved *POSTCARDS ON PARADE*, didn't obfuscate it with "literary" smog—it's a "show"— an entertainment. Period. They wrote wonderful things on cards—like a sneak preview film—which the sponsors sent me a copy of. Positive Feedback, ah!

I seem to be in a reconnecting mode. Last weekend, I restored contact with Big Sis Viv [Elmslie], after a one-year hiatus. She's single, shares my taste for irony, 71 years of age, in fine physical shape—still a nice Vassar girl[7] in many ways. All went well, helped by showing emotion more honestly & directly than ever before. So, this coming weekend, Cynthia [Elmslie Weir], my Big Big Sis, is arriving from Cambridge. Viv went to see Joe's boulder,[8] in a field uphill where his ashes were strewn, so now Cynthia wants to do the same. She has a brace, a bad hip, a yappy dog, and quite jagged personality lunges & mood shifts exhausting to respond to. She's 81 going on 82. I guess she's entitled, right?

Fingers crossed. I dreaded Let Down, post-Standing O, but, so far, it hasn't attacked me.

Yesterday, Karole Armitage[9] phoned from Firenze. She's, I hope I hope, my new Collaborator. Choreographer. Her own company.

She's asked me to write the words for a full-length dance piece about [Michael] Milken, Junk Bond Roi. I'll get to confab, face to face, Oct. 18—in NYC. Her synopsis keeps skittering off the page into Danse

---

7   Vassar College. "Vassar girl" is defined by UrbanDictionary.com as slang for "any very well-educated woman who always gets their [*sic*] way."

8   A granite boulder in a field on Kenward's Calais, VT, property, where Joe Brainard's ashes were scattered. The walk up the forest path to Joe's stone was a ritual upon arriving in Vermont and a routine walk throughout the summer. Kenward told me that Joe had chosen the rock himself, from another location on the property, and the boulder was moved after Joe's death to the field uphill among a cluster of pine trees.

9   Karole Armitage, American dancer and choreographer, artistic director of Armitage Gone! Dance company, b. 1954.

Symbolique Meaningfulness, but I watched her work on a video, and it's most inspiring—never seen such fast-paced aggressive leg work. The human bod turns into an astonishing implement. I hope to get to write a postpostpostmodern musical, words, in which her dance troupe stars, plus three actor-singers to deliver my stuff. I don't know the person who'll set my lyrics, pray he's as good & enjoyable to collaborate with as His TruBlue Worthy Steven Taylor.[10]

I asked Bill Bamberger[11] to edit a collected of my poetry, as is appropriate to someone of my years, if not poesy world clout, and we've been battling lists back and forth, badminton style. He's thought up a title—*ROUTINE DISRUPTIONS*, which I like a lot. He's the one person in the world who thinks I'm a terrific writer & he goes to the trouble & expense $ resultant dollars down the drain & publishes me (every poet should have ONE such support system. One small-press publisher once said at Naropa[12] gabfest, a few years ago, or else they're kaput!). [. . .] He has a few small presses in mind to send my collected to, in the vain hope. . . . And I do mean vain. But—you never know! I've forbidden him to publish it himself. He needs a new car. Number One on his list—is Alicia Von Cornfleur of Mocha Mug . . . Coffee House Press to you, homegirl.

Deer mosey across my mown lawn, looking wistfully at the house—so close to its windows, trusting, high on a bumper crop of still crunch and tart apples, slow to dart off. They want to wear high heels, watch Jane Russell on cable, stomp out Bambi stereotyping, head for a mall, buy Ferragamo boots the better to stomp their way to tropical sunsets and anteaters slithering along the arroyo.

Glad your students are a lift, hope your autumn goes well, & that breath comes and goes without causing you concern.

---

10   Steven Taylor, American musician and poet, b. 1957. Friend and collaborator with Kenward on projects such as *Postcards on Parade.*

11   William C. (Bill, W. C.) Bamberger, publisher, b. 1951. Bamberger Books published a bibliographical profile of Kenward in 1993. Bamberger edited Kenward's new and selected poems, *Routine Disruptions* (Coffee House Press, 1998).

12   Naropa University is a private university in Boulder, Colorado. Home of the "Summer Writing Program" of the Jack Kerouac School of Disembodied Poetics, where Kenward and Lucia first met in 1994.

NAW [*New American Writing*] was sent me by Maxine Chernoff,[13] so I got to read your story last night. You and Paul Auster absolutely dazzle me, how you both know how to write pages that don't seem "written," and yet are such a delight to read. Like James Cain, further back. Or Barbara Pym. Or Elizabeth Bishop as poet.[14] Is a puzzlement, one I relish. Sort of like singing so naturally, the song doesn't seem sung.

Keep in touch. I think of you often, & I'm glad you're there.

Love from your Calais chum,
Kenward

BOULDER, CO
SEPTEMBER 29, 1995

Dear Kenward—

Your letter made me very happy. You sound so good.

I read the paragraph about the deer in both of my classes. One student asked, "Is that a poem or a prose poem?" I said it was just part of a lovely letter, that it was simply an example of how a great artist sees the world.

I'm glad you sent money to Ivan.[15] In addition to feeling rotten, he was quite sick about moving & hospital bills. I haven't seen him to see the collage you made. (I loved the collage print you sent to me.)

I will write a proper letter soon. My ex-husband died.[16] I was in Oakland for a week. It was sad & sweet. My sons are so fine and loving to me & one another. He (Buddy) was an immense presence

---

13   Maxine Chernoff, American poet and writer, b. 1952. Close friend of Kenward's. Coeditor of *New American Writing* with her husband, Paul Hoover, American poet, b. 1946. Lucia's story "Mama" was published in *NAW* #13 (1995). *NAW* published many of Kenward's poems over the years, as well as my poetry in several issues.

14   Paul Auster, American writer and film director, b. 1947. James Cain, American author and journalist, 1892–1977. Barbara Pym, English novelist, 1913–1980. Elizabeth Bishop, American poet and writer, 1911–1979.

15   Z Press Foundation grant to Ivan Suvanjieff.

16   Lucia married jazz musician Buddy Berlin in 1961. They divorced in 1968 but remained good friends.

in our lives. He had called me every day since I moved here. It wasn't until I got back that I felt his loss. Sweet thing about death is that all you're left with is tender memories and new ones that you had forgotten.

Thanks for comparing me to James M. Cain & Elizabeth Bishop. When I was 7 or 8, I saw *Mildred Pierce* five times—changed my name to Sherry. I loved it when Mildred Pierce answers the question, "What will you have to drink?" She says, "I'll take sherry—home."

> *I love you,*
> *Lucia*

BOULDER, CO
DECEMBER 26, 1995

Dear Kenward,

Well, I got one of these mysterious poetry grants[17] again. And again, pretty spooky—not just because my car totally died this time but I didn't even care about that. I had finally graded all the papers & read the dissertations & only one 10-page letter to write supporting colleague for tenure.

Thinking to myself—will I use this time to write? Have I forgotten? Do I still have anything to say? Just sitting around feeling museless . . . Last time I was so ashamed—oh, I have done so little work—I don't deserve it, etc. This time I look upon it as a sign from above, the face in the tortilla.

What was that song, "I found my million-dollar baby at the five & ten cent store?" I remember all the words to "Paper Doll." Do you? It's pretty weird, actually . . . A doll that other fellas cannot steal.

Well anyway, I am very very pleased. My new computer turned out to be part of a Bad Batch so had to go back to the factory . . . but I have a story I'm going to work on in this notebook—if I can read it later—sorry to put you through my handwriting.

The Mazda man who put in transmission last spring advised me to

---

17   Lucia was awarded a grant from Z Press Foundation, a press/nonprofit organization founded by Kenward and others to allocate funding for artists.

get rid of it on the spot. Well, I'll do that now. Not now, tomorrow—& with much gratitude.

Had sweet Christmas at Dorns with Hollos, Sidney Goldfarb, Dorn's daughter. Old dear friends.[18] Had lunch with Bobbie, who is happier than I've seen her in years. [. . .]

My youngest son & family were here for Thanksgiving. Wonderful. Then a two-week visit from my dear niece Monica & boyfriend. Now her husband. They got married here. That visit was nice but too long & they are Mexican & used to dinner at 10 & maids, etc.—so very very exhausting.

My sons were with each other & then families in California. I wasn't even (very) homesick. It made me feel good that they all love each other & are all fine—not just fine—joyous & funny & loving.

I missed Buddy—to talk to him and our kids—gossip about his sister & my niece Monica marrying H. He's German, schlocht, alphabetizes the spice cupboard.

Thank you for helping me & for coming into my life.

All my love.

> *Happy New Year—*
> *Lucia*

BOULDER, CO

FEBRUARY 1, 1996

Dear Kenward,

The new computer that came with my contract was a lemon, spent three months in the factory waiting for parts. I am now trying to learn how to use it. I still write in longhand before I transfer stories to these new-fangled contraptions. I have a machine problem. Once some nurses where I worked were talking about vibrators and one of them asked me if I had a vibrator. God no, I said, I don't even have a vacuum cleaner.

---

18   Ed and Jenny Dorn, daughter Maya Dorn, Anselm and Jane Hollo, Sydney Goldfarb, Bobbie Louise Hawkins, among Lucia's close Colorado friends and University of Colorado colleagues, all writers.

Collaged postcard from Kenward.

My cat jealous, just walked across and wrote you a paragraph.
I deleted it. I am still opposed to these machines, because of the
DELETE. It's too easy to take back what you said. I remember when
if you got a sentence REALLY wrong, you'd have to take out the
whole page, get carbon all over a white cashmere sweater and retype
the entire damn page. I'm sure I was more careful to begin with and
suspect the writing was much richer. "Minimalist prose" is simply the
result of the self-destructive pulsating cursor.

What a negative word, cursor.

Spoke with Ivan this morning, and of course (see I almost said curse)
we talked about you. I wish I were going with him to New York and
the three of us could sit around and laugh, talk. What I love about Ivan
is that we can chatter about baseball, shoes, snow, cars . . . but beneath
it all, like sub-titles, is an understanding of what's actually going on,

and an empathy. He is Really working hard, pulling this whole project[19] off. Trivializes his achievement, as usual. He's having a party for Irish Nobelist at his house tonight. I can't go . . . is hurt that I'm not going. I'm wiped out after office hours and seminar, soon as I write this I'll be in bed. As hard as being sick is, people don't like sick people, don't get it. Ed Dorn[20] thinks I'm addicted to oxygen, for example.

It's snowing again! My old car wasn't getting up hills before the snow. Thanks to you I was able to lease a solid Jetta, with heater, defroster, snow tires. It is so great, especially since I have a short leash of O2,[21] so I don't get scared about not getting home on time. Thank you, again, so much.

I was in two wonderful Manhattan blizzards when cars couldn't run. In the fifties. In one I put my two sons on a sled (on 13th Street, I think, just around the corner from you) and we went in the middle of Fifth Avenue all the way uptown to the Museum.[22] The Rothko show had just opened, but because of the snow only a few people were there. But also because of the snow and clear clean sky, the light that came through the skylights was literally a divine light and the paintings throbbed with color. My (two older) sons remember this as vividly as I do.

The next snow was the day of the [John F.] Kennedy inauguration. ("in-agua"? Do those guys get immersed, like a Texan Baptist? Beats the puff of smoke.) I felt like a Writer. Had lunch with Peter Davison,[23] my editor at the Atlantic Monthly Press. (They gave me $ for an option but

---

19   Organizing PeaceJam, an international youth education program, with Dawn Engle.

20   Ed Dorn, American poet and writer, 1929–1999. Lucia's mentor and close friend.

21   Lucia relied on a portable oxygen tank, especially in high altitudes like Colorado. One of her lungs had been punctured by her spine, a result of double scoliosis.

22   The Museum of Modern Art's Rothko show was held January 18 to March 12, 1961.

23   Peter Davison, American poet, editor, publisher, 1928–2004.

didn't do the novel.) Then we went to the Harvard Club to watch the inauguration with all these Harvard men furious at old Robert Frost.[24] I don't think the word deconstruction was invented yet, but they did it to the whole ceremony in very witty, nasty Harvard way. I was thrilled, by everything, them, the television, the ceremony, my being there, the snow.

Oh oh . . . something's happening, sort of ee cummings effect on my screen. Think I'll quit and hope it prints normally and does the job . . . which was to say hello and send my love.

    Lucia

BOULDER, CO

OCTOBER 20, 1996

Dear Kenward,

Never heard from you. Thought to myself, "Oh oh, I've offended him with that story[25] I sent. Now he can't stand me." Then the other night, Ivan said, "I can't reach Kenward—I think he must hate me."

"God, Ivan, don't be so neurotic," I said.

I know you don't hate us. Either things are going very well or badly?? Did you sell your apartment? Are you in Tasmania? Are you writing? Please know I hope all is well with you.

I'm so-so. Classes going great. I love teaching. Health is lousy, very weak & tired. Can't walk far, etc. So work going slowly. And not very good what I do write. Illness makes one so self-centered. (How nice that my handwriting is bad; I wrote "one" but it looks like "me"! It makes me self-centered!)

But when I do think about people I care about, you are there. Send postcard. Pronto.

    Love,

    Lucia

---

24   Robert Frost, American poet, 1874–1963; Frost was inaugural poet in 1961.

25   Lucia sent him a copy of a new story, "Let Me See You Smile," from *Where I Live Now* (Black Sparrow Press, 1999).

Dear Lucia—

Today is my last day alone, until—I'm just not sure. Mid-Feb? It's dark most of the time, bitter cold out, and tomorrow I head for my Vermont boondocks casa, to spend six days with my niece, Vivien Russe,[26] and her control freak hubby, very sweet control though—Willie. They've turned into The Folks I Never Had—"dress warmly" stuff. Well now, it'll be pioneer conditions up there—I guess the last time I was up there, in winter, was with Joe (years and years pre-AIDS)—and the town snow plough came through & made big banks so the car was impossible to get to, also the toolshed. So all we had was frying pans, kept whacking at the drifts, when Ralph[27] drove up, our looker-after. That he should see this: so shaming. Dilettantism.

I don't have a laptop, and the plane's so tiny, I don't feature hauling my Apple Classic II up there, which means I'll be cut off from all writing. Handwrit, impossible—frying pan backwardness. Which is why I feel so impelled to get back to you, right away, having just heard your phone voice—it's almost 6 AM, Sunday, along with Ivan's, scares me awfully, thrusting me into the Role of Beloved like that, for this Feb visit. He looked so Prince Valiant last time he was East, downright embarrassing. I revert to childhood good manners, distancing, clambering onto the high ground where one is safe from being sought after frontally, muting Belovedness Angst.

Thanks so much for the invite. Dutch lad CW[28] returns December 30th from his Other Life in Amsterdam, and it says here we're tootling

---

26 Kenward's niece Vivien Weir Russe, daughter of Cynthia Elmslie Weir.

27 Ralph Weeks, friend and handyman of Kenward's in Vermont.

28 CW was a significant other, assistant of sorts, to Kenward for several years. Kenward went through a series of helpers that didn't work out very well: CW, Mr. Yu, and Mr. Oz among those discussed in this correspondence. Those helpers' names are included in the letters as Kenward and Lucia referred to them, but their identity isn't revealed because of later accusations. That previous helpers had taken advantage of Kenward was chief among the reasons Lucia later mentioned that I should move to New York and become his assistant.

about as couple, till mid-Feb, which includes The Rockies Ascent. CW loves cats that enter and exit. Me too. But would one corpulent oldster and one skinny Dutch lad fit into your guest room? We bed share. He has good manners, makes good strong coffee, worships poetry books, as books, and sometimes also as poetry. It's a bit sitcom, the relationship, a word his Dutch "tutor" uses, long distance. "How iss ze relationship?" So, be honest. I'd (we'd) love to be your guest, three nights, if couple-dom wouldn't be stressful for you. [. . .] Wherever we stay, B&B, you, I do want to hang out with you.

The reason I'm coming to Boulder is this: my sister Cynthia [Elms-lie Weir] died last October, age 82. Cynthia's daughter, Vivien Russe, and hubby, have taken it into their noggins to commission a work in memoriam to Cynthia, to be written by me. So I thought *NIGHT EMERALD*, the Wilde musical[29] with Steven would do nicely. I need to confer with Steven, who wrote me a rhapsodic Dad letter, which Patty Padgett[30] attributed to babe-driven sleep deprivation. Is zat so? Our theatre works never seem to "get on," not counting fringe areas (parking lots, flea markets, forgotten subway tunnels). But I do love working with him, and, as *POSTCARDS [ON PARADE]* keeps proving, if orchestrated "theatrically," his music holds up beautifully. So—one more time.

I've been writing poems again—they're fun—there's no audience to fret about, so it's possible to write for oneself, guilt-free. I wish I had the nerve to do what you do, write so tellingly about seeming actualities, so the "writing" disappears into the work itself. I just don't know how you do that, artlessly artful. It's so rare. Maybe all that time devoted to Chekhov (two librettos)[31] enabled me to be so open to your actualities, I just can't call them "stories," not that they're not.

---

29 Kenward was writing a musical with Steven Taylor about Oscar Wilde titled *Night Emerald*.

30 Pat Padgett, wife of poet Ron Padgett, both very close friends of Kenward's. The Padgetts had a house downhill from Kenward in Vermont and also made seasonal moves between Calais and their apartment in New York City.

31 Kenward wrote *The Seagull* and *Three Sisters* opera librettos based on Chekhov's plays.

"Well now"—a wonderful poem line starter-offer tapped at me yesterday. Well now, happy holidays. The enclosed photo is my Mama, Constance Pulitzer (TB, hence Colorado)[32] & her chumette, Alice, mother of a poet childhood chum of mine, Gerrit Lansing,[33] who sent me the photo I had xerox-enlarged. Do you think they drank booze? From the same glass? And are the pictures hung so erratically to cover wallpaper stains?

> *Much Love,*
> *Kenward*

Dear Kenward,

Dear Ivan . . . One reason he loves us both so much is that we have Belovedness angst. So does he. He may be telling me he loves me all the time and asking me if I love him. But if I would just call him up and say I love you, I wouldn't hear from him for weeks. He's only been to my house twice since I moved here! It seems very important to him that you and I should Love one another.

I became your friend before I knew your work, one afternoon when we sat at a little metal table outside of Naropa.[34] We spoke a little. And that was what was so nice, how we were quiet together, sitting there.

I'm answering YOU so soon to thank you for the priceless photograph of your mother. She's so beautiful, shameless! shiftless! or surely she was shortly before the picture was taken.

As for staying here . . . that was Ivan's idea too, so you'd feel at home. I'm afraid you might feel too at home. I don't have a guest room. I sleep on the couch and any guest sleeps in my bed. Usually the next day the

---

32   Kenward's mother, Constance Pulitzer Elmslie, was the daughter of American publisher Joseph Pulitzer. As a result of her diagnosis of tuberculosis, the Elmslies moved to Colorado Springs for the high altitude and dry climate.

33   Gerrit Lansing, American poet, editor, critic, 1928–2018.

34   Naropa University "Summer Writing Program," where Kenward and Lucia met in 1994.

guests are begging for the couch because cat goes in and out all night. (I open the door in my sleep.)

I thought it would be fun to have you here, but it would be crowded and un-private with C.W. (I prefer calling him that, like in old novels or diaries, for discretion.) We'll see, after a night or two in B&B, and you can check out my Facilities. Nabokov and Henry Green[35] are my favorite guys. My son took a lot of N. while he was here . . . Gone is my favorite *Laughter in the Dark*, which I used in a class last year. These mountain-climbing carrot juice crystal head students Hated the book, thought it was cruel and immoral. Poor kids . . . how can they rebel? Our generation, and their parents' generation, did all the drinking, sex, drugs and rock and roll, so all they've got to do is excessive recycling and anorexia. (I have several male anorexic students now. New to me.)

I'm having Big problem writing from my life, about the love affair with Terry.[36] The actuality just doesn't disappear into the writing. The simple fact was that he was seventeen and I was thirty-five. I lost my teaching job, got evicted, my ex-husband took my sons away . . . My friends were scandalized, thought of it as child abuse, as will my readers, especially because he committed suicide. I can't "seduce" my readers into sympathy for the woman (me) but I have to just write the darn story before I die. I like your word "actualities."

I do love you. You make me so happy. Once it was your description of deer and now it is the vision of you and Joe with frying pans in the snow. And the problem of why the pictures were hung that way. Perhaps stains. Lumps in the wallpaper paste? Beds used to be under them

---

35   Vladimir Nabokov, Russian-American novelist, 1899–1977. Henry Green, English novelist, 1905–1973. I would become Lucia's student the following month, and she assigned our class to read Green's novels *Living, Loving,* and *Party Going.*
36   Lucia is referring to her story "Let Me See You Smile," which she'd sent to Kenward in October about her relationship with Terry (named Jesse in the short story). The relationship was dramatic and tragic; both were arrested for public intoxication and assaulting police officers, and Lucia was fired from her teaching job, as written about in the story. In real life, her sons weren't taken away but spent the summer with their father, while Lucia attempted to get her life back together, including separating from Terry. After months of struggling with breaking up, Terry committed suicide.

while children lived at home? To catch the sunset color in August? To miss the hot sun in August?

>*Well, now . . . see you soon.*
>
>*Love,*
>
>*Lucia*

NEW YORK, NY

JANUARY 1998

Dear Lucia—

4 AM. CW asleep, upstairs. Cat movement sounds. Clump. Clump.

Monday. Jean Boulte[37] sick, Brazilian artist-chum who has looked after my digs, for ages, lives on top-floor. AIDS for eight (?) years. He caught cold from a lunch visitor, which is a disaster for his depleted system. He went out yesterday (CW heard him on the stairs) which means his fever-icy shudder combo is lessening in intensity, I hope I hope.

Xmas & New Years in Vt was fine. My niece Vivy and her catalogue-prone hubby Willie, like being practical-helpful, a rare trait in my immediate fambly, which enabled me to be carless, thereby escaping Icy Roads Malaise. CW got his blizzard, I got P&Quiet to work on my dreadful SELECTED,[38] my Albatross, which keeps flapping its dusty wings and landing back on my shoulders, digging its talons into my harried lobes. A fancy way, big deal, of acknowledging receipt of first set of proofs, and spending two weeks—long long hours—rectifying a truly stunning aggregation of errata, computer-generated, yeah, but [. . .] I had recourse to Paste Up, the proofs were so bad. For starters, titles are left margined, as are all short line poems, so out-of-whack visually—I'm still in deep book design shock, and furious it takes so much much much time to clean up Coffee House mess.

[Coffee House] had the nerve to send me a totally dippy Production

---

37   Jean Boulte, Brazilian-American artist, former assistant and friend of Kenward's, lived in a fourth-floor apartment in Kenward's Greenwich Avenue townhouse until 2004.

38   Elmslie, *Routine Disruptions: Selected Poems & Lyrics* (Coffee House Press, 1998).

Questionnaire, just rescued from my dump-it bin, unanswered, which included the following queries—I kid you not:

What colors do you associate with this book?

Puce and magenta polkadots. Polkadots essential.

References (religious/cultural or images (colors)) that you feel should be avoided? Why?

I hate puce and magenta polkadot dagos. They smell bad. And they're lazy and steal puce and magenta polkadot art objets God wants me to have. I hate God. He's self-centered. And I hate you, because you're a puce magenta polkadot idiot control freak with terrible table manners. You fart loud, and your mouth bacteria is outa control and smells like mongrel dog breath after canine's gorged on putrefied coyote flesh from Mongoloid Swamp, ND.

Please list any word associations you have for this book.

Puce. Magenta. Dagos. Stinky bod with slimy tentacles [. . .]

Collegiate humor, sorry 'bout that.

Ten-day Xmas in Vt included a huge organic turkey brought from Maine & baked by niece Vivy, which CW and I ate off of, for days and days. I made leftover turkey soup, delish. [. . .]

Holiday logistics were amazingly stress-free, plane up met by Harold Camp,[39] who looks after The Place, and me. Old style Vermonter, 74, married 51 years to a huge misshapen lady, Pauline, beautifully askew—they live in a trailer with her incontinent 90-year-old Dad [. . .].

Harold remembers my place[40] when it was a working farm, with cows he helped with, and a barn, long since torn down. He's retired, used to drive a truck for the Capitol Candy Co, distributing foodstuffs and beverages to Mom & Pop grocery stores in Northern VT, from border to border, NY to NH. He repairs bikes on the side, recycling spare parts culled from local dumps. Word has gotten out, so it keeps him

---

39   Harold Camp, longtime caretaker of Kenward's VT home.

40   Kenward bought the Calais, VT, property in the 1950s with his partner, American lyricist John Latouche, 1914–1956. American poet and biographer Brad Gooch wrote about Kenward's Vermont property in the November 1986 issue of *House and Garden*.

busy, evenings, working in his shed, and spending time away from Pauline, whom he is devoted to, adores. She, too, must weigh around 200, and he refers to her as "a big girl," respectfully and fondly.

[. . .]

I hope your time off from Schtudents is working out well, and that you enjoyed some Sons time, wherever, and are back in a story-making mode.

6:30 AM, time to head for greasy-spoon[41] coupla doors down for waffles. I didn't gain one ounce—despite heavy gorging. The last few days, I've cut back. Pink grapefruit taste real good.

Write soon, so I know what you're up to, ensconced in '98.

Perks me up—crack at a fresh start. Just trimmed most of Rilke's nails.[42] A breakthrough—he used to fight trimmage fiercely.

Much Love,
Kenward

BOULDER, CO
JANUARY 10, 1998

Dear Kenward,

I spent many hours, as a child, wondering about the meaning of "It's a long road to Ho," "Little pictures have big ears," and "Mind your P's and Q's." Finally, in the twilight of my life, I learn that P and Q stands for Peace and Quiet. Now, when they elude me more than ever. Manuscripts and requests for letters piling higher and higher. Ex-students waited until my grueling semester was over. Oh. But, then I feel guilty for resenting them. I should be proud, grateful, etc. Ahkmatova has a lovely little poem, something to the effect, "I urged each one to Write! How do I make them stop?"[43]

Then too is the panic that if I do get some P's and Q's, what if I have Nothing to write anymore? I had started thinking about different essays

---

41 The Den diner, corner of Greenwich Avenue and Twelfth Street.
42 One of Kenward's two cats, Rilke and Satie.
43 Pen name of Russian poet Anna Andreyevna Gorenko, 1889–1966.

I wanted to do when John Martin[44] decided my book of stories is too short . . . wants 100 more pages. It seemed Finished to me. The stories made some kind of whole. Well, I won't complain. ("I can't complain" is such a silly expression . . . of course I can!) Thank heavens he never changes or even challenges a word, and books are typeset by dear friend Graham McIntosh,[45] who has been setting my stories since late seventies with "Angel's Laundromat." He knows that when I say things like "a earring," it's because that's how the character says it. [. . .]

That Production Questionnaire would be disgusting if it hadn't generated your wonderful responses. Kenward, each Paragraph in your letters is a perfect little story. The sad first one about Jean Boulte, his fever-icy shudder combo. Your hope. [. . .] It is insane to ask an author what word associations he has for his own book. He WROTE the word associations he had. That's the book.

Now though I'm going to be wondering what colors or religious images should be avoided. It reminds me of the photo of the man with a club who smashed Michelangelo's "Pieta." The caption read, "I thought it said 'Piñata.'"

But, hey . . . good news is that soon you will have a new book! [. . .]

I hope I will have news, etc., next time I write. I'm pretty much of a shut-in. Biggest excitement around here was last week when we had such a hot day the wasps came out of their nest on the porch and through all the open doors into my apartment. That same day the battery ran down on smoke detector so it kept chirping. So with the lazy droning of the wasps and crickets and sunshine, it was like July in Alabama. It's snowing now. 2 below last night. So much for global warming.

Happy New Year. Love to you and CW,
Lucia

---

44   John Martin, publisher of Black Sparrow Press, b. 1930. Publisher of many of Lucia's story collections, Black Sparrow Press also published Kenward's collaboration with Joe Brainard, *The Champ*, 1968.
45   Graham MacIntosh, book designer and printer, collaborator with Black Sparrow Press.

*[In the following letters, Kenward describes collaborating with composer
Claibe Richardson and writes of plans to publish his mother's diary, over his
older sister's objections. Lucia shares fears of her sons' and readers' reactions
to her upcoming collection.]*

NEW YORK, NY

FEBRUARY 7, 1998

Dear Lucia,

In midwinter, some well-brought up folk succumb to the vapors,
and their penchant for sinking spells slows them down something terrible. They take lie-downs, return to their desks restored, only to find
themselves staring at some memorandum or other, zonked out of their
skulls, even though they haven't partaken of any refreshment that might
prove mind-altering or mood-swing enhancing.

In good times and bad, they're liable to pack their steamer trunks,
lists of necessary accessories neatly checked off, and head for balmy
climates that defeat this malady of the spirit they refer to as the Winter
Blahs.

Once there, they come alive again, put on glitter-gold encrusted
beanies with jaunty slogans—*'Nuff Guff*—*If It's Broke, Try Coke*—*I'm a
Gook Kook*—and sign up for Shuffleboard King & Kween Kontests &
jaywalk & play possum, sneaky oglers, savoring tan young musculature,
schlurping up bizarre Dairy Creem flavors: Piss Poor Pistachio, to cool
their tongues, other moufs, unmentionable orifices only found beneath
the steely follicles Ice Age monsters, happily long since extinct, were
blessed/cursed with.

[. . .]

My immediate task, after CW has showered, is to proceed down to
the Basement, which I have a phobic terror of. Down There, are all the
Unsolds, mostly LP albums I brought out ages ago, via Z Press, hoping
against hope they'd "catch on," which they didn't. Claibe Richardson,[46]

---

46   Claibe Richardson, American composer, 1929–2003. Close friend and collaborator of Kenward on musicals such as *Lola* and *The Grass Harp*.

composer of *The Grass Harp*[47] and sweet old pal, came by last week with a CD man, who has a tiny label, no money. He'll release a CD of a show Claibe & I wrote, and produce an LP of—about Lola Montez,[48] named *LOLA*.[49] Somewhere, in the awful depths of the Basement, may or may not be the original studio tapes of this musical play, with topnotch Broadway voices, luscious, full orchestrations—string section, not synthesizers. If found in the archival detritus down there, Claibe & I'll each put up $2,500, and the man will add this title to his still small catalog. Pat Padgett, a smart lady, advised me not to be "hard on myself" & to go ahead, & wake up this "dead" work and shell out the two-and-a-half grand.

Next plaint: I've been having an awful time "culling" stuff from a work that may or may not resurface, rewritten pretty totally, in a lit mag called *ARSHILE*[50] I'm rather enamored of—so nicely put together. I'm stuck in the first section—a monologue by one Lady O'Higgins, whose persona may or may not be to blame for the first bit o' this rambling thorny rose of a letter. So I'll head back into Lady O'Higgins, who longs to be in a Marx Bros flic, and then see what happens.

I'm a bit anti-family right now. A ruckus erupted when my goofy spinster sis in L.A. (Vivien #1) was told by my sweet confidante artist-niece (Vivien #2 of Maine) that our Mom's diary[51] was going to be published. Lee Ann Brown,[52] Steven Taylor's ex, has a teeny-tiny feminist press, TENDER BUTTONS, & decided to bring out my Mom's Diary, come May, in tandem with a family memoir by me—even though I, as I pointed out to Lee Ann, do have a dong. No matter!

---

47 *The Grass Harp*, musical by Claibe Richardson, book and lyrics by Kenward, based on Truman Capote's 1951 novel. Broadway premiere November 2, 1971.

48 Lola Montez, stage name of Eliza Rosanna Gilbert, Irish dancer and actress, 1821–1861.

49 Elmslie and Richardson, *Lola*, first Off-Broadway performance March 24, 1982; soundtrack by Harbinger Records, 2001.

50 *Arshile: A Magazine of the Arts*, literary journal founded in 1993 by poet Mark Salerno.

51 Kenward's sister Vivien Elmslie, 1924–2017, and his niece Vivien Russe. Kenward was trying to get his mother Constance Pulitzer's diary published.

52 Lee Ann Brown, American poet and book publisher, b. 1963.

Anyhoo, V of L.A. threatened legal action, no kidding, as she felt "left out," and went into a blind fury at having heard of this prospective publication via V#2 of Maine, whom she was jealous of, as V#2 of Maine . . . usurped . . . pecking order. Dreary. Have you fallen asleep yet? All very "Young and Restless" soap opera fodder minus the amnesia plot twist to make it workable. The upshot is: Lee Ann, I think, has decided to bring out her Granny's diary, rather than tangle with this rich white trash dysfunctional bunch of loonybird boobs.[53] And I'm loathe to subject my words to a DNA broth I've found a partial release from by—you guessed it—writing words as freely as I can, and to hell with The Folks. End of plaint. The project is on ice, for now, and maybe I'll get to batter down my block re Oscar & lyrics for patient, patient Steven.

End of plaints. I hope your sabbatical is leading to new stories. I turned to your oldies, for sustenance, as your last big letter meant the world to me, had the same voice as your stories (weeks ago) and, as I knew they would, they hold up like gangbusters, the stories. It can be a tough test, rereading after time has lapsed and taste does shift and evolve. Waugh[54] doesn't hold up so good. Babs Pym does. Confession: this particular tough old bird reaffirms—you're tops. Honest & honorable work, so forthright & free of both fault-line artifice and word tricks to camouflage the black holes. No black holes—amazing feat.

I grew to love [Chekhov's] work so much, writing two librettos[55]— and there you are, much to my surprise, side-by-side with Anton. Anton, meet Lucia. Lucia, meet Anton. So: I hope I get to read the new works, whenever, but sooner is better, then again, no, the good stuff is always worth waiting for. And I hope you don't get pushed into changing the over-all shape of a collection to please someone else. The CD guy wanted Claibe & I to add songs to *LOLA* (dump

53   The Pulitzer family and its internal politics.
54   Evelyn Waugh, English writer, 1903–1966.
55   Kenward's opera librettos based on Anton Chekhov's plays, *The Seagull* and *Three Sisters*.

demo stuff?) as CDs can squeeze in more time than LPs. As CW'd
say—"Ridiculous."

Stay well, hope Feb treats you well.

Love,

Kenward

Dear Kenward,

Thanks for your wonderful lavish letter. I'll never be able to answer
in Kind . . . Monastic situation here (Lovely . . . I'm working.)

Don't pay any attention to Vivien #1. Lordy, we spent all those years
having to worry about Parents, ("Ooh, what will they say?) then it's your
kids or siblings. I once had to smoke outside MY OWN HOME so as
not to contaminate any visiting grandchildren. My husbands never read
my work so I never worried about them. But I seriously have to worry
about my sons. They used to get mad if I had a narrator with only one
child . . . how come you wrote about Mark? Duh. It's too complicated
to write about four children, you have to feed them, dress them, etc.
They got hurt because I wrote a story about a woman that runs away
from home. How could I even Think such a thing, when they and my
grandsons love me? To their credit, they aren't bothered by sordid tales of
my drinking days. But I am petrified about how they will react to a story
about woman 36 with a very young lover, 17, in new book.[56] Several good
friends find it shocking and immoral. I didn't even tell the "Real" story
. . . Not because of what anyone would say, it was just too hard.

But hey, that is so great that Tender Buttons [Press] would do your
mother's diary! What business is it of Vivien 1's anyway? For Lord's
sake. I shudder to think of Her diary, how dreary. We like Vivien 2 better. You must reason with V#1. Your mother's photo is in my bedroom
now . . . each time I see her I wish she could Speak. Lee Ann's Mama
must have had a pretty nice one. I love Lee Ann. Have only talked
with her a few times but we had great giggles on both occasions. She's

---

56   "Let Me See You Smile."

the only other person I know who used to go visit the hedgehogs in the pet shop, and who agreed that we didn't want One hedgehog, but the whole cage. I am inspired to try to copy MY mother's diary from Kentucky, where we lived in a boarding house. She had a crush on a bricklayer who turned out to be a bad lot. She quoted me, at 3, saying, "Look Mama, the wind is reading my book." She was a bad person, but brilliant and funny . . . like Oscar Levant.[57]

So, I am writing some light, so far, pieces for the book, which will be out in the fall. They won't hurt it, maybe give it some needed softness.

I am in love with William Hazlitt[58] . . . essays. Sharp and witty. Unhampered. By his time, his dorky sisters, tradition. I think for the most part I am . . . except for the Dozens of stories I can't write, because to do so would damage the memory my sons have of their father(s) (Buddy adopted my older two sons.) And some scary stories from when I worked as a counselor in methadone program in New Mexico. Still some of those mafiosos living, argh.

My problem now is that I am sober, have a good job, my sons are all well and happier than most people I know, with good marriages, I have fine dear friends. I think I've "written out" all the painful areas of my life. Not much to say about my cat, really. I'm afraid I don't have any stories left. I do have essays I want to write, about alcoholism, incest, etc. with a very different way of looking at those things.

I feel sad for Monica L.[59] She didn't do it for the money. She was a poor, once too-fat neurotic kid dying for attention. Whatever the outcome it will be Horrible for her to have had public know so many unflattering things by friends, lovers, presidents, etc. Plus, where is she going to get a job? And she wants a real job, to impress people, not money from the *Enquirer*.

Just spent an hour trying to change the ink of the printer. Finally

---

57   Oscar Levant, American pianist, composer, conductor, 1906–1972.
58   William Hazlitt, English essayist, 1778–1830.
59   White House intern Monica Lewinsky. Coverage of President Bill Clinton's impeachment trial was underway.

went to the manual, where the last line said, turn the printer back on. Enough of this hi-tech business for today.

> *Love,*
> *Lucia*

Dear Lucia—

A pretty weird spring, so far. Thunder last night, so unusual for NYC—torrential rains, end of Jakarta-muggy hot spell. I'm wearing the favorite sox of Rilke, fat cat adopted last June in Vermont, nearing his first age year. He pretends the sox are . . . I don't dare think what . . . licks them, claws at them, rests his head and paw on them. A sort of parody of what goes on in executive suites, in the old Hollywood: desk sex a la Clinton B. MGM.

I was thrown, last week, by an invite I heard about, last Jan, but it was supposed to be confirmed, and wasn't, so I assumed it was off. The invite was to do my one-guy version of *Postcards on Parade* in an honest-to-God alive-and-well regional legit theatre in Providence, RI, called Trinity Rep—one-shot deal. April 13th, day after Easter, that's what I'll be doing—300-seater, free, so no one "discriminating" will come. The boss finally reached me yesterday—and I lit into him, aggrieved as I was by the lack of follow-up.

In the pretty brochure, listing the entries in this "new play series" *Postcards* is described as a "charming musical travelogue . . . nostalgia . . ." or something repellent (sunsets in Bali in the Sixties?) . . . [composer] Steven [Taylor]'s name is left off, and the work is never properly identified as a Musical Play. The Impresario, one Oskar Eustis,[60] is probably used to divas flying off the handle. He took it well, apologized, & the rest of the conversation, about his approaching Daddyhood in two weeks, was friendly and civilized. The god-dad will be Tony Kushner,[61] who wrote

---

60 Oskar Eustis, American director, dramaturg, b. 1958.
61 Tony Kushner, American Pulitzer Prize–winning playwright, author, screenwriter, b. 1956.

Angels in America, a two-evening marathon that lasted on Bdwy awhile, lost a bundle, and snowed the critics, so I thought. Some brilliant writing in it. Reading about this play spurred me to write *Postcards*. Oskar gave *Angels* its first birthing in California, had a falling-out with Kushner, so another director, a genius, George Wolfe, brought it in. Genetic loop history. I'll start rehearsing "me" tomorrow, when the final leg-work is done: picking up fresh cassette tracks. This time around, there'll be slides (not of sunsets in Bali!), around a hundred of them, all in order, cued into the script. I hope the performance, and the response, is persuasive enough to brainwash Oskar into the huge risk of taking it on as a full-scale production, with eight solid pro performers. [. . .]

In early May, I've been hired by the Poetry Project[62] to sing at a cocktail party, for deep pocket supporters of this worthy institution, at a swank uptown apartment that belongs to Dianne Benson. Fashion Woild. 20 minutes, $250, very decent pay. And I'll be a character in a play by Kevin Killian,[63] coming up late April, at the Poetry Project. I'll use my awful nasal Truman Capote voice[64]—truly repellant, enerve fag whine, underneath hard-as-nails. Hope your Sabby is going fine 'n dandy. Oof! Time for zzzzzs.

LOVE,
KENWARD

[In the following letters, they write of a new opportunity via an investment banker friend of Kenward's, which both turns into a small grant for Lucia from the Annie Rensselaer Tinker Association for Women, and begins a fantasy narrative of the mysterious "Nancy" and the "Tinker Belles" that Kenward and Lucia develop for years. They continue discussing Kenward's and Lucia's

---

62 Poetry Project at St. Mark's Church was founded in 1966 in New York's East Village.

63 Kevin Killian, American poet, author, editor, playwright, 1952–2019.

64 Truman Capote, American novelist and playwright, 1924–1984. Kenward imitated Capote's voice perfectly and sometimes answered the phone with it, and he told me a story several times of when he once used that voice to answer the phone and it was Capote himself calling in regards to Kenward's adaptation of his novel *The Grass Harp* for a Broadway musical.

forthcoming books, and upcoming performances of Kenward's Postcards on
Parade. *Lucia reveals some of the true events behind her short stories "Carmen"
and "Strays," and writes of a bus accident witnessed from her front yard.]*

BOULDER, CO
JULY 2, 1998

Dear Kenward,

What a tonic, a sweet breeze, your letter and *SCREEN TREAT-
MENT.*[65] Thank you. *S. T.* is fabulous . . . I too laughed out loud, as
much from sheer pleasure as humor. By the "azaleas' assiduous frottage"
I had begun to take it all for granted, was jolted back with "His grandson was a pharmacist's assistant in Ypres." Witty, dazzling book, much
more than that though . . . it is beautifully crafted, like a musical piece
full of lovely refrains and echoes and implications. The rhythm and
pace is terrific, just rollicks along, one great image after another. The
kicker is that it is, in spite of its sophistication, so much fun. [. . .]

I am currently low down and blue, hating my work, sure I'll never
write again and the only BAD part about your (nicely made, also) book
is that I feel how can he like MY simple-minded stuff? But I know you
sincerely do and can't possibly tell you how much this means to me.
And thank you, too, for mentioning me to Wall Street and the world
of finance.[66] I am seriously broke and just had to pay huge amount for
false teeth. Another indignity of old age. It's getting to me this summer,
emotionally, being so fat and old and tethered to this [oxygen] tank. I'd
love to jump into a stream or a pool. Money worries have added to bad
mood dog day so . . . well, thank you.

I don't know *Arshile*, but will find it and subscribe so I'll be sure to
get fall issue. It's true— it is usually unwise to share work with writer
friends. I'd mutter a little on this topic (dear friend just got huge grant

---

65   Referring to a collaged chapbook Kenward made for her that included a
poem, "Screen Treatment," later published in Kenward's collection *Blast from the
Past* (Skanky Possum Press, 2000).
66   Referring to Kenward's reconnection with Dyke Benjamin, who was on the
board of the Annie Rensselaer Tinker Association for Women, which ended up
awarding Lucia a small literary grant.

for something I began, showed her, ETC.) but your book put me into such a good mood. I don't want to spoil it. Writers are actually as bad as critics. I just read the Bronte letters (forgot to send in the damn card to book club.) I only love Emily, but she didn't write letters. Only time Charlotte perked up was when she Trashed dear Jane Austen, just ripped her up. Provincial, superficial, petty and boring, etc. etc.

I'm glad Ron Padgett[67] is your friend, I'd share with Him anytime.

Several interruptions since I started this, so missed the postman. But both were caused by your magic and my decision to enjoy this balmy weather. First friend called, good news about biopsy . . . he had prostate removed last year, chemo, etc. Doing very well. Undaunted. He's using an impotency drug called The Muse, which gives me all kinds of ideas for cartoons. The poet saying to the lady on the lyre on the cloud . . . "No for god's sake, not another poem, I want a hard-on." He said the only side effect is that it makes the penis Cold. Now in this three-digit weather that sounds delightfully refreshing and balmy. Oh, and to answer your question, Whatever happened to coitus interruptus? Nothing. Get it? Ha ha.

Then just as I was moving my hose, wham bam, a Special Transit bus ran into an Oriental lady in a SAAB (black windowed) right on my corner. The bus was full of Special i.e. retarded adults with other infirmities going to the re-hab at hospital across the street. I offered to drive them the rest of the way but driver said they had to stay there until they were Evaluated. There was a delightful little spectacle as fire truck, ambulance, police, the Oriental lady's husband in a Mercedes, Three Special transit busses arrived.

Best part was that the passengers (none of whom were hurt . . . they had Said they were—that's why he called an ambulance) were all howling and yelling away and hanging out the windows because it was so hot. The fireman borrowed MY hose to wash the spilled antifreeze away "so it wouldn't harm pets." (It all got washed to the pets down the block.) When he handed me back my hose, I offered a Down's

---

67   Ron Padgett, American poet, author, editor, b. 1942. Close friend of Kenward's.

syndrome fellow a drink, so he drank. Then all of them wanted a drink. It makes me wildly happy to do something, anything, I've never done before, like give four or five strange looking people hanging out of bus windows drinks from my hose.

"Remain seated! Do NOT remove your seat belts!" the poor driver was shouting, worried about lawsuits, his job. He was definitely in the wrong, ran a stop sign . . . but the ones he should worry about are the Saab and the Mercedes.

Exhausted by all this commotion I came in and made myself some ice water. Cosmo, my dear deaf cat, was complaining about the heat too, so I dropped two ice cubes into his water dish. He took a drink COLD just as the ice cubes cracked loud enough to hear. He jumped a foot, hissing and spitting like a cartoon Halloween cat. It terrified Cosmo. He's on my bed with his face to the wall. Life is fraught with peril.

Sending some magazines. Hope I didn't already. One, "Carmen,[68]" very dark.

> *Thanks for making me happy,*
> *Signed,*
> *Balmy in Boulder*

CALAIS, VT

JULY 14, 1998

Dear Lucia

Happy Bastille Day. Sunny out, and Harold Camp, The Mad Mower, just tooled up in his pick-up, 8:30 AM. Green license plate, costs extra, Personalized—spells PAPPY. His huge wife, Pauline, whose body sprawl is formidably free form, has had Stones removed, is recovering. Harold did the housework—his pec problem is improving, and his "prostrate cancer" has been licked (operation this spring). Downhill, Ron is back on the tennis court, which means his foot ailment is in

---

68   Berlin, "Carmen," a short story collected in *Where I Live Now* and *A Manual for Cleaning Women*.

remission. Patty, his Missus, who was once engaged to Ted Berrigan,[69] who went to New Orleans & eloped with a girl he'd just met, named Sandy, has a new "butch" hairdo—close cropped, no more bun, no more long hair. No more dye. She's recovered from a mystery childhood malady named The 5th Disease—a body spots 'n' fever deal. My diabetes sugar numbers have been high, for me, lately. I watch cable TV, old movies full of smoking and gowns that glitter a bit in black-and-white. I eat non-sugar sweets, wafers, popsicles, that really aren't non-sugar. Today—new leaf.

Patty and I go for walks, two so far, gentle start. The fields and woods are wet from incessant rain, so we keep to the dirt roads. Patty's smart, keeps her smarts hidden from the outside world. Catholic girl-hood, Tulsa, pre-lady-lib? My stiff knees are responding to all this attention. I think a bod is supposed to look after the person, not the other way around. HAH! This brings you up-to-date with us oldsters' health concerns.

Yesterday, I got a postcard from Coffee House book designer, with whom I've been out of touch for a couple of months. [. . .] There are still some problem areas, including the front cover, but I feel a heap sight calmer now about the book ending up as—a book.

Today, my printer has run out of ink and my old computer, the Mac Classic, has decided to die again. So I'm working away at CW's Compaq, peering out at the big pond, with waterfalls engorged from weeks of heavy rain.

I've set up a November trip to Boulder, one show with Steven at El Teatro Judy, Boulder Art Musee,[70] and a reading at Naropa, some songs with Steven as a closer. I hope I get to spend some real life time with you. [. . .]

Thanks for sending the two stories. "CARMEN" is so strong, I don't know what I make of its emanating from you. Its quieter compadre lured me into remembered (and still extant) grief shallows and

---

69   Ted Berrigan, American poet, 1934–1983.
70   Boulder Museum of Contemporary Art, BMoCA, where Judy Hussie-Taylor was artistic director.

dark places, stillnesses. I was struck by the ghost section, and the smallish detail that balloons into a memory take-over, obliterating time divides.

Your account of the bus accident was so hilarious I took it to my niece Vivy and her hubby Willie, to read it to them after dinner. They've bought a huge New England mansion once owned by a cook-book writer (Mrs. Appleyard[71]) who died ages ago. I sat in a Lazyboy in a long long front parlor, empty of furniture, just three seats, and read it, badly, as the laughter I'd held back alone kept welling up, unbidden. High point of eve. I hope you turn it into part of something, a page work.

The Wall Street Man phoned the other day, just after I got your letter & stories. He wanted your address. He said the Thing was All Set.[72] My role (I'm innocent!) was this. Once a year, he takes me to uptown lunch (big fees) and this time, I recounted how Lee Ann Brown has feminist press, and I was to be published (Mom's Diary plus my family memories, a double-bill). This was pre-Sis Threat of Law Suit. And he topped me by chatting about being Foundation Head . . . and I ended up sending him some of your books, which CW tracked down, which he liked very much. End of gesture. I hope he's come through, and if it's a lottery, great, and if it's a Round The World junket, great, so I won't feel I'm a dumb Referrer, my role, this time around.

Noon. Time to print this second page, and see if the tech magic works.

Whew! It does!

Love,
Kenward

PS. Enclosed an Arshile. *Hope you send them a W.O.R.K.*

---

71   Louise Andrews Kent, American author of the Mrs. Appleyard cookbook series, 1886–1969. Friend of Kenward's.
72   Dyke Benjamin, Wall Street financier friend of Kenward's and board member of the Tinker Association.

Dear Kenward,

Thanks for sending *Arshile*. Really fine publication, perfect for your piece. Have only read the excellent translations and the essay on Joanne Kyger by Alice Notley,[73] two of my favorite women. I called Joanne, she was really moved by it. I wish I HAD something to send. Although I don't think I'm sophisticated enough. Ivan [Suvanjieff] talked me into giving him last two stories for a single issue [of *The New Censorship*]. That will be nice though . . . a good combination. One sweet and one sour. Another murder. Actually there are several scattered about my work . . . some disguised, like in "Strays." The dogs were killed but so were two of my colleagues in methadone program, so almost was I . . . so as not to testify in Grand Jury. Sent my kids to Mexico and I used assumed name in California until finally they all went to jail or died. In another story a drug dealer dies.[74] I did stab him but he didn't die.

I am a woman with a past! With lots of them. Most of "Carmen" was true except of course I never would have lived in a trailer. I didn't murder my husband. He did hit me and then he gave himself an accidental overdose. I drove myself to the hospital, thinking he was dead. My son Dan was born 2 1/2 pounds. Doctor thought he wouldn't live, said not to name him. (This baby is the same dear noble Dan, 6' 3" and in fine shape, who was just here with his son.) I did say that there was nobody home. That's how my marriage ended. Berlin finally got off heroin, only way I'd let him near our sons. They went to see him in Mexico every summer. We all loved him actually, even through a later cocaine period, which took most of his fortune.

He was semi-invalid, off drugs for past eight years and we all took care of him. He called me every day in Mexico and later in Colorado. I really miss him. The story "Carmen" surprised me. I wrote it after the

73   Joanne Kyger, American poet and writer, 1934–2017. Alice Notley, American poet, b. 1945.

74   "La Barca de ilusión," published in *Home Sick* (Black Sparrow Press, 1977), republished in *Evening in Paradise* (Farrar, Straus and Giroux, 2018).

will when his sons got $100,000 each, but all had to give it to IRS for his back taxes. I never got child support, my insane choice, but ridiculously low trust accounts for their college. He never once helped them, even when he spent $20,000 a month on drugs. They were none the worse for the lack of money, still love and miss him. I never told them negative things about their father. I didn't know I still Felt them until I wrote that story.

So the Coffee House book is coming along! Great. BEST news for me is your trip to Boulder. Steven had told me . . . I can't wait to see you and CW—AND the show. I've been eating popsicles too. HOT here. I'd love to be transported to Calais, meet Vivy and Willy and Ron and Patty. And Harold and Pauline. I wish you would think about a novel. Or several novellas. I love your prose. Even your letters open up to me the place, the characters. I look forward to your family memories. Tell me that you will be doing your Mom's Diary in spite of bad sister.

Wasn't that nice, the accident of the Special.Transit bus? I had never paid any attention when the busses passed. Now though when I'm watering watering watering or sitting in porch swing they all wave when they go by. Sweet . . . They must think of me as the lady with the hose in her nose and the water hose for drinking.

I'm cheered up . . . not sure Why. Nothing changed and it is so hot. Maybe a story is coming. Wish I were in charge of the kaleidoscope that turns some days so hopeless and others full of joy.

I even felt kindly toward my oxygen and not being able to get about. It has given me an exquisite dream life. (My biggest pet peeve is people telling their dreams, sorry.) Nothing HAPPENS in the dreams. But I'll be a child in the back seat of a car driving through pines. Intense pine scent, blue jays, wind in my hair, hair stuck in my mouth. Or in the ocean in the Yucatan, tasting it, floating, looking at sky. Or in a freezing mountain lake, walking on sharp mossy stones . . . finally plunging in. Many other lagniappes. I love that word—don't think it quite fits, but in any case, they are pure sensation and with no context.

A very dignified elderly lady called me and asked for my address. Said she was from the Tinker Society. That they were going to send me $100 a month. I asked why and she said, "Because you are a woman, my dear," that she would be writing to me. No, this wasn't a dream, perhaps it's from the Fountain, er, Foundation Head?

I wish I had a Lazy boy. I watch baseball lying on the couch, my knees bent, feet in bucket of ice water. I'm going to get headphones so I'll look like Chacmool.

Much love,
Lucia

BOULDER, CO
JULY 24, 1998

Dear Kenward,

I received a check from the Anne Marie Rensselaer Tinker Foundation, $500. I paid my Visa bill so I hope I qualify. Had to fill out detailed questionnaire. If I pass, they will send me $100 a month ($500 was for back months).

I don't feel quite right about this. I make a good salary. I do spend about $800 a month on oxygen & medical insurance doesn't cover—so am always short. But still . . . sure there are working women needier.

Also I have the idea that this is a perpetuating sort of thing—since they asked so much about my savings, life insurance, etc. I have been denied life insurance all my life. I have one now that didn't require exam or medical history, $100,000, for my sons. And that costs a lot & won't pay if I die before 2001. It seems so little to leave my sons. I'm sure not going to leave any to the Foundation.

So we'll see. $100 a month would be great, so I hope I pass. I'd love to meet these ladies—the one I spoke to was out of Henry James.[75]

Maybe I'll strike it rich—those cloned mice cheered me up. (What do animal rights people think about that?) I'm getting the patent for cloning minks, will make a killing. Ha ha.

Love,
Lucia

---

75   After speaking to Nancy Houghton of the Tinker Association, Kenward and Lucia began inventing personalities and characters for "Nancy" and other Tinker Belles, sending each other letters and postcards from these imagined identities.

[In the following letters, Kenward describes a fourteen-piece series of small paintings artist Ken Tisa is creating as a portrait of Kenward. Lucia remembers some negative reactions to her 1990 collection, Homesick. *They begin inventing a character for "Nancy," based on one of the women in the Tinker Association.]*

CALAIS, VT

AUGUST 3, 1998

Dear Lucia—

A spate of perfecto days—cool, blue skies. Vermont summer days at their best. Ken Tisa,[76] collaborator and good ol' boy pal, is visiting artist, and works down in the cabin, by the big pond—it looks like a Creemie stand, but has a big worktable, and privacy. He's doing my portrait, which will be a mix of small oils of stuff that relates to me. He asked for a Muscle Man, provided, and a photo of Joe Brainard, also provided, and he's redoing two of my *Postcards on Parade* collages, one, a male nipple work. Last night, I stayed in my outbuilding, sorting through postcards, for the first time since arriving in May. Riffling through them is a form of visual therapy & inner replenishment I'd foolishly ignored. [. . .]

Loved your account of the Tinker Belle episode. I was hoping for Vegas bucks, a cream convertible, a ladies' maid, vacations in a palace, all yours, on the Klondike. Drat. I believe the stipend-honorarium, whatever, is For Life, so, by the time you hit 150, there'll be a zero-000–000 pile-up. But, cheez, Me-Generation-wise, that's not a very sparkly support system.

I've done no writing. But relations with Coffee House have resumed, and even stabilized. The front-cover is as I wish. I'm starting to look forward to [*Routine Disruptions*] being a book I can hold without growling and fuming. I'm taking your counsel re a novella very seriously. My memory is terribly porous. Maybe I can start trailing it. My

---

76   Ken Tisa, American artist, b. 1945. Friend and collaborator of Kenward's. Tisa's collection of small portraits of Kenward's life and Tisa's ceramics and visual pieces were on proud display in Kenward's New York and Vermont homes.

stress pile-up is much less oppressive these days, and I feel bouncier re CW's return, for six months, Aug 11th.

Love,
Kenward

BOULDER, CO
AUGUST 4, 1998

Dear Kenward,

Oh dear—they sent me another check, $100, & I spent that one too.

This is dangerous. Some similar ladies in this Hi-Rize Apt all decided I was witty in the sauna & then I told them my name. Then one of them read one of my books. Something scandalized them. I was ever after that sola in the sauna. Awkward silences in the elevator. Eyes averted at the mailboxes.

I could make it a variation of Dr. Faustus. This woman sells her soul for $100 then she has to get white gloves & a hat & go to matinees at Lincoln Center, turn blue in the beauty parlor.

Oh dear. I'm truly not sure what to do. Not exaggerating. I was fired from two jobs after people read my books . . . I can tell that Nancy [of the Tinker Association] is not prepared for my work. I really like her. I know I would like them.

Oh!

Confused in Colorado,

BOULDER, CO
AUGUST 14, 1998

Dear Kenward,

Porous memory. Lovely way to express this problem. I spent excruciating hours at ToysRUs getting birthday presents for [grandson] Truman, 5. Thank heavens I didn't mail them because—only because another son called and asked when Cody's birthday was, did I remember that it was Cody's birthday. [Grandson] Cody is 6. Alas, whereas Truman likes action toys, gory exploding videos, weapons, armor, etc., Cody likes chemistry sets, astronomy books, intricate puzzles, science experiments. As I recall

. . . Bobbie[77] (years ago) actually went to a hypnotist trying to recall details about Guatemala for a book she was writing.

That still is one magic of writing. I'll remember some person or event and only after I'm into the story do details emerge and surround the sentences. People and songs come in.

Went with Ed and Jenny [Dorn] to hear wonderful fiddler and guitar player, the Cantrells. They reminded me of you, and of old postcards and motor inns.[78] Played things like "In my Adobe Hacienda" and "Slow Boat to China."

[. . .]

Ivan [Suvanjieff] said he had talked to you . . . that you thought I was upset about the amount from the Tinker Belles. Au contraire. It's a lovely amount that I can look at as for books or, as Nancy says, the beauty parlor. Ivan thinks I'm bothered to be in a group with old ladies. No, no. Problem is I love these old ladies. My ambition was to retire and live in a hotel in New York and go to Schrafft's with other old ladies. Even now as an old lady I get into trouble. Maybe it is my voice, which is sweet, and the writing voice is sweet and open too, so some people, all old ladies, are Shocked and feel they have been betrayed when they read about sex, drugs, murder, etc. Even you were shocked by "Carmen." I have two WORSE shockers in the new book. How can they pass that book around? Nancy already likes me . . . we talked at length on the phone. She is Dear. I couldn't help myself . . . I wrote her a nice letter, told about the deer who spends every morning under the apple tree, etc. Twice I have said *Send back the money*. But it was spent! I am going to have to stop soon, because it IS a relationship I have got myself into and they will be hurt by me.

This has been a problem several times. I had a fine job with vascular surgeons who were training me to be a Physician's assistant. Great job.

---

77   Bobbie Louise Hawkins, American short story writer, monologist, and poet, 1930–2018. Close friend of Lucia's.

78   Among their vast correspondence are hundreds of postcards (both were avid collectors).

The woman who ran the office read *HOMESICK*,[79] convinced them that I was dangerous, probably seeking drugs or prescription pads. Oddly enough people I have sort of used as characters have not minded at all. It is a definite ethical problem. I would never Really write about my sons, for example. But, as Bobbie says about her husband: "he shouldn't have done that to a writer."

I was really offended by Paul Theroux's nasty portrait of [V. S.] Naipul in the *New Yorker*. Bad Form. Bad karma. I canceled my subscription to NYRB when they printed scathing essay on Pauline Kael by Renata Adler.

Your letters are fun and bring me all these people. Each letter, though, is shot through with the purest and most exquisite and lyrical poetry.

So when is the book out? Those were very good reviews, perceptive views, not just positive. Glad you like the cover. I have to go with [Black Sparrow Press publisher John] Martin's wife's cover, whatever it may be. *HOMESICK* was so awful, but I loved *SO LONG*.[80] I'm starting to get the panics about book. Ivan and I trade insecurities and baseball stats. Last week he was worthless. Unspoken rule is that we both can't be worthless at the same time.

How is your portrait coming? You sound really, well, happy.

> *Love,*
> *Lucia*

CALAIS, VT

LATE AUGUST–EARLY SEPTEMBER 1998

Dear Lucia—

Great excitement! I've met Nancy!![81] She was at the Farmer's Market last Saturday, in front of the Montpelier jail where the booths are set up. Craftspeople are moving in on the Growers. And there she

---

79   Berlin, *Homesick: New and Selected Stories* (Black Sparrow Press, 1990).

80   Berlin, *So Long* (Black Sparrow Press, 1993).

81   This is the first invention of their Nancy "character" based on the Nancy of the Tinker Association.

was—with her own table of dried wreaths. Some, I confess, were a tad bizarre—the skull-and-crossbones made of desiccated red rose petals and thorns: with a tacky silk banner attached (message: I LOVE LUCIA in lettering reminiscent of the Lucille Ball sitcom)—a bit arch for me. She's taking a rest-cure in the same, er, "state establishment" that James Schuyler[82] spent several months at—in Waterbury, a town about twenty miles from Calais.

The therapy is first-rate, I hear, and many experiments are being carried out for the future good of mankind. The experimenters, mostly non-accredited, from foreign lands and obscure belief systems, pay for this privilege so the institution turns a slight profit for The State—and of course helps the Not So Almighty Dollar hold its head up as a currency. The trade deficit is sapping the national will via Consumerismo, in my humble opinion.

Back to Nancy.

Meat once a week is guaranteed, and a freshly laundered sheet once a month. The locked dorms and barred windows (it was a prison actually, built to incarcerate witches, warlocks, Civil War pacifists and 'nancy' camp followers) provide excellent security, both for the inmates and nervous townspeople, who have had their share of hallucinating nakeds urinating on their gladiola beds. The therapy is primal, and makes good use of "channeling" and "shock treatments" that wreak havoc with the electricity bills. Her "shop" hours—she wasn't allowed the use of sharp implements and her request to make Scalpel Art was summarily refused—have been a lifesaver.

Her wreaths are eye-catching and she's allowed "out" every Saturday as a reward for good behavior, to sell her wares for pocket money—those wrinkles have started to really show, and while cold cream and generic moisturizers don't do the trick, they're better than nothing. Her new hair-do is a daring experiment—it juts out to one side. Looks like it weighs a ton, but she manages to keep her head straight. It does

---

82   James Schuyler, poet, 1923–1991. Close friend of Kenward's, who is here referring to Schuyler's hospitalization after a mental breakdown while visiting Kenward in Vermont.

bobble when she gets excited, but maybe the old, Golden Pond Hepburn[83] is a visual icon for Nancy—"Bobble Homage"—rather touching that.

I couldn't get all the details, but Nancy did hiss out the word "stress" meaningfully. Dupe[84] has been acting up again and the rattle of tire-chains in the boudoir is not conducive to the focus Nancy needs, and is accustomed to, while applying lash glitter, eye shadow, blush cheek resonator, and her very own wrinkle concealant formula flown in weekly, pre-incarceration. Barracuda sperm degenerates into useless mush all too quickly. Ocean micro-temperatures are hard to replicate.

[. . .]

Enough about today. The trip was jam-packed with doings. In LA, I did my radio interview with Michael Silverblatt[85] (who loves your work)—spoke my new poem, *Cyberspace*. Third or fourth time on his show. Two-thirds of the way through, he'll say something about the work that is, well, oracular. It makes such good sense, puts the work in perspective, and I always kick myself—why didn't I know that? I wrote the stuff, after all. So the interview went well, and so did the solo show at Beyond Baroque, an ex-town hall with a performance space, a library/bookstore, and upstairs, a large room where my collages were on display, about thirteen strong. On white walls, well lit, they looked great, I thought. Plus, to fill out one wall, three rows or page-size collages from *Postcards*.

Post-performance, by the time I'd changed back into civvies (I went clowny garb for Part II)—there were only four people at the "reception." They were—CW's Dutch "tutor," an ex-professor of I forget what (ethics? law?) and three S&M leather guys, one said Tutor'd met via Internet, and had made the trek to SF to, um, do-what-they-do, slash slash, ouch ouch. They were OK—I was glad the galleria wasn't empty. One day off, then a workshop ($35 fee) in Performance Art,

---

83   Katherine Hepburn as a character in film *On Golden Pond*.

84   Dupe is a character they invented for "Nancy's" husband.

85   Michael Silverblatt, American critic and broadcaster, host of the long-running radio program *The Bookworm*, b. 1952.

since I'm haughty about no honorarium for gigs. The solo went well, my voice still there, and while the second half dipped—"Cyberspace" too long—a few people came up afterwards and were bowled over by it, but it is a toughie.

[. . .]

Talked to Vivy [Russe] of Maine yesterday, and they're OK now. Simple scenario—sell Maine house (real estate market terrific still, so big moolah bundle) and move to Calais Palais. Fix it up a bit, so winter living is comfy. Whew! Money vibes pretty much back where they belong in the sub-basement of small print, so we all can get back to being easy & affectionate etc. [. . .]

Cherry on Family Sundae is: when I didn't show up at a Calais Palais lunch my diabetes doc nephew [Gordon Weir] attended—I wanted to vent disapproval—lack of family support re. Mom Journal Should Be Published—Doc went into action. When my litigation-prone Sis [Vivy Elmslie] came for a visit to their Vermont vacation home, he got her to write a permission letter to me. So now I can go ahead with Mom's Journal—and a "time travel" account of my own, started last fall. Burden removed—except for the writing, which I enjoy.

I keep laughing; 3 AM, in bed, washing dishes, kitchen, wherever—your Soap Fantasy, to home, lawn sale ads.

Hope your students treat you right. Nancy too.

Much Love,
Kenward

BOULDER, CO
SEPTEMBER 12, 1998

Dear Kenward,

What a delightful surprise, to hear that you saw our dear Nancy, and how priceless, heavenly, the wreath, with its message to me. When I opened the box a (welcome) gust of wind came in at the same moment that it began to rain. The first rain in many weeks . . . Tiny bits of dry blue and red petals blew all about the room in little tornadoes. I took it as a sign that she was at her Ouija board in Waterbury, trying to contact me, so I hope she heard how much I love her. I also tried to let her know that the dry dairy creamer they give you in those places works very so well as a wrinkle concealer. I'm sure she'd prefer that I didn't know she was there . . . perhaps I could send her anonymously a tube of hemorrhoid crème, for a mini facelift, to get her through this period. Kind of you to refer to that little bobble of her head as a Hepburn Homage. I rather like to think of it as Nancy's way of marching to the tune of a different drum.

I have been looking everywhere for the sweet letter she sent with the check. She is truly a lady. There aren't many such genuine ones left. My fears about her reactions to my little stories have vanished. Nancy simply could never see anything unseemly. Even unseemly things would acquire her grace and become acceptable.

She invited me to sewing group that meets three times a week, where they make things for less fortunate people ("this gives us such joy"). And the fall luncheon is November 13 at the Junior League. Oh I'm so sorry I can't go. (Really.)

I would have loved to have been in Waterbury with James Schuyler. (He is one of my most favorite poets. I heard him read in San Francisco, an historic event.)

I was one of those alcoholics who only periodically got very terrible, usually combative or near death and/or suicidal and needing medication against seizures. Invariably ended up in straightjacket or four-point leather restraints in psych wards. Alas, these are not the wonderful places they used to be. In the old days, before all these wonder drugs, before Thorazine and Haldol, everybody in there was mad in his or her unique way, but it was ok to be insane, everyone accepted completely the others' bizarrities . . .

We were all safe there. Intense friendships, kindnesses. All night laughters. Only bad part was that you had to stoop to a little grid in the wall to hold your cigarette to it, clamped steady between your teeth, in order to light it, and you had to take bath in two inches of water, with an attendant who held the soap. But in later years everybody just sat in the wards with Georgia O'Keefes and Monet's Waterlilies on the walls, drugged, waiting for the trays of the medication cart. Five-hour chess games. All afternoon watching bowling.

Leafers! Sounds like a description of Latino felons or those guys that hang out in 7–11's. It is like that lovely British expression "day trippers." I never heard of leafers until I came to Colorado, where I also, I suppose, became one. Oh oh. The maple tree on the corner of 5th and Alpine is turning. Better than leafing here is bugling . . . going up to listen to the elk. But you must have done that, heard the sweet plaintive calls. So you are waiting to leaf and then return to New York? It must be wonderful up there now. [. . .]

I recently read about and saw lavish photographs of that motel in Las Vegas. I'm happy to know someone semi-imaginable is actually Going there. Who would choose to go there? I mean, I can imagine people wanting to go to Las Vegas. I would, but I'd want to go to the hotel where the volcano erupts every four hours. God, sometimes this world seems so crazy, I get caught up in the Apocalypse-millennium fears. How come nobody brings up Janet Reno?[86] Her hair should be impeached. The whole Clinton/Monica situation just pitiful, just plain pitiful. Coming in the sink is too tacky to bear. Can you imagine Thomas Jefferson coming in a sink?

I loved the latest Calais chapter, saying goodbye to Ron and Pat so early in the morning. [. . .]

You need a column, daily or weekly, in good publication.

Sorry if my letters slow down. I am in bed by 7. Slept all day Friday. I am Swamped with work. Three required office hours have grown to seven. Classes going great, though. Students responding with pages, pages. Former students sending novels, screenplays, story collections. Nobody doesn't do their homework. God, when I was in college we'd be out necking in the "boondocks" or drinking beer at Okie Joe's. But these kids? They all say "Present." They even bind their homework. They take notes. (On ad-lib insanities that occur to me). A few Wonderful Born Writers, a few god-awful students.

Ivan just called, got a little jealous because I said I had to go, was writing to you. "Well go ahead. Go write your letter." He sends his

---

86   Janet Reno was currently the U.S. attorney general presiding over President Clinton's impeachment trial.

love. Spent the day working on his serve. Desmond Tutu is coming in November. Ivan and Dawn [Engle] want to ask him to marry them. I don't know her, but I know she has been patiently in love with him for a long long time, finally got him to believe he was lovable and could love her, so I think she's pretty great. She also saw how good he could be if his talent's channeled. They are doing positive, actually innovative programs with these PeaceJams and young people.

Oh oh. It's 7 pm. Cinderella time.

Thanks for making me so happy with the wreath and news of Nancy.
> *Love,*
> *Lucia*

[In the following letters, Lucia writes of a publication delay and responds to receiving another grant from Z Press, substantially larger than what the Tinker Belles are sending. They write of the televised "Live from Lincoln Center" New York City Opera production of Kenward's opera Lizzie Borden.*]*

BOULDER, CO
JANUARY 10, 1999

Dear Kenward,

First I must tell you that I had a really rotten winter break. Not working did not ease pain in back and I didn't get the cortisone shot in my spine. Dr. kept sending me for more and more tests, finally hospitalized me . . . because of coumadin they couldn't do myelogram, which involved 12 sticks to find space between vertebrae . . . had to be weaned off that and onto heparin for other tests. Good news is I am going to get surgery in March (need to get students in order, substitute, and to coordinate with spring break). They are putting in some kind of struts or props and screwing them in somewhere, which will take the incessant pressure off of nerve. I am tremendously relieved that there will be a relief from this. I had been Seriously down, unable to write or go out etc. Huge billowing gusts of self-pity. Usually spend Christmas with the Dorns, but they were in England, only one son called (others understandably with children and families). I was homesick, broke because of spending $ on acupuncture and massage, which felt good and took care of sore muscles but never addressed nerves. Neither covered by insurance so savings gone and Visa maxed. Woe Was Me . . . and I wouldn't be able to go home in summer. Haven't written a word.

(And my book . . . the galleys didn't come. Man who was setting the type died and [book designer] Graham McIntosh not finding a replacement yet, so lord knows about That.)

I don't think you can imagine how happy I was to receive the grant.[87] I am not even going to feel undeserving or embarrassed or any kind of Thought, that I had had previously, of not accepting this unbelievable manna from heaven. Thank you from deep in my heart. I'll need help at home, have to co-pay hosp . . . I need to go home and see my family in the summer. We talk and write. I think feeling lonely and sick this break made missing them very acute.

It is not a bad thing that money should mean so much, it is a simple fact that money eases many cares. I feel a huge relief, an immense gratitude. I don't even feel uncomfortable about any confusion about whether it is for my work or because you are a friend. Your letters and your work have given me so much joy and love these past years that this seems part of the gift of your friendship.

Anyway I am very heartened . . . ready for school tomorrow. New notebooks. New eraser and socks. Lunch-pail. I received great letter from the dean confirming my reappointment for four years.

Off to Xerox syllabi while no one is using copier (Sunday). Hope you are both well. Did you see your doctor? My new year's resolution is always the same (diet) . . . Broken. Last year It was to read Faulkner and that was a pleasure. Dante this year, and not to discuss my health (broken, see above) or the weather.

Did you see *Shakespeare in Love*? What a delight. I want to see it again, with my eyes closed, for the great dialogue. How it "got" writing, and the theatre. The silence when the play was over.

[. . .]

---

87 A grant from Z Press.

Dear letter from Nancy.[88] They're all going to the Botanical Gardens next week.

> *Thanks again . . . I love you,*
> *Lucia*

Dear Lucia—

In ten minutes, the oatmeal will be ready, CW sez. Warm out, Friday. *Lizzie Borden*[89] is gearing up—the stress of which I just adore. Next Tuesday, a benefit I get to free-load at, as librettist. All I have to do is get up from table when Jack Beeson, the composer, mentions moi. I'll get to hear the mysteriosa diva, who plays the Step-Mom from Hell, Laurie Flanigan,[90] sing some aria samples, along with our Lizzie, who is terrific, and who I saw summer before last in Cooperstown, NY, where the production was tried out.

Today, I talked to a lady who is in charge of a promo program, next weekend, two nights back-to-back at the Guggenheim Musee. I'm part of Discussion Panel #1, composer, librettist & someone called Dramaturg. I just hate the word dramaturg. Turgid. Turgid drama: that's what they either slavishly enforce, or slavishly pretend to get rid of. Dramaturgs are lowlife: esthetic cops. Boo!

[. . .]

Oatmeal break. Deelish. CW conversation about Ginsberg versus Ashbery[91]—"value" of poetry for betterment of sassiety as an expectation, overt or covert.

Back to the op'ry.

---

88   The real Nancy Houghton from the Tinker Association also enters the letters and it is sometimes difficult to distinguish Lucia's and Kenward's invented persona of her and the Tinker Belles.

89   Elmslie and Jack Beeson, *Lizzie Borden*, opera. Premiered at New York City Opera on March 25, 1965.

90   Laurie Flanigan, opera singer, b. 1959.

91   Allen Ginsberg, American poet and writer, 1926–1997. John Ashbery, American poet and art critic, 1927–2017. Friends of Kenward's.

In 1966 (?) when our opera was launched. Jack got so baffled by the foreignness, non-Waspishness of the Greek surname of a prestigious theatre director then on a roll, Cacoyannis, that he contacted the wrong Greek, Psacharopoulis—who had only done summer stock, was startled at this plum job being offered, & turned out to be just perfect for *Lizzie Borden*.

Jack is bound & determined to stick a mirror back in a scene—a mirror Lizzie can actually smash, on-stage, so that blood makes its presence palpable for the first time, pre-murder. The director & scene designer (super on the whole) have their visual concept—abstract space with minimal real-life clutter. Summer before last, at first I was thrown by the minimalism, but Ann Lauterbach,[92] my date, talked me into accepting this shift. Which built tension, scene by scene, so that, when Lizzie headed up to the Murder Bedroom—the lighting created scary stair shadows that took over the empty "living" room—a visual triumph, so basic—and absolutely terrifying: encroaching labyrinthine shadows.

So the conflicts will start to heat up—rehearsals start Monday. Whether they're "open" or not isn't clear, "open" meaning accessible to the writers. Hey, that's us. I love rehearsals dearly—but I feel strangely passive so far, this time around. In a way, I want to go opening night, period, and not get involved. I've seen it through several productions, through the decades, plus its initial TVing. I'm happy it'll be done & done well, but part of me doesn't want to feel responsible for it anymore. I'll probably end up wangling my way into rehearsals, later on. Jack & the director, Rhoda Levine,[93] don't get on (i.e. mirror or no mirror). But he's a good theatre man—not necessarily true of composers (iffy for poets too) & deserves being listened to. End of opera scuttlebutt.

Thanks for the big V, so nice to get a snap of you—very good one too. I showed it off to Patty, who'd surfaced for spinach salad from basement archiving. She thought you look as she thought you'd look.

Finished off transcribing another Mom Journal, denser & with more

---

92   Ann Lauterbach, American poet, critic, essayist, b. 1942. Close friend of Kenward's.

93   Rhoda Levine, American choreographer, opera director.

going on than its predecessor. One page is really strong: bro of Joseph Pulitzer commits suicide. Her governess (referred to only as "Madame") shows her a newspaper account which mentions burial: Jewish rite. First, deep shame at "everyone" knowing. Then deep fury at prejudice.

I hope the back op goes easily for you . . . & that you had a fine V-Day!

Much Love, &
Happy V Day!
Kenward

Dear Kenward—

I hope you're not tired of me writing to you.

I have friends who write & write all the time & even tho I love them and letters I feel guilty not answering & when I get another letter I am cross—God, Another beautiful letter?

It's about Nancy. Somehow this could be a story, but alas, of course, I couldn't even write it. There is Nancy herself—& there is Your Nancy & there is the Nancy that makes me feel like a little girl & she is the kind mother. So God knows what & how I write to her & I truly am sorry to miss the next outing Friday to Philadelphia, the botanical gardens.

She wrote me a special note asking is she could publish (in newsletter) (without my name of course) my letter about the joys of Christmas (?) & the one about the best semester I ever had (?) & I was so pleased!

We have a new Tinker Belle, lady of 96 who does lovely woven colors of flowers.

What if my entire . . . what, Poetics? . . . becomes transformed? I have an urge to write about summer camp . . . sitting around a campfire on a moonlit night singing *Row, Row your Boat* in rounds . . . I never went to camp. Now I regret not having gone to camp & never being homesick or getting poison ivy, no crush on archery instructor . . .

I never had a nanny . . .

Love
Lucia (Laughing Chickadee my camp name)

NEW YORK, NY

MARCH 8, 1999

Dear Lucia,

Lizzie did good, last night. The opening went as swimmingly as is allowed, in real life, as opposed to hallucinatory kid dreams of fame and glory. And I had fun, spotlit, first pre-show, from Row A of mezzanine, seated beside my crotchety composer, looking down at the huge sold-out (or "papered"?) orchestra section as the producer man, diminutive, cute boyish, and devoid of control freak attitude, made a speech in front of the curtain, quoting from Mayor Giuliani's proclamation, not Lizzie Borden Day (the Police Dept is having a tough enough time as is these days) but New York Opera Day. Impresario outed me as poet, got my name right, & Jack & I stood up, to much, much applause. I blew a kiss. Tacky?

For the curtain calls at the end, Lizzie fetched the composer & I from the wings. The decibel level of the applause, considerable to begin with, went up, up. Jack wore his customary red jacket, a carry-over from the successful German production two years ago. He looks like a bandleader from the Fifties, hotel ballroom—very Lawrence Welk. I lost my Byron cameo last week. So around my neck, a gypsy gold medallion glittered, a golden dollar surrounded by more gold, for a Higher Up in the gypsy hierarchy. Joe [Brainard] found it, originally. We used to play a card game. Pounce, and put up stakes—jewelry. Back and forth they'd go. First a duo bow. Then we stepped back, joining the line of the cast of eight, plus Rhoda, the director, and John Conklin,[94] the scene designer, and the conductor. One group bow, everybody together. Curtain down. Curtain up.

Second group bow, everybody together. And that was that. Opening finito.

The audience was so quiet & riveted as the Lizzie net tightened. 2,700 people in NYC in 1999 quiet & collectively riveted.

The Shakeresque set, a room, sort of, has clapboard walls, so it isn't "inside" or "outside," but both at once, with proportions askew. Not

94   John Conklin, American theatre designer, dramaturg, b. 1937.

3/08/99

Dear Lucia,

Lizzie did good, last night. The opening went as swimmingly as is allowed, in
real life, as opposed to hallucinatory kid dreams of fame and glory. And I had fun,
spotlit, first pre-show, from Row A of mezzanine, seated beside my crotchety
composer, looking down at the huge sold-out (or "papered"?) orchestra section as
the producer man, diminutive, cute boyish, and devoid of control freak attitude,
made a speech in front of the curtain, quoting from Mayor Giuliani's proclamation: not Lizzie Borden Day (the Police Dept is having a tough enough time as is
these days) but New York Opera Day. Impresario outed me as poet, got my name
right, & Jack & I stood up, to much, much applause. I blew a kiss. Tacky?

For the curtain calls at the end, Lizzie fetched the composer & I from the wings.
The decibel level of the applause, considerable to begin with, went up, up. Jack
wore his customary red jacket, a carry-over from the successful German production two years ago. He looks like a bandleader from the Fifties, hotel ballroom --
very Lawrence Welk. I lost my Byron cameo last week. So around my neck,
a gypsy gold medallion glittered, a golden dollar surrounded by more gold,
for a Higher Up in the gypsy heirarchy. Joe found it, originally. We used to
play a card game, Pounce, and put up stakes -- jewelry. Back and forth they'd
go.

First a duo bow. Then we stepped back, joining the line of the cast of eight,
plus Rhoda, the director, and John Conklin, the scene designer, and the conductor. One group bow, everybody together. Curtain down. Curtain up.
Second group bow, everybody together. And that was that. Opening finito.

The audience was so quiet & riveted as the Lizzie net tightened. 2700 people in
NYC in 1999 quiet & collectively riveted.

Letter from Kenward, March 8, 1999.

The Shaker-esque set, a room, sort of, has clapboard walls, so it isn't "inside" or "outside", but both at once, with proportions askew. Not "Expressionistic". There is a calculating intelligence behind this space. It is severe -- but, as structure, quite beautiful -- if seen on a wall in a museum. But, to live in -- no.

A long long window in one wall, the longest window in the world, too narrow to look out on anything worth looking out at. An opening in the rear wall leads to another space, undefined, with one portrait: the Dead Mother -- the only touch of Victorianism. A few armless wooden rocking chairs. Steep stairs project into this room-that-isn't-quite-a-room space, stairs leading to a door soon established as the entrance to the Master Bedroom, unimaginable as a recognizable room with bed & creature comforts. There, Father & Stepmother cohabit. The audience is infantilized. The door, so high up at the top of the stairs, leads to an out-of-bounds nothingness, from which one hears the stepmother's voice tra-laing, hectoring. The stairs are the longest stairs in the world, to or from Hell? Good question.

The stage lighting keeps shifting. Shadows materialize & vanish, so subtly, one doesn't ever notice the imperceptable changes of color and darkness. Nothing is blatant, overtly surreal. The structural minimalism bespeaks rectitude, but the rectitude has been dehumanized, is unhinged. It is like meeting a stranger, with sensible-seeming attributes and surface correctness. Discrepancies keep undermining this wrong first impression. One realizes the person is in peril, at the mercy of deep, artfully denied derangement.

The setting gives the viewer no recognizable time of day or night to anchor to. What is even more disorienting is the total lack of claustrophobic closure. The dreamlike space opens onto other spaces, perhaps like it, so the viewer confronts a sense of infinity -- an infinity of replicated structures that enforce unseen, totally internalized strictures. The family, four in number, become shadows too, at times, their human shapes projected disjointedly, caught in this pristine order, set in a New England with elements of familiarity conjoined to a daunting strangeness, hallucinatory and yet purposeful.

This is the visual support system, a concept realized with exactitude, that enables the opera to prevail. I hope so very much you see it, on the boob tube, March 24th, or whenever...

Much Love,

Kenward

"Expressionistic." There is a calculating intelligence behind this space. It is severe—but, as structure, quite beautiful—if seen on a wall in a museum. But, to live in—no.

A long long window in one wall, the longest window in the world, too narrow to look out on anything worth looking out at. An opening in the rear wall leads to another space, undefined, with one portrait: the Dead Mother—the only touch of Victorianism. A few armless wooden rocking chairs. Steep stairs project into this room-that-isn't-quite-a-room space, stairs leading to a door soon established as the entrance to the Master Bedroom, unimaginable as a recognizable room with bed & creature comforts. There, Father & Stepmother cohabit. The audience is infantilized. The door, so high up at the top of the stairs, leads to an out-of-bounds nothingness, from which one hears the stepmother's voice tra-laing, hectoring. The stairs are the longest stairs in the world, to or from Hell?

Good question.

The stage lighting keeps shifting. Shadows materialize & vanish, so subtly, one doesn't ever notice the imperceptible changes of color and darkness. Nothing is blatant, overtly surreal. The structural minimalism bespeaks rectitude, but the rectitude has been dehumanized, is unhinged. It is like meeting a stranger, with sensible-seeming attributes and surface correctness. Discrepancies keep undermining this wrong first impression. One realizes the person is in peril, at the mercy of deep, artfully denied derangement.

The setting gives the viewer no recognizable time of day or night to anchor to. What is even more disorienting is the total lack of claustrophobic closure. The dreamlike space opens onto other spaces, perhaps like it, so the viewer confronts a sense of infinity—an infinity of replicated structures that enforce unseen, totally internalized strictures. The family, four in number, become shadows too, at times, their human shapes projected disjointedly, caught in this pristine order, set in a New England with elements of familiarity conjoined to a daunting strangeness, hallucinatory and yet purposeful.

This is the visual support system, a concept realized with exactitude, that enables the opera to prevail. I hope so very much you see it, on the boob tube, March 24th,[95] or whenever . . .

> *Much Love,*
> *Kenward*

Dearest Kenward,

I am honored that you sent me the beautiful, beautiful Lizzie collage and poem, & the letter,[96] which should be published as chapbook itself. I have read it over and over. The poem is lovely, the shape of it exquisite. The artwork is delicate and dreamy and catches exactly what I thought most haunting about Lizzie . . . her lyrical tenderness, as when she protected her sister and especially that incredible scene, with language like leaves falling, sweet sweet, just before she quietly slips into anger.

I am so glad to have seen the production and then to read it again.

I hate this getting old and forgetting. That's truly now the only part that is unacceptable. I would have been able to quote your lines to you, for pages. Wonderful refrains . . . the father, damn! and Lizzie's so ~~beautiful~~ *fine* (*I have o vocabulary*). Magic, her beautiful visions changing into madness with such subtlety.

I wish you had thrown a pie in Beverly Sills'[97] *(Shrill's)* face. Or

---

95   "Live from Lincoln Center" presented the New York City Opera Company's televised performance of *Lizzie Borden* on March 24, 1999.

96   A letter too long, twenty-five pages, to include in this selected correspondence, but a detailed account with collages and poems of the *Lizzie Borden* opera and TV broadcast and interview.

97   Beverly Sills, American opera soprano, 1929–2007. Sills hosted the "Live from Lincoln Center" TV broadcast of *Lizzie Borden* and interviewed Kenward and Jack Beeson, as well as the opera's stars, an interview that was aired at intermission.

just soaked that unfortunate hair-do of hers. Sorry, but her deaf child is one of those sick details that please me. What a diva . . . she didn't really want to hear any of the other women either, who were quite interesting.

I loved the ambiguity of the father's and Lizzie's last kiss. This play has All-American dimensions of repression and loneliness and sin.

I love the opera of *Lizzie*. It is a real American opera and our American heroines are wild as Medea or Aida. Loved Jack [Beeson] on "America," all the sleazy places he mentioned! Our country! But *Lizzie* is so American and played over and over daily . . . women I taught in prison were Lizzies. Our puritanical sick lovelessness calls out for forty whacks. Oh . . . at first I thought that the ending shouldn't be there, that it should have ended with die screams, but the sing song childlike ditties were exquisite dreamy pathos. Perfect ending. The set was divine, colors perfect. [. . .]

Well, I enjoyed it immensely, was very moved by it. Thank you again for letter and the poem, richer for me now that I saw it.

It was so wonderful to watch that interview! You with that very interesting medallion and devilish grin. Jack was great, but every time he got going she trilled in again.

My name always has been a problem. My mother, from Texas, wished she had been an actress and when I was born she named me Lucia Barbara. *Lu-chi-a* as in di Lammermoor, Barbara for Barbara Stanwyk.[98] My Father got home to Juneau from Nome and said he wouldn't call me Lu-chi-a, but Loosha. So both called me their version for the rest of my life, with "little Lu" as nickname. In El Paso, and later, in Chile, Latins all called me Luceea.

My first husband and second both reverted to LOOsha form, which is why many old friends, Bobbie, Creeley,[99] etc. from that period still call me Loosha. Then [Buddy] Berlin, who lived many years in Spain,

98   *Lucia di Lammermoor* was a 1835 Italian opera by Gaetano Donizetti. Barbara Stanwyck, American actress. 1907–1990.

99   Bobbie Louise Hawkins. Robert Creeley, American poet, writer, 1926–2005.

and with whom I lived years in Mexico, called me Luceea. Since I answered to all three names in South America I never had a problem, so many Italian friends or opera lovers call me Lucheea, and Swedish etc. people call me Loosha. I love the way you write LOOSHA, and it sounds friendly and intimate, like Loofa or Mushy.

I've been a supporter of Michael Price, Dale Smith and Hoa Nguyen[100] for years. D.S. has been putting out consistently good magazines of new writing.

I'm still not up to par, not even up to snuff . . . In fact I've been up too long.

Want to get this off. Will continue soon.

All my love,
Loosha

[In the following letters, Lucia and Kenward react to the publication of Where I Live Now, *and Lucia reveals details behind her stories "Evening in Paradise" and "Let Me See You Smile." She sends updates of friends at Naropa University's Summer Writing Program and writes of a surprising trip to a wheelchair repair shop. Kenward reports of a new connection with the York Theatre interested in producing his musicals* The Grass Harp *and* Postcards on Parade. *The potential director of* Postcards *turned out to have known Kenward's longtime partner Joe Brainard, and Kenward shares details from these meetings and the memories they provoked.]*

CALAIS, VT
JUNE 13, 1999

Dear Loosha—

Pre-dawn, bird twittering starting, kitty bros rambunctious night chases, conked out at dusk, so wide awake at 2 AM, resolved to straighten outbuilding muss.

---

100   Michael Price, Dale Smith, and Hoa Nguyen, poets and writers, editors of *Skanky Possum* literary journal and press.

The NYC impresario phoned (answering device works again thanks to Ron Padgett)—where is that script? All he has is the *Postcards on Parade* CD songs + the "Suicide Rap," no dialogue, so he still hasn't a clue about the story. For starters, how Tim & Kevin meet.

So, finally, building on my one-guy performance version, I've expanded it to include "bare bones" material from the published version, which is just too dense to trod the boards. I'm a bit ashamed I was so self-indulgent, nothing edited out. The stuff "looks" OK printed, has page energy, but it would drive a theatre audience crazy, me too, all that verbiage. It's the poet's besetting sin, prolix words out of actor mouf. Mea culpa.

Finished the overhaul yesterday. Very satisfying to clear out the excess, which, at some points, allowed the remaining text to gather force, as theatre. Surprising—unexpected. End of techno-shop blah-blah.

Two naked molar places with implants imbedded have kicked up (gums) so I'm going to NYC to have the implants "uncovered"—but actually to find out if something can be done about the swole-up gums & soreness + slightly wiggly upper falsies. Such a tiny problem health area, BUT . . .

I've had to do a lot more leg work, household chores & town shopping, and I've taken to swimming in the pond. Which is the best part of the day—immersion. Mind tensions go away. Quiet wawa bliss. Sugar level down, normal.

Tomorrow, off goes the *Postcards* script. Fed Ex, and I hope I hope, while in NYC—I can meet with the impresario and the director he's thought of, whose name is Worth Gardner.[101] He comes from Tejas, that's all I know, and I wish you were at my side, to give him your Tejas once-over. Hope & Pray the new script WON'T cool their positive response to the songs on the CD.

Ron Padgett is reading *Where I Live Now*, loaned downhill. He's tough, and his advance word is: good stuff. Specific praise for the ending of the doc office cover-up tale[102] — Ron liked the hubby meeting

---

101 Worth Gardner, American director, playwright.
102 Berlin, "A Love Affair."

the cover-up nurse, and being jealous of all the things his wife & lover-cover did together.

The placement of the tales is, I think, masterful. Your Body of Work, by now, is so strong. Who else has a continuum of short fictions that hold up like—like Gang Busters—as my Tejan collaborator-composer Claibe [Richardson] would say. Your very own niche. In ancient times, Kathy Mansfield. Dotty Parker. And Tru [Capote]. But he expanded into noveldom, crime fiction & could write a good lyric—i.e. "I Never Has Seen Snow" (music by Harold Arlen, from their flop musical, good score, *House of Flowers*,[103] based on his short story about bordellos in Haiti. And Innocence).

You're so strong, I just can't read another word of Elizabeth Bishop—prose stories. Unfair to her. So I've switched to Ivy Compton Burnett.[104] My oh my, so good. Dippy Anglo tempi, very funny and droll. About a boys school, teachers. Pastors & Masters. Dialogue terrif. Like the story of yours that started as a play. Ach, forget its title. Your dialogue pace so fast: amazing. And so funny! Anyway, Ivy makes me want to read more Henry Green.

Poem accepted by *First Intensity* guy,[105] sent it to him really because if he prints you, he must be OK. Nice acceptance letter—Easter 2000 Issue. He'd heard from you (I dropped your name, in my send-out, congratulating his taste)—he was so pleased by that.

No boating, since CW left a week ago tomorrow. But walks with Patty, and solo swims. One late afternoon, I went to A Single Pebble. Chinese food. The owner-chef is a perfectionist genius, so all the dishes are amazingly refined—with crest-of-civilization complexity. I'm taking Ron and Patty for Ron's B-Day, Thursday, pre-NYC. Maybe everyplace has these rural treasures now, but I don't think so. Vermont, theory

---

103 *House of Flowers* is a musical by Harold Arlen (music and lyrics) and Truman Capote (lyrics and book), based on Capote's short story. Broadway premiere 1954.

104 Ivy Compton Burnett, English novelist, 1884–1969.

105 *First Intensity* literary magazine was founded by artist/editor Lee Chapman in 1993. Both Kenward and Lucia were published in *First Intensity*, but they debate in the letters whether her name, "Lee," indicated a gender.

only, attracts oddities who do what they do with great skill. And, so far, not so high rent that they have to package, and do marketing dress-up, to do what they feel the call to do.

I go into deep pleasure trances in restaurants (and sometimes in the theatre, at musicals)—rarely, alas—and that's what happened at A Single Pebble. Solo dining entranced is unbeatable. I don't recall the pleasure trances being as hypnotic if I'm with someone, unless it's a Love Trance, which is great, but distracting: front burner overload.

[. . .]

Now it's afternoon. Nice walk with Patty, this time up into the woods, where Harold has made walking trails, cool and shadowy from the branches overhead. A downed pine blocked us, turned back, walked uphill to Joe's stone. And back.

Patty looked on my computer at an archive list. She was searching for *Beggar's Holiday*, a musical (40's) John Latouche[106] wrote the words for, music by Duke Ellington.[107] The impresario who may (or may not) tackle *Postcards on Parade* puts on three musicals a year (book-in-hand, two performances, staged reading)—forgotten blasts from the past. I mentioned the Latouche-Ellington collab to him, and he wants to see the script, which at one point, ages ago, I revised.

Lunch of burger & local strawberries. Lay on the grass a bit.

What a benevolent Sunday. Must tidy up! I've propped up the Lotteria Bird against the Eiffel Tower collage my mysterioso SF poet-publisher sent—along with a beautiful collage now framed, and in the place of honor over the fireplace. I noticed its many Sevens, and the Zeros, formally, but didn't look for "meaning." Showing the work off to the Padgetts, finally, finally it dawned on me:

70, dummy. 70. Birthday present. 70. Get it?

Mucho Love,
Kenward

---

106 John Latouche, American lyricist, 1914–1956. Kenward's mentor and partner.
107 *Beggar's Holiday* is a musical with a book and lyrics by John Latouche and music by Duke Ellington. Broadway premiere, 1946.

Dear Kenward,

Truly exciting, all that talk of impresarios and directors. I don't like the sound of you worrying about being "self-indulgent." You Can't write verbiage, so don't go and cut too much. On the other hand, maybe I love your writing because you have cut all but the crispest . . . How good you sound, working on all this. Aren't we lucky to have this torment and joy in our lives? (I mean if we were baseball out-fielders we wouldn't be fretting about impresarios or points of view now). We'd be too old to fret about baseball!

Good news that you are swimming in the pond. Swimming is the best exercise for us. I am too embarrassed to disrobe in public, and a long [oxygen] hose gets tangled up in children, beach balls, etc., so I was looking for a lonely pond the other day, outside of Boulder. Got completely Lost. Down in a gulley where there are woods and marshes. I kept turning, randomly, thinking I was going west, toward the mountains, because what was disconcerting was that I COULDNT SEE A SINGLE MOUNTAIN. Finally I came onto a vast stretch of green green pasture with fifteen or twenty thoroughbred horses galloping or just standing majestic. Blue Cloud Ranch, which I'll never find again, alas. Took me about an hour to SEE the mountains and they had been transformed, pine trees and log cabins. I was in a place called HYGIENE. Old train station where tuberculosis people just got off and got into rocking chairs. I would have lingered but was out of gas and air, so it was scary long ride home. Sorry to write so long to say I never found a pond.

Then the miracle drug which helped arthritis pain did something awful to coumadin blood thinner. Was on the way to Joanne Kyger's reading when my nose began to bleed. Everywhere . . . looks like I ran around the room several times and picked up every object, bent over every book. I'm just going to put yellow crime scene tape around my kitchen. All the phone numbers got bloody! Hours in ER. They kept packing it and packing it and spraying cocaine, which kept me awake for two nights. Dear Bobbie Louise came and talked with me until they

Snapshot of
Bobbie Louise Hawkins,
Anne Waldeman + me
listening to Andrew
Schelling read his
poetry.
    So difficult... not
to hanken back to an
olden, sweeter time...
        Loosha

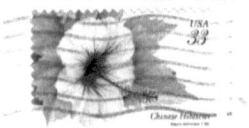

Kenward Elmslie
P.O. Box 38
Calais
Vermont
05648

Postcard from Lucia.

finally admitted me . . . Nice people but it was terrible. I promised that
I'd stay in bed so they let me come home last night.

So I have missed some good things at Naropa . . . Lee Ann Brown,
Kevin Killian, Creeley and Ondaatje. Joanne and Donald, Bobbie[108]
came to lunch on weekend before, lovely afternoon, with fond mentions of you.

Thanks for the wonderful postcards and the kind comments on my
book. Some people are finding it "tough" or "rough." Many shocked, as
I was afraid they'd be.

I adore Henry Green. I teach *LIVING-LOVING-PARTYGOING*
almost every year, but also Elizabeth Bishop. I've read her books over
and over that the names are worn off the covers. What I do is just start
at the far left and read through them all every few years. I'd give anything to write with her subtlety, or to be able to spell it, also. In one of
her books (a widow meets the man on the train from Italy) she is going
up the stairs and her dead husband goes up too. That odd remark the
Only reference to her continuing grief anywhere but still her pain is
True and present. I'm so heavy-handed, wish I were like Bishop. I'll
check out Ivy Compton Burnett.

You do know that Max, in *PARTYGOING*, is the Prince Aly Khan?
This pleases me because as a nymphet in Chile I met him partygoing
there, and he did light my first cigarette (borrowed for the occasion).

I can't tell if *First Intensity* LEE is a guy or a woman. Is nice, and the
magazine is good. I'm not going to brood about not writing. Health is
the project for the summer. Damn if I could only find a pond. I'll let
you know . . .

I like solo dining and solo museum looking. Nothing worse than
solo theatre or movie though. Getting lost solo was exciting. The Arabian horses loping . . . I could watch them as long as I liked and not say
a word.

---

108   Writers participating in the 1999 Naropa University Summer Writing Program, Robert Creeley, Michael Ondaatje (Sri Lankan–Canadian writer, b. 1943),
Joanne Kyger, Kyger's husband Donald Guravich (Canadian-American poet,
artist), and Bobbie Louise Hawkins.

Best of luck with your script. I hope your teeth are healed. Glad you are walking with Patti.

> *All my love,*
> *Lucia*

Dear Kenward,

Thank you for your divine cards. Been ailing and blue, mail comes and I smile, change my pace.

Met the very lovely Ann Lauterbach but unfortunately missed both an excellent, I hear, talk, and a reading. Went to one reading Tuesday . . . why do they have so many people read, and for so long? Could not get out of bed the next day. Yesterday went out in the morning to get new tires for my wheelchair . . . preparing for son and Grandson next week. Zoo, Ocean Journey, etc. Did I tell you about getting lost trying to find the Boulder Reservoir a few weeks ago? Well, this was lost on the Same Road, but in the other direction. Last time I ended up in Hygiene, Colorado, this time in Lafayette, hungry and tired and lay down for nap, woke up at nine p.m., missing her reading, also Clark Coolidge, Bill Berkson, etc.[109]

Today I got a map. Oh. The wheelchair place forgot to say turn on Spine Road. Weird enough to have a wheelchair store . . . only one with new tires . . . way the hell out in the country, but I took a right off Jay Road (halfway to Longmont . . . cows, horses, old pickups on blocks by barns) then took a left on Spine. Drove and drove and there, like something from OZ, an Oasis from David Lynch[110] was, this subdivision CHERRY ORCHARD LANE ESTATES. A convoluted maze of pale aqua two-story houses EXACTLY ALIKE on streets that circled around and around and crossed one another. The streets were named Cherry Orchard Street, Cherry Orchard Lane,

---

109 Clark Coolidge, American poet, b. 1939. Bill Berkson, American poet and art writer, 1939–2016. Friends of Kenward's.
110 David Lynch, American writer, filmmaker, artist, b. 1946.

Cherry Orchard Circle, Cherry Orchard Drive. My sheet of paper said Cherry Orchard BEND.

Now I had imagined a strip mall with Medical Supply store or Something but 5778 was identical to all the other ones, same petunias by the porch, big SUV in driveway. Not a soul in sight, hadn't been during all my circlings. Eerie. What are they all Doing in there? I rang the bell, expecting a typical suburban living room and housewife, but this Floozy in a 70's blonde teased up-sweep opened the door. "You're the one who called, thought you'd be here yesterday. Shut up, Rock!" The back half of the living room opened out onto dog runs, not with French doors but with an opened ceiling garage door . . . in the back of the living room were four cages with pit bulls in them. A chair and a computer on a desk. An astoundingly lush and tall geranium, about 60 wheelchairs, and of course all four pit bulls barking at me. "He'll be down. Sit in that chair," she said, so I did.

Wow. When he came, I thought, Oh my god this is all a front for some huge methamphetamine laboratory. Unshaven, bleary-eyed, tattooed, long hair biker type stamps down the stairs and says, "I open at 10."

"Well, it's eleven."

"So, today I open at eleven. What do you want?" I showed him my wheelchair, which I had pushed with Much difficulty, hauling [oxygen] tank also. "I need new tires. The bike shop says they're too old and keep coming off of the rim."

"All they need is air," he said.

"But he put air in."

"Well, put some more in . . . nothing the matter with these tires."

So I thanked him for his time, but asked him if he would mind helping me take the wheelchair out to the car. He nodded as if to say anything to get her out of here. I went out and waited by my car. He didn't come . . . so I walked back. He had opened the (real) garage door, and was filling the tires. I was quite touched by this gallantry. "Why thank you very much."

"Fuck, these tires come right off the rim. You need new tires, these are worn out."

So we agreed that he would put them on. He said to come back in the evening. Can't, how about Monday? "No, Fourth of July. Come Tuesday." But meanwhile this fiend and possible chain-saw murderer became Transformed right before my eyes.

In his garage were wheelchairs of all sorts . . . really complicated ones for quadriplegics, with computers that function, can make talk with a stick on their forehead, chairs run by something held in teeth, all kinds of intricate and sophisticated contraptions that he makes for people all over the country. People who couldn't communicate, much less drive around, can do all kinds of things, telephone etc. with his chairs. I didn't get much of a chance to look around . . . enough to see that he was a serious genius. The Real Thing. Wow. "I'll see you Tuesday," I said, but he had already gone inside and was shouting at the dogs.

The houses all around all looked exactly the same . . . I got out of there, took a left on Spine onto Jay Road, thinking it would get me home, but I drove and drove and there were No Mountains anywhere. I was headed toward KANSAS.

Did arrive at Naropa for their wrap-up Colloquium. Ann [Lauterbach] was great, gracious. I didn't speak with her, or even attempt to tell her why I had missed everything.

Did meet Elaine Equi, who I have adored for years, and Jerome Sala.[111] Fan of them both since they were in *Barney*, other LA magazines. So will hear Elaine read tomorrow, along with others too numerous to mention. It isn't poor health that makes these events so difficult. I think if I were Healthy they would really seem too long. Elaine said many interesting things about Joe Brainard today, speaking of him not as a painter or a poet, but as a philosopher.

Oh, I wish I were drifting in the lake with Willie, or on a walk with you and Patti. Shelling peas on the stoop. Canning okra.

Very happy that Dan (my youngest) and Cody, 6, will be here next week. I'm feeling lonesome, unreasonably, but family will help that. Don't you miss C.W.?

> *All my love,*
> *Lucia*

---

111   Elaine Equi, American poet, b. 1953, and her husband, Jerome Sala, American poet, critic, b. 1951.

Dear Loosha—

Happy 4th Update. 5:45 AM, cloudy, heating up already, though freshets kept the night air coolish. Slept good. Replenished energy.

6 PM—Ron & Patty Padgett are coming uphill to dine on Vt peas, Vt small red potatoes & chili con carne, Tejas origin, black beans. Farmers Market lettuce salad, dessert yet to be decided on. I'm thinking of Flan Mix, if I decide to contend with caramelized sugar top, i.e. creme brulee sorta. Tie in, read on. Traditionally, it should be salmon. But chili Tejas is hard to beat. Especially as the weather has been amazingly non-Vt—Deep South muggy, hot nights.

I seem to have stumbled into careerdom, a temp position I don't know quite what to make of. My niece sees it as a morality tale: patience, perseverance, reward system kicks in. Non-theatre folks think it's like all those backstage stories where the understudy, etc. T'ain't so. I've been to Theatre Hell & Back. T'ain't easy, McGee. And if it is: watch out! It's Slumber Party time. The above is my attempt to Think Tough, ward off complacency.

This starting gun huff-puff is like nothing I've ever experienced. Two weekends, ensconced in my deluxe room, Palace Hotel, the guys come see me. The guys are Jim Morgan,[112] started off as set designer for the York Theatre, off-Bdwy org that does musicals, has done two I wrote the words for—*The Grass Harp* and *Lola*, about Lola Montez in Grass Valley, Ca, her memories of past triumphs and amours thrown in. The pretty blonde ex-chorine who once was in John Latouche's masterpiece musical, retelling of Homer epic in American terms—*The Golden Apple* (1954)—& who kept the York Theatre going, died of cancer two years ago. The hardest audition I've ever done was singing *Postcards on Parade* for her, debilitated by chemotherapy, hard of hearing, exhausted. She told Jim Morgan—"not for us." But he picked up on the CD, as did the director he chose, as did the actor he chose. From "Don't call us" to acceptance that includes Steven Taylor 100%. That's Showbiz.

---

112 James (Jim, Jimbo) Morgan, York Theatre director and collaborator with Kenward on staging several musical productions.

Here's where the goings on get a bit real life "fictional." The first weekend at the Palace, us three qu——began to get along great, right off. Jim Morgan watched us bond. Doesn't always happen—theatre folk, uh uh, tricky. Various kinds of baggage. Complex hierarchy. Attitude that projects in very big barns, to the last row in the balcony. The actor confesses what it's like to physically deteriorate so drastically, you feel cut off—friends say, I know what you're going through. No, they don't. I screen out that what he's talking about is AIDS. I chip in with the anger I felt after Joe went—people's shy nice-nice gestures infuriated me.

The actor asks Joe who? Brainard, I tell him. Brainard. The writer? One & the same. As plot, a bit long arm of coincidence prone. Turns out he knew Joe, as waiter. In fact Joe, learning it was his birthday, got up from table, came back with one dozen roses. Some other diners asked: why the roses. Birthday Boy. So they get him more roses. It's a terrific birthday.

Joe was part of the time on his own in NYC, balancing nonstop four months of total togetherness with me in Vt. Had restaurants he was faithful to. This was one of them. Week later. I'm back at the Palace to meet with the guys some more re *Postcards on Parade*, which, the first weekend, Jim Morgan, surprising himself, committed to, April 2000.

It's what he's always wanted to do: new stuff, not just Golden Oldie musicals. And, a second really weirdo coincidence, he decides to do another new work—a revue of Latouche lyrics, very tentative title, his biggest "standard"—*Taking A Chance on Love*.

" . . . But now I'm taking the game up,
And the ace of hearts is high."[113]

That's always weighed on me, John [Latouche] forgotten. And his work was the best. Led to Saint Sondheim.[114]

Second weekend, second installment in the Joe-Waiter saga.

Patty Padgett and I pieced this together, the sequence, after my

---

second return to Vt. For many months, Joe knew he had AIDS but couldn't tell anyone, not a soul, as he didn't want to worry near and dear ones until he began to go downhill. So he linked up (still in limbo, closeted) with AIDS guys such as the waiter. Who wanted to go to Australia, surrogate for an AIDS chum, too sick to go back to his homeland. Joe promises him the fare, round-trip, just like that. The waiter, future star of *Postcards on Parade*, written partly about Joe & a closeted AIDS situation, goes to Aussie for his chum, who tells him not to worry about payback (impossible!) to Joe.

Actor/waiter comes from Cleveland, smokestack blue-collar folks. Stringency. He's never travelled. He comes back changed. Joe begins taking him to restaurants in search of the Best Creme Brulee in the World. The summer Joe took sick, up here, the problem was his innards. He couldn't hold food down. A huge malevolent tumor . . . so, back in NYC, he couldn't go to his restaurants, see his waiter pals who "depended on him"—typical chivalry.

Back to *Postcards*. I read them a bit of *Bare Bones*,[115] my remembrance of Joe. That's what they want. Maybe it's a frame.

To my total consternation, and I mean total, the guys (star & director) go for my "heavy" stuff. The suicide rap. What they don't go for is musical comedy window dressing I've worked into the structure to compensate for the far-out stuff I just HAD to write, but feared any audience would rebel at, unless they could toe-tap some, have "regular" amusement songs wriggling in their laps as a reward for putting up with the rough stuff. And because what good is a musical if it doesn't bonk you with funny words and gorgeous melodies you can't stop humming, plus cute guys and gals who can emulate dreamboats in action. I rest my case.

The guys want the work to tap into Joe more, Joe and me, and the loss. And that's it. It's 1999, and life is short, and they'd love to make big bucks & have old-age security, but what they want is a work, me at my best, not me conniving to create a theatre piece that sugarcoats the tough stuff so it won't all be too too dense, too "Far out." The audience. That's a mistake, I guess, like worrying about The Reader, like a fussy

---

115   Elmslie, *Bare Bones* (Bamberger Books, 1995).

governess. Imagined Deep Pocket customers who can come up with the scratch, $40, these days, for off-Bdwy—deserve a Good Time. Forget 'em, the guys are telling me.

Good grief.

Felt like writing you to celebrate Independence Day. Goal, what I needs must do—reconceive *Postcards*, my ornery independence intact.

I have a month till CW returns—the solitude now seems a blessing, so I can get into this headset, and let the needed words out. It could be a very visceral & affecting theatre piece, as the CD is, &, for whatever reason, my one-guy performance version—but with the work's intensity upped, pro performer at the wheel.

Exemplar is a play about a Donne professor who is dying of ovarian cancer—*Wit*.[116] Won the Pulitzer this year. It should win every year. Basically a one-person play, with supers (Doc, nurses) tooling about as back-up. That's what the guys want: one person & Joe, and everyone else a carom echo.

Thanks to the collapse of the musical as theatre (biz is great, esthetics shitty)—Sondheim, oh Sondheim, where are you, its savior & executioner—there's a dead area you could drive a truck through. *Oklahoma!* radiance doesn't work post-Nam. Sondheim pissy post-modernism gets him deeper and deeper into an attenuated "art" musical, more and more cut off from its primal energy sources.

Same deal (mum's the word, pretty please!)—recent Ashbery, Poet King. From dowser to drowser.

Lordy Lord, enough shop talk. Steven Taylor & the director (Worth Gardner, Tejan) are now in the loop via e-Mail. I'm still exclusively Snail.

I hope you're doing OK re Rocky Mountain heat, Naropa invaders on top of your regular school chores, & new wheel necessities. Loved the part of your letter where you took off, alone, what guts. Made me think of me, solo on a mountain rockscape in Nepal, split off from

---

116   Margaret Edson, "Wit," Pulitzer Prize–winning play, 1999. Premiered in Costa Mesa, CA, in 1995, playing regional theatres until moving Off-Broadway in 1999.

my fellow hikers, too much dope, chewed wad of hasheesh, lay back, forever, sky gazer, jolt of paranoia panic, lost, lost, silence, just—rocks, mountains, whole ranges of them, huge vs minuscule me. Struggle up, catch up with my party. Scairdycat panic recedes.

Any chance of a "Selected" Tales a year or so from now? Did I write you CW thought Babs Martin's cover[117] would be perfect for an instruction manual for Clown School?

Freaked out getting back last weekend. Newark Airport went into chaos worthy of Calcutta exodus from Plague—passenger zoo, two hours on the runway, four hours late arrival at Burlington. The system's so max, the least iddy-biddy storm somewhere—implosion strikes.

I'll get to stay put, till I get some *Postcards* revamps on paper. Very peculiar to have theatre artists so accepting of my words, more than accepting, really—hongry for MORE!

The Padgetts have returned you[118]—between covers—& both think you're terrific. Back it goeth, safe home, bedside support system.

> Love,
> Kenward

BOULDER, CO
JULY 9, 1999

Dear Kenward,

Twilight shining on the glitter from your great letter. Green sparkles on my shirt, on Cosmo the cat, and even on a bowl of cherries, which are disappearing fast into my grandson's carmine little lips. Writing this while watching *Most Disastrous Sports Videos*, 6 yr old Cody's TV show. He also likes *COPS*, for same reason I do . . . all the people's heads are blurry and everybody runs around backyards. Last night we watched *Most Dangerous Cop Chases*. One guy drove for miles and miles, in and out of lanes, running lights, up onto sidewalks 90 miles an hour . . . terrific driver. Cody was very upset that I was rooting for the driver, who was a bad guy.

---

117 Barbara Martin, book cover designer for Black Sparrow Press.
118 *Where I Live Now.*

When apprehended he said, "Well . . . bleep it . . . this town could use some excitement." I cheered that, which shocked Cody even more. (His born-again mother has already told him that her ex, my DEAR dear son, and I are sinners.) He is confused, poor kid, because he does love us both and I don't just LET him watch this disgusting show but watch with him. [. . .]

I don't think violence is bad for children to watch, but stupidity and vulgarity are . . . I am aghast at the dreck this child watches for hours every day. He and my son Dan have done some great things this trip though, camping out and hiking, kayaking. He is bright sensitive kid, loves being read to. I remembered that I really prefer to read children's books. Beatrix Potter's *The Tale of Pigling Bland*, best love story ever.

Thanks again for reading my book and saying nice things. I continue to get very negative responses, now I hope it doesn't get reviewed. I would like a "selected" from some place, would like to retire before my four years are up. Until I retire I'm not even going to think about writing. I just get mad because I'm too tired, have no time, etc. So I don't write, at least I'm not muttering. Since I made this decision I've become much calmer and ZEN-like . . . I think maybe I told you this already, well, I'm still in better frame of mind not plotting for a stretch of writing time, just going along in my days, and I do enjoy those days.

I'll hate to see these two fellows leave. We've had fun, laughed a lot. Dan is my youngest and definitely the "sweet one." Kind and affectionate, sentimental. So is Cody. It's a dilemma, being such a solitary person, don't think I could live with anybody again. But it's so nice to kiss people goodnight and in the morning say "Good Morning."

I loved your letter. Terrific news. It sounded like a screenplay for a forties musical, with great cast of characters. I am so very happy that they want you to do the writing about Joe, the most beautiful of your writing. It is a sweet caressing blessing that this work will have come out of all that you shared with him and the terrible loss of him. This is exciting. *Bare Bones* is painfully beautiful. I am very glad to think of you working on it.

Kenward, it looks like this year will be even better than last year. I can hear the crackle of your energy and I can get really corny with metaphors and say that it flies out of your pages just as the glitter did. Wonder if it is poisonous? (glitter) I'd love to shake it over Cosmo every day.

Next morning: We're off to the Boulder reservoir, which I didn't find the day I was looking for it, but did find when I got lost on the wheelchair day. I went to pick up my new wheels. The man really fascinating. Dog food and dog poop all over because, in addition to the caged pit bulls, he has a 6-month-old Great Dane, already huge. While I was waiting for the man to write up an invoice (His first attempt on new computer and, No he didn't want any help) the puppy got a grip on the stairway carpet and yanked it so hard it all came loose, so that one can only slide down from upstairs. That was cool, the man said, he'd have to get rid of this carpet anyway.

Ok, we're ready to go. Do have to say Dan pushed me around in the wheelchair at children's museum, aquarium, etc. I HATE it.

Where are Viv and Willie?

> *All my love,*
> *Loosha*

[The following letter from Kenward became one he edited and read publicly in several venues. I read the abbreviated version of this letter at his 75th birthday celebration at the Poetry Project in 2004. The revised "Vermont Letter to Loosha" (296) was also part of Kenward's musical revue, Lingo-Land, in 2005.]

CALAIS, VT
JULY 11, 1999

Dear Loosha—

It's midnight, insomnia time. Stars are out. Absolutely still. There's a tiny dead bat on the front porch—invaded the downstairs a few nights ago, swooping its way around and around, much to the delight of [cats] Rilke and Satie—repeated lunges, as it nestled high up on a wall. Mystery demise. Found it on the bedroom floor, scooped it up, still quivering, hoped it'd fly away from the porch.

I've been turning into a couchless couch 'tater, watching cable movie after cable movie. Today the remote went on the blink, mid-prison movie. So I retired early, the Sunday *NY Times* a wonderful sleep-inducer—though it was exciting to read about Frank O'Hara[119] (museum show, LA) and about Joe [Brainard] "essential eccentric" (huh?) Frank collaborated with.

Patty Padgett is away in the big city for gum intervention, & so Ron volunteered to be my Walker—down the dirt road a bit, yesterday afternoon at 4, over some mowed field, ancient apple trees, to the path that leads uphill, where Joe's Stone is.

To the right, halfway up—pine needle-soft path, freshly gone over by the Mad Mower, Harold Camp, "prostrate cancer" survivor. Vermont weather has returned, cool nights, dry air days, blue skies, zephyrs—all the perks that got lost in the shuffle of Jakarta-intense mugginess and an exhausting heat wave. But that was last week, and the week before that. A twin-trunked fallen pine blocked this path, removed by Ron, who sawed its trunk into rough-hewn seats, by the side of the path!, low one for Patty, higher one for long-legged me. Ron and I sat a bit, and indulged in poetry biz talk. And some show biz problems of mine got voiced.

Oh dear. More "shop talk" inflicted on you. Claibe [Richardson], Tejas composer of *The Grass Harp*, wrote me, objecting to a few words in the "new final" version that will be performed next October in SF by a tiny, tiny company that calls itself, endearingly, Forty Second Street Moon Theatre. Did I write you—the director is most enthusiastic about this revised script.

Claibe objected to "lounge lizard," "halfway house," and "cutesy-wootsy" & the placement of a new song, never before heard—Judge Cool, a retired widower, sings of Irene, his dear departed wife, to Dollyheart, who has left her sister Verena's house to go live in the woods, in a treehouse, in company with her black companion, Catherine Creek, and her teen-age nephew, Collin. The Judge is drawn to Dollyheart, as they settle down to sleep. Claibe worried: why would he sing about Irene to Dollyheart?

119   Frank O'Hara, American poet, playwright, art critic, and curator at the Museum of Modern Art, 1926–1966. Friend of Kenward's.

Answer: tendrils of intimacy. Trust. Sharing the baggage—his past: a breakthrough. I *never* write this way, figuring out "motivation" ahead of time. So, to justify my words to Outsiders, I make it up, the motivation, but something in me regards it as a really foolish way of thinking. But to others, actors especially, it's a safety net.

This is the dark side of writing words for musicals—justifying everything. I'm an unashamed word hedonist. I love a word, phrase, paragraph, I stick it in. And then I needs must explain the why. Weird.

[. . .]

Anyway, the new CD of *The Grass Harp* arrived (sent by Claibe, the composer) & I hope to listen to it tonight. Bill Corbett, a fan of the LP, is coming over with Bev, his wife, and I'm taking them out, with Ron, bereft of Patty, to a topnotch eatery. I just don't dare listen to it alone. CDs of old LP "cast albums" always add bonuses—this CD tacks on two songs from another album, songs that got dumped from the Bdwy version. Ever heard Elaine Stritch[120] sing? She has a great vibrato-free cutting-edge "belt" voice that zings a mile-a-minute past inner ear barriers. I'm very curious to hear the remix of her "I Trust the Wrong People."

First time out with Steven [Taylor], Poetry Project, he sang it, guitar accompaniment gem-like simple. Made Allen [Ginsberg] weep. Me too, almost.

It's Doc Week for me. Results of last week blood-tests. That's tomorrow. Then colon videoing—drink awful sludge the day before. That's Thursday. Then the skin lady too. More cancer fear, all those youth years baking. Ron insisted on going with me for the colon thing. What a pal. Two years ago: some polyps got snipped, otherwise fine. My Mom died of it—at 48, and her bro. Genetics. So lucky, so far.

Starting to get restless, solo. Month went by blissfully stress-free. Another month to go.

CW another quandary. He's there, then he's not. So hard for him to give up enticing possibilities, saddled with "a relationship." Hard work for me, too—most days, "us" getting through the day without drop-offs

---

120 Elaine Stritch, American singer, actress, 1925–2014. Played Baby Love in *The Grass Harp* on Broadway in 1966.

& black holes I'm not used to. He's a kid. Rebellious! His Basics fine. Very smart, Starveling heart.

Patience.

First Shop Talk. Then Relationship Crud. Some letter!!! Particularly after your last—extraordinary hallucinogenic realism of the expedition to the wheelchair freakhead genius. It's a new story, I hope. Lift off force, off the page.

Last week, rustled up a memory work for a submission request from a nicely done mag—*Fence*, deadline "now." Haven't heard back, so—

A) Maybe the fax didn't make it there.

B) Contents too "raw."

I'll let it set awhile, and if it holds up, send it your way

To complete the Walk Loop. After the level pine-needle stretch, the path meanders down, harder walking, onto a property line cleared area, where snowmobiles turn in from the road, in winter. Level back on the road, uphill to the Padgett manse, and then, steepish, uphill to Home. 40 minutes.

Walk Date this morning with Ron—9 AM.

Still not sleepy.

Hope you're having a good time with your kiddies. Do you have a CD player? Claibe sez I'll get a bunch—& I want to send you one, so you can listen to "The Babylove Show," in particular, but also Elaine Stritch, and Barbara Cook[121] singing "Chain of Love."

Love,
Kenward

BOULDER, CO
JULY 15, 1999

Dear Kenward,

Beautiful letter, the starlit night with bat and walk with Ron in the woods.

Hope all the tests came out fine and that you are well. I had hoped to get strong and fit this summer but didn't. Do yoga and stretching for an hour but anything strenuous gets to my back, sends me to bed

---

121   Barbara Cook, American singer, actress, 1927–2017. Played Dolly Heart in *The Grass Harp* on Broadway.

again. Just about everything seem too tiring to contemplate. Seriously working on this problem, the shut-in blues. I would be in big trouble without baseball. Yankees playing today and tomorrow on TV.

Once I've written something (like wheelchair man), even in a letter, I can't "use" it again. That's why I don't keep journals. I can't revise or re-write either.

So now, to me, the whole *Postcards* project sounds like a nightmare. I loved the idea of focusing on Joe, but not at the expense of rest of it. And once you cut "lounge-lizard" or "cutesy-wootsey" the balance will be disturbed. Tell those people it is Beneath you to explain motivation or "justify" anything. If a writer has purity of intent to begin with, the right words will come out. Of Course the Judge likes Dollyheart because she's the kind of woman he can talk to about Irene. Tendrils of intimacy. C.W. Starveling heart. The quivering bat. If anyone in this whole U S of A gets *le mot juste*, it is you. [. . .] I'd love to just get on the plane and go boss somebody around in New York, defend your genius, tote that barge . . . oh that's a different musical. Well, Steven will get it, thank heavens you work with him. He is an angel. His play-ing and singing with Ed Saunders[122] was divine. He doesn't need words, just his voice can make you weep.

Yes, I have a CD player . . . will love to hear *THE GRASS HARP*.

Computer has died. Dear heart was failing. Let me print this page & then all went dark.

I suppose I'm not as down as I thought. It makes me perversely happy that I renewed the warranty! What a shame if nothing had gone wrong . . .[123]

> *Love*
> *Lucia*

Dear Kenward,

Thank you so much for *The Grass Harp*. I loved it of course. "Dropsy Cure Weather" & "Marry with Me," but most of all . . . The one and only and Divine "I Trust the Wrong People"—Elaine Stritch

---

122   Ed Saunders, American poet, singer, editor, activist, b. 1939. Member of the band The Fugs, with Steven Taylor.

123   Italics are handwritten additions to the computer printout.

is wonderful. (Have we talked about Mabel Mercer? I loved her &
Stritch has the true style & depth. Trumpet great too.) Super song &
"Brazil"—I loved already when you and Steven did it in Boulder. Have
played it over & over, dancing to "Brazil," which disturbs Cosmo.

Cosmo has become querulous & moody in his dotage . . . we leave
petty arguments . . . (Well are you going in or out? I'd appreciate some
consideration . . . Well, Stay out, see if I care! Oh so now you want
in.) He stands in front of (inferior) cat food, thumping his tail and not
speaking . . . I think we need separate vacations.

Good times & lyrics, *Grass Harp* super—those last songs especially
. . . Lovely lovely words to "Dropsy Cure Weather." I'm so impressed.
I mean, I think you're a genius, but it's so fine to see you & Truman
Capote together. I love his work, him. I've said this before, but still am
mad at how unrecognized he is in the American "canon"—anthologies,
college courses, etc. [. . .]

I am so glad I have people like you in my life.

Loosha

Keep me posted on *Grass Harp*—I didn't remember in time to tell
more people about *Lizzie Borden*.

PS *Publisher's Weekly* gave my book a rave! First review . . . may others be so kind.[124]

CALAIS, VT

JULY 27, 1999

Dear Loosha—

I'm so happy about your news—THE review. I know it's an awful
chore, but, next time you have Xeroxing to do, please, pretty please,
pretty pretty pretty please send me a copy. For some reason, I'm afraid
to articulate WHY I'm so drawn to your stories, as if that'll entail
proving I'm a really smart critic. Because I'm not. So it remains a private matter, this strong feeling for your work, connected to Chekhov,

---

124 *Publisher's Weekly*, March 1, 1999, review of Lucia's collection *Where I Live
Now*.

that much I know, and a blissful summer working on a libretto of *The Seagull*. Now they're on their own, they hold up like "gangbusters" as Claibe Richardson'd say.

You mentioned in a letter an adverse response, which just terrified me! I know there's very little justice re writers & taste & intellectual rigors & post-modernism & book biz 50,000 titles per annum etc etc etc—so I'm vastly relieved.

Your wanting to come to NYC & Fight For My Words has stiffened my resolve about *Postcards on Parade*. I've figured out the sequence that's been baffling me for about a month now—

A) Vast relief this kinky orphan opus has been let into a respectable home of risk-taking professionals. I owe them "everything"!

B) Having just read the published version, I was horrified at my indulgent word riffs on the page. Fine for reading eyes, but much too dense and meandery for a theatre audience. Musical theatre is such a complex spectrum. Space has to be shared. Felt in dire need of Guidance & Discipline.

C) Fear of being cranky, egomaniacal in front of strangers. I just hate having to "push" my work and myself, having seen too many pushers who have nada to push.

D) Hubris as writer. Proving I can satisfy others' needs. Tell me what you want. I can do that! Gauntlet, Tilt At Windmills Syndrome. Also, being a captive writer is a marvelous way to escape responsibility if the work ends up a mess.

E) Abandonment angst that dates back to childhood. If I don't behave, toe the line, please those in control (Producer, Director), fulfill their needs, I'll get rejected: just fate! Too weird & "special"! Back to the Poet Ghetto.

Anyway, the Producer may or may not contact me today, and I'll have to tell him I can't redo it, linked to Joe, his death—my dire reasons for writing the work are separate from the work itself. And must remain separate. The characters must be allowed to come to life on their own, not as phantasm projections of a Griever. OK. That's that.

I've been disgracefully easy on myself, the past week and a

half—haven't written a blessed thing. Movies on cable, and an incredible amount of sleep. Food gobblings. Focus comes and goes. Patty keeps me sane—we walk an hour, slow pace, just about every day. Harold Camp has made paths through the woods, so there are varied routes. A boondocks version of Proust. The way to Joe's Stone in the upper pasture—that's where we went this morning. My legs worked OK. The ledge where Joe and I (and Anne Waldman etc etc etc) used to sit and smoke pot & look at the sunset, can't find it. Pines have grown up, so the view of the mountains is cut off.

Dinner downhill with the P's last night. Ron is a tennis maniac, midsummer tournament (doubles) has kicked in. So far, he & pardner have won two matches. Patty, trying to help me lose weight, served a sensible meal: chicken breast, tarragon from my plot, salad and string beans from their garden plus a few small potatoes, and a round eggplant (like a sports ball Mayans might have used) sliced, drizzled with olive oil. I'd brought it from the Farmer's Market, Saturday in downtown Montpelier. I love conjoining "downtown" and "Montpelier" as it's a T—blink and you'll miss it. Two blocks one way, and then the leg part, three blocks continuing on to the state gov't bldgs, the golden domed capitol, granite office bldgs, some redstone Victorian, with signs, ground level: BEWARE OF FALLING ICE.

The two copies of your book I ordered just a few days ago, Bear Pond Bookstore, had tooled in, so I picked them up, after stocking up on peas (just about over) & fava beans, and the round eggplant, and beefsteak tomatoes. One copy is for Vivy, my niece. The other is for Jeff Clark,[125] the SF Angel Poet who has adopted me, or have I adopted him, who knows—he writes me amazing letters, handwritten, with visuals interwoven—it's a little like being back with Joe (dreamt of Joe today, erotic stuff, so weird, coming back to the surface, and re-confronting the still hard-to-believe fact he's gone for good)—Jeff Clark's visual invention is All There. Did I tell you he sent me a collage for my birthday, with the Sevens and the Zeroes so artfully positioned, I didn't even get the point, 70, 70, till a few

---

125 Jeff Clark, American poet and book designer, b. 1971.

weeks ago, showing it off to Ron and Patty, in the place of honor, over the fireplace, wham! Am I dumb! Joe's work was the same way, the "point" artfully worked in—no eye clobbering or grand-standing allowed. You find your own way to the Bonus. Like *your* work, Loosha.

Glad you liked the CD. Hope you found *The Babylove Show* redolent of Tejas. And again, congrats on the *PW* accolade, and on your PC acumen & zip.

Much Love,
Kenward

BOULDER, CO
JULY 31, 1999

Dear Kenward,

Thank you for the Jeff Clark book and the minty leaves from the forest? Your garden? I already like Jeff Clark, just from what you have to told me, (the collage, his letters) look forward to the book.

Downtown Montpelier! One sentence and the little town is fresh clear, right before my eyes. Now I'll mutter "downtownmontpelier" as a soothing mantra, with the sounds of shattering icicles refreshing in this dog-day heat.

I too have been watching old reruns. *Dog Day Afternoon*, one of my favorites. I think I told you several times that I have Seriously stopped writing. Maybe I'll write after I retire. This has been a huge relief . . . I can listen to telephone bores without rancor, read student mss, and be glad that they are writing during the summer, etc.

Loved especially that V for Victory postcard . . . and also Beaumont Hospital, at Fort Bliss in El Paso. My mama was a gray lady at Beaumont, played bridge all day with one-armed wounded soldiers. All those El Paso years full of Fort Bliss soldiers. We used to hang out at USO I think because there was so much kissing going on, and once we got the job of counting the soldiers who came in. For an hour, I think but it was still very important. The woman who usually did it went in to dance with a soldier.

I am very glad you came to a firm decision about the *Postcards*. Oh,

I so understand all the a, b, c, d, and e's of how difficult this part of writing it. I THINK I have no self-confidence or ambition at all, can't sell myself, etc. On the other hand, whereas I couldn't care less about recognition or fame, I do want to be immortal! You describe perfectly the combination of fear and hubris. And the fear of hubris, the hubris of fear. Knock Knock. Who's there? Hubris? Hubris who?

Two women, not Readers, said they found the book disturbing and dark. This depressed me for days. If they had loved the book, I probably would have felt that I had sold out. Amazing how all of us fragile people are the very ones who become writers and actors.

Joe was one of those spirits who will never be gone for good. I feel love for him and never met him. He was mentioned at least six times the few times I was at Naropa this summer . . . in different contexts, but always as an illumination in the speaker's life or work.

For years after Terry (Jesse)[126] died, his parents and I would call or write to tell about ways it seemed he was There. Once I was writing to his mother and a Flock of butterflies came into my kitchen. My favorite time was one of the many times I drove by our old apartment in Oakland, top of a downtown tenement. Maybe eight years after he had died I was on a bus, feeling his presence so intensely . . . as the bus passed our apartment, I looked up as always, and the kitchen was in flames! Firetrucks, etc., bus had to detour.

Love to think of your walks, your Swann's Way and Harold's Way . . . I did read all of Proust this summer. I still prefer the "old" translation. Did you read *Proust and the Stars*? I enjoyed that. There were many quotes in French . . . I felt I could read French again, but had just read the English so often. I had been reading Shakespeare, and Hazlett on Shakespeare, but, alas, now it's time to be preparing for the fall and I'm teaching RECENT fiction. Alice Munro oldest of the writers I'm teaching, closest to Chekhov.

My Fitness program is erratic. I can go two or three day and then laziness and ice cream sneak back in. I wish I had a personal trainer.

---

126 Terry was Lucia's lover, written about as "Jesse" in her story "Let Me See You Smile."

The Padgetts seem to be keeping you in good health. Patti's menu sounded wonderful. You do have a way with words. I'll feel kinder toward eggplant now that I see them as Mayan footballs . . .

Peter Michelson,[127] a colleague, nice man, took me to the mountains, to Brainard Lake! Wheeled me in my chair over mountain paths. I'd walk when it got steep or rocky. We sat an hour by cold loud creek, quite heavenly. His sunroof was open. On the ride home, I got sunburnt on exactly half of my face so I look like a before and after picture.

Still enjoying the CD. Enclosed is that review.[128] Not really a rave but I like the last sentence. Everything about the movie stars is true, even the bill of sale stuck to Ava [Gardner]'s breast.[129] All I made up was the bartender, Hernan! The beach boys true too. Saw Tony in 1991. He's still driving La Ava for water skiers, still handsome. One of them now has a spa-ashram for $1000 a day. American women go eat fish and papaya, sleep on mats, bathe in the river, do yoga and chant (i.e. zero overheard). Huge devoted following. He, Alfonso, has changed his name to Love, pronounced Loof. He's the one that stole the woman's teeth. He did make pre-Colombian figures to sell. Once he came running into our house yelling "Los idolos! Los idolos!" leapt over our back wall and kept on running. We assumed, as one did in those days, that he was having a bad acid trip. Turned out the federales were after him for his fake idols.

Rikki DuCornet[130] wrote good review, coming out in *Rain Taxi*.[131] Alas, I do like . . . need . . . praise and thanks for your elegantly extravagant praise. I truly value your opinion, which makes it even sweeter.

My postcard source is on vacation. Hope it is to someplace scenic.

All my love, dear friend,
Loosha

---

127   Peter Michelson, American poet, b. 1935.

128   *Publisher's Weekly* March 1, 1999, review of Lucia's recent collection *Where I Live Now*.

129   From her story "Evening in Paradise," *Where I Live Now* (1999) and *Evening in Paradise: More Stories* (Farrar, Straus and Giroux, 2018).

130   Rikki Ducornet, American writer, poet, and artist, b. 1943.

131   *Rain Taxi is* a Minneapolis-based book review and literary organization founded in 1996.

[In the following letters, Kenward writes of a new musical revue of the work of his former companion, lyricist John Latouche. He tells Lucia about their relationship and shares stories of other composers, such as Leonard Bernstein and Aaron Copland, to which Lucia responds of her friend in Chile, Felicia Montealegre, who married Bernstein. Kenward and Lucia talk about politics, politicians, and changing times, as well as reactions to their own writing. Lucia replays a substitute teaching experience where the poem assigned to discuss was about Lucia, as written by former friend Denise Levertov.]

CALAIS, VT

AUGUST 6, 1999

Dear Loosha—

Fast-paced daily round lately. One day so much swirl—I told Patty on our morning walk I felt like a Station Master. [. . .]

Today, CW & I drove to Plainfield, nearby, to a sort of 60s Hippie cafe, with very good fried catfish, and had lunch with Bill Corbett, unofficial Poetry Pol Boss of Boston.

Much remembrance of Rudy Burckhardt,[132] who ended his life a few days ago, by slipping into his pond (Maine) one night. A while back, Edwin Denby,[133] Rudy's buddy, ended his life, 80ish, same house, via pills. Bill Corbett had interviewed Rudy only last week, and the night before his demise, Rudy'd sat beside my niece, who, even stressed, looks very appealing & accepting, and somehow John Latouche, my mentor and beloved way back, came up. Vivy was astonished to learn John Latouche was short. Significant phantoms heard about ought to tower.

I'm thinking of John Latouche a lot, these days, as the four-person revue of his songs that the York Theatre has scheduled for mid-season (off-Broadway, NYC) is coming together, thanks to the dedicated guy, Erik [Haagensen],[134] who thought up the idea. He came to visit me,

---

132 Rudy Burckhardt, Swiss-American filmmaker and photographer, 1914–1999.

133 Edwin Denby, American poet, critic, and writer, 1903–1983.

134 Erik Haagensen, lyricist, playwright, director. Wrote "Taking a Chance on Love," a musical review of John Latouche's life and works.

for a few hours, back aways this summer, and I liked him and his "husband," gulp, that's what he calls his, er, pal. But I worried a bit about Erik being Show Biz prone. Wasted worry, turns out.

Yesterday Erik sent me pages from an extraordinary journal John Latouche kept, one summer, on Martha's Vineyard, when he was collaborating on a musical, *Candide*, with "Lenny" Bernstein & Lillian Hellman.[135] I'm "K" or "Ken"—and it's very odd to read about this phantom youth I have such a tenuous connection with, 40 odd years later. The year was '55, the summer before he died. I was 26.

Some of the writing is amazing, some lifts off into philosophizing that tries too hard to be "important." I was cordoned off, a bit drippy, concerned about not being "anyone," surrounded by very high-powered people, intensely competitive & clawing seductively, for top place every second, often in a beguiling courtly way. John's has much more "voice" than two journals I read recently—Elizabeth Bishop & James Schuyler, who saved their best for poems.

Erik has been to the Library of Congress, and to Richmond, VA (where John's relations live) to research his oeuvres, and gain permission from the family for the revue (no problem). I'm very touched that Erik's written me in such detail what he's doing, and seems to want to include me as a sort of heir apparent, which, in a way, I am. But nobody knows this—so I'm very happy about being treated with such forthright elegance.

He mentioned, lovingly, the "signature" work of John's that obsessed me (teenage years on)—*Willie The Weeper*, based on a folk ballad about a reefer smoker, and his doll, Cocaine Lil. It's a work I'll never calm down about. A dream piece—it follows Willie from rich to lonely to powerful to abject poverty and nothingness ("Mr. Nobody From Nowhere Town" is one of the songs) to a dope bash with Cocaine Lil that ends when the "dope gave out" . . . and he's left alone to confront himself. The music by [composer] Jerome Moross[136] is both quite

---

135 Leonard Bernstein, American conductor, composer, author, 1918–1990.
Lillian Hellman, American playwright, author, and screenwriter, 1905–1984.
136 Jerome Moross, American composer, 1913–1983.

sophisticated (one song is actually "atonal")—inspired by boogie-woogie. A gorgeous great work that is quite unknown. Bless Erik! He "recognized" it, and wants to use as much of it as is feasible in a revue which can't bog down, which needs to spin from song to song. Erik wants to use fragments from the diaries, interspersed with songs and dialogues. So smart! If the collaging is adroit, and the performers and direction adept—a tall order—this could be an amazing theatre piece.

Cool out, rainy, so no boat ride with CW, who has been really sweet so far. Tonight, he offered to make oatmeal again for supper, a ploy to help me lose a bit of weight. But, seeking variety, I've made a salad (cukes and local tomatoes) & a mystery dish from Susan's, a take-out vegetarian hole-in-the-wall with a different third world menu every night.

I gave a copy of *Where I Live Now*, to Vivy and Willie, who kidnapped it to Maine—and went nuts for it. I mean nuts. As did Willie's computer assistant. I have a hunch the book really circulated in that house. Tomorrow I'll ask them for coherent feedback.

So glad to see the [*Publishers Weekly*] review. *Rain Taxi* kiddies (I ate Chinese with some of them in Minneapolis) are so smart & caring about words, so you should get a very fair shake in its pages.

[. . .]

I can't end this letter without including a snippet from John Latouche's journal.

Lunch with Leonard* and Aaron Copland. Aaron more like a jungle bird than ever, but warmly reminiscent of "our eighteen years." Leonard told us: "I bet they've already built civilian detention camps for over a million people in Colorado . . ." He was disturbed about the Joint Anti-Fascist Committee still using his name on their letterheads. And similar chat. After lunch, back to his apartment, where frantic phoning began, in an attempt to find some housing in Martha's Vineyard.

Back home and slept an hour.

K. woke me at seven for dinner: [. . .]; we departed al nine for Jerome Moross's sordid atelier, [. . .] and he full of woes, as usual, but both looking very well if a trifle humid. We played bridge until 1:30, with their winning streak interrupted by persistent bickering. Raw nerves.

K and I home sound two.

About to go to sleep when a sudden transformation in K changed the
anatomy of the night—a thundering heart, a surge of archetypal tenderness.
The constant surprises of the familiar.
* Leonard Bernstein, ** John's mother, *** Jerome's wife. Jerome Moross
composed the music for BALLET BALLADS & THE GOLDEN APPLE.

Hope your August is a breeze with no fan meows necessary.

Love,
Kenward

BOULDER, CO
AUGUST 16, 1999

Dear Kenward—

Note to say hello. Out of postcards & my computer screen faded
away with a slight hissing sound. It's in the shop with many hours of
lectures, syllabi, etc. that I need for school—inside of it, still I hope.

I love it when you talk SHOW BIZ! The revue of John Latouche's
work sounds terrific. *Willie the Weeper!* I don't know his work but loved
hearing about him & reading the exerpt (I can't seem to spell today.)
Gorgeous line about the surge of archetypal tenderness, "The constant
surprises of the familiar" will keep me happy for weeks.

I knew Leonard's wife Felicia Montealegre[137]—although name then
was Cohn. In 1946—in Santiago. Her father was my father's predecessor in American Smelting & Refining Co (Guggenheim one of buyers).
Chile was such a new world for me. She gave me very sage (& snobbish) advice about how to behave, who to know. Actually it was very
good advice. Because of her I entered Chilean & English society instead
of sticking with US Embassy & military kids, & I learned a great deal
as a result. Leonard B perfect husband for her—gave her exactly what
she wanted most!

[. . .]

Saw Anne & Andrew at a party Saturday.[138] They both seemed

---

137 Felicia Cohn Montealegre, Chilean actress, 1922–1978. Married to Leonard
Bernstein. Friend of Lucia's in Chile.
138 Anne Waldman, American poet, b. 1945. Close friend of Kenward's and

nested, sunburnt & glorious, had been camping. This is the week when we have meteor showers. I set my clock for 1 AM, went out, with Cosmo. Sure enough shooting stars all over the sky. Anne asked if I had heard from you—and to send her love if I wrote to you.

I'll stop. I can't read my writing.

P.S. Lovely for you I imagine to come across yourself in those journals. I have to tell you of bizarre experience I had: When I lived in New York with jazz musician husband,[139] our upstairs neighbors in Greenwich Street (downtown) loft were Denise Levertov & Mitch Goodman.[140] Denise I were close close friends—we all were. She tried to talk me out of romance with Buddy Berlin &, when I eloped with him to Acapulco, she refused to speak or write to me. Many years later, after Buddy & I were divorced—in Albuquerque, N. Mexico—I was working as a substitute teacher. The class I was to teach one day was high school literature class & the lesson plan was to read & discuss Levertov's "Melody Grundy,"[141] which was an (angry) poem about ME! We talked about the poem. I didn't say anything about our friendship, etc.—but did impress them by knowing so many of her (early good) poems by heart. I had them all write a page describing Melody Grundy. . . . Very strange.

> *Love,*
> *Lucia—Loosha*

[In the following letters, Kenward recounts family money troubles and travel plans for a California production of The Grass Harp *and a Frank O'Hara festival. They both write of getting older and medical worries. Lucia shares the grace of poet Ed Dorn's failing health.]*

Lucia's. Andrew Schelling, American poet and translator, b. 1953.

139 Lucia's second husband, Race Newton, jazz musician.

140 Denise Levertov, English-American poet and writer, 1923–1997. She and her husband, Mitch Goodman, American writer and activist, 1923–1997, were Lucia's neighbors in New York.

141 Levertov, "Melody Grundy," *Poetry Magazine*, 1963.

CALAIS, VT
AUGUST 18, 1999

Dear Loosha—

Turbulent week. Fambly. My adorable niece, Vivy Russe, Maine artist, and [. . .] her day-trader hubby, who now heads three companies, the result, my guess, of exhilaration via Prozac + off-the-couch zippety-doo-doo—termination of analysis, a few years ago. He's a very eccentric gent, that's for sure, springs from Dostoyevsky pages, the brilliant blunderer, with a ricochet hidden agenda, due to familial deprivation, emotional starvation as kiddo + horror sojourn in Nam: saw human heads on fence spikes. [. . .]

This morning I figured out the Dream He's Caught In, and is driven to keep repeating the outcome of—he's the Victim, always, deprived of what's rightfully his (will moolah) by relatives, who fail to recognize his capabilities, try to force him into a mold. His grandfather, who raised him (parents were dead, auto accident, I think)—a Kansas City millionaire—disinherited him, as Willie refused to become a lawyer. His one sis, filthy rich, years and years later, offered him one million, which he refused. No tipping policy! From "his" share, she'd made multimillions in the ensuing decades, which she didn't proffer. Festering injustice. [. . .] Meanwhile, Vivy's bros, being guys, came into big Pulitzer moolah[142] (me too)—sometime in the Eighties, I think. Being a girl, she was left out, a 100% non-person.

Vivy is now caught in this dream too, has gone to her bros, and her mom (Cynthia, my nun-like octogenarian widowed sis) who departed several years ago for a slim & non-aggrandizing pie-wedge in the sky. Vivy raked in moolah from her Dad, a Cleveland baby doc, who left her his modest fortune. Then came Cynthia, who left her half her modest fortune—her three sons, the other half. This summer, my turn. So I agreed to up the Vivy amount in my will, promised to my Sis a decade ago. But Vivy wanted Willie included in, directly! Not promised! I said Yes, hoping that'd solve The Problem. But inside, red flag warnings

---

142   Kenward is a grandson of newspaper magnate Joseph Pulitzer.

went up: I'm caught in someone else's dream, Willie's, now Vivy & Willie's, now Vivy & Willie's and Kenward's. And not only want out, NEED out as, aside from my quirky fondness for self-reliant independence, I've learned what a danger it is to try to fulfill other human being fantasies of oneself. It's just about impossible to do. One's feet get so cramped. One develops an iddy-biddy, lurchy walk.

One is a child again.

All this Will and Moolah Tension is definitely against my religion, which has been, ever since I attained my majority, to create my own fambly, as best I could, and not feel hemmed in by tree diagrams involving corpuscles & DNA patterns. It works! I've adopted you, and great pleasure has ensued. No heavy-duty baggage to contend with, unasked-for ghost voices, burbling away of the same old wrongs that need to be righted, night after night. Edenic, our unstated, sensed boundaries, and taken-for-granted vistas onto reality.

[. . .]

The good news is the director of SF *Harp* has written me positively about the considerably revised script I sent him, so at least that's "on track." Can't wait to hear the new speeches, particularly a new phone monologue for Verena Talbo, who is now fleshed out, a "stick figure" villainess no more. I chatted with Claibe, its composer, and he backed down from his objections to certain words in the revision, and grudgingly accepted le placement of a new song for Judge Cool. I'd forgotten how rough-and-tumble it is, writing book-and-lyrics, versus librettoing.

Today came a letter from my one booker-inner in LA, a rather gaga guy who runs Beyond Baroque,[143] a cultural outpost, always about to go under, in far-flung Venice.

Fred Dewey's[144] his monicker, and he initially phoned me to invite me to a Frank O'Hara Fest, to read O'Hara. Gratis! Travel three thou miles, huh? It's ended up, he's supposed to give me a solo at Beyond Baroque, an exhibit of my Ott Woiks, and, to rake in plane fare to L.A.-for-two via workshop scam in Performance Art. Which, last time,

---

143   Beyond Baroque Literary Arts Center, Los Angeles, CA, founded 1968.

144   Fred Dewey, writer, activist, 1957–2021.

I enjoyed thoroughly, my shtudents were most varied & most apprecia-tive of my efforts to help them tap into performance energy.

I'll "book-in-hand" Frank's wonderful Grade-B movie of a play, "The General Returns From One Place to Another,"[145] as I did at Hahvahd, at a Gay + Lesbo student-sponsored O'Hara Fest five, six years ago.

Then we (CW and I)'ll head up to see a performance of *The Grass Harp* in SF. CW hates LA, loves SF, which has temptingly terrific rare book bookstores.

8:15 AM now. Coolth hath returned. Walk with Patty, then a post-card dealer, good eyes + a very nice guy, is paying me a house-call. He lives in NY, opposite Bennington (southern Vt). Riffling thru postcards is my great escape hatch. Hope to find some to wing your way.

Hope you're OK, Professor—facing up to Back to School. I've loved your postcard shower.[146] I know you're hard-pressed by groves of A duties now, so—forgive the above lengthy recap. I haven't even touched on Erik, the Latouche putter-togetherer, sending me some xerox pages of Latouche's diary, kept one summer month on Martha's Vineyard, when he was at work on a musical version of *Candide*. His collaborators were—Leonard Bernstein (music) and Lillian Hellman (book—dialogue and dramatic structure). He was so caring, & for-gave me my dumb youth-hoodedness.

Mucho Love,
Kenward

BOULDER, CO
SEPTEMBER 19, 1999

Dear Kenward,

40 degrees, with snow flurries! Strange day, anniversary of Buddy Berlin's death 2 years ago. My oxygen machine siren went on when the lights went out, total darkness, with ghostly pietas at every window,

---

145   Frank O'Hara, *The General Returns From One Place to Another (A Play)*, first published in *Art and Literature*, 1965.

146   Both collectors and lovers of postcards, Lucia's and Kenward's correspon-dence comprises hundreds of (often hand-decorated) postcards with individual and continuous messages.

turned out to be full-leafed branches broken by heavy snow, leaning sadly against the windows. Several new teacher's pets, who fell in love first day of class, came to help me get snow tires out of cellar, some other odd jobs. Big breakfast and nice conversation. Dear kids. She's from Liverpool, Kristy. His name is Yuri, parents from Macedonia. Most young Americans in Relationships affect an ironic stance, combative by-play (and fore-play for all I know) but these two very courtly and courteous with one another. Sweet. They also brought up suitcase of winter clothes, so I have on flannel pajamas, am in bed reading student papers, writing never ending letters of recommendation. Taking break to say hello. Wet cat Cosmo just came in from the now pouring rain.

Hope it is gently autumn where you are, that you are not in N.Y. filling sandbags or rescuing cats in row-boats. Another student of mine is Seriously Mormon, believes that Y2K will bring Armageddon. I called him when the tornado hit Salt Lake City, thinking that this must only confirm his fears, but no, he said, "The Temple was spared."

The Poetry Project asked me to NY to read. I was so pleased. Thanks to you I could even have afforded the trip . . . Made reservations with train, hotels, arrangements for oxygen etc . . . At least I learned it was Feasible. And not so daunting now that I use the walker. It would have been Dec 15. I had to cancel though. Last two weeks of school I'm there all day every day for theses defenses, which usually puts me in bed for a week . . . I'm scared I couldn't handle it physically.

More important though is that Ed Dorn is very ill. Of course he has been for years now ever since diagnosis and projected few months. Please don't mention this to anyone. It is strictly my evaluation of situation. Both of them continue to make plans for spring and for when he is feeling better and strong. I think Jenny might need me around in next few months. Well anyway I'm not going. Maybe at spring break. REMIND ME AGAIN when it is that you go to California . . . I also could catch your act and visit my family. Now that I have looked into train travel I'm not so daunted. I do want to go to New York. I could even go to the Thursday group[147] with Nancy! See you in situ!

---

147   The Tinker Association meeting.

I hope I didn't offend you, talking about $, etc. That is such an awkward subject . . . I may have seemed ungrateful or uncouth.

Nice dusty smell and clanking sounds. The radiators came on. I've been using them as desks. better go move things off and get back to work. I just wanted to tell you how happy I was thinking that I was going to see you.

> *Love,*
> *Lucia*

NEW YORK, NY

OCTOBER 22, 1999

Dear Loosha—

Back in NYC. I wake up, so far, thinking I'm in Vermont—the city noises transplanted to country road, still woods. Alarum! Disorientation! So I am nowhar. Uncentered, but gaining, as Harold Camp'd say.

Weird, the annual packing up and out and the unpacking: reassembling this-goes-here, this-goes-there, reforming a norm. The drive to NYC in Jack [Graves]'s van was E-Z-Come-E-Z-Go. We left a tad after 7, arrived home by 3, CW in a state from no pitstops for ciggies. *Friendly's* breakfast only halt.

Last night, home-cooked dinner with Ron and Pat Padgett in their teensy apartment. Ron has a mysterious Balkan connection, one trip to Albania, one to Bulgaria. Their Bulgarian lady guide is travelling through the US—a bit brusque-honest ("too small": her verdict re their apartment). Ron ebullient about showing her the city: Staten Isle ferry, etc. Ron had an awful time finding me Beyond Baroque flyer re my gig, unseen by me.

So we talked about the Special Place problem. You put the essential paper in the Special Place. But where is the Special Place when you need it? The flyer is great, as my mug is bigger than Kenneth Koch's,[148] which will give him a red-faced envy attack—he's a maniacal fame buff,

---

148 Kenneth Koch, American poet and playwright, 1925–2002. Mentor and friend of Kenward's.

and I'm supposed to be relegated to obscure Permanent Neglectoid Status on the postage-stamp sized Poet Dance Floor.

Tee Hee.

Patty made chili, avocado slices, salad, creme caramel for dessert, and lemon macaroons. Which regurged me of one of perhaps two childhood jokes I remember:

There were two sisters who shared the same set of false teeth, the second sister asked the first sister if she could use the false teeth for a bit. The trade made, the second sister exclaimed, "Yum Yum. Macaroons."

Went over like a lead balloon.

I'm still in deep denial re West Coast jaunt. Tuesday departure? Diary sez today is Oct 22, Friday. Yup, Tuesday L.A! Diary sez so. Sez so. Sez so. Mild out. Patty's agreed to take me shopping for clothes today. No raincoat, no overcoat. Moths get at stuff. Need long pants. Look like a bum. I've never learned to maintain a proper tasteful rich person wardrobe.

Dark area. Ron back from three-day Ann Arbor fest for Ann Mikolowski,[149] died of cancer. U of Mich did right by her. Ken M, bereft hubby, may keep their *Alternative Press* (postcards!!!!!) going. Ron gave Anne Waldman high marks in Mich, got past initial career spiel, and out came the old Annie we know and love. Ed Dorn bad off, I hear. Hard on you, no?

Back to work, slide cues, music cues, haven't even rehearsed yet to find out if my canary chords can still tweet tweet.

Hope you're not swamped by Kiddie Work Load.

Made some new collages for lobby sale at Beyond Baroque: pleased how a couple or three or four came out. I'll send you a sample, post-Ca. *First Intensity* took one as mag cover, next yahr. Very pleased to be cover artiste. That show of Joe Brainard's (SF starting gate) will tool into Boulder, thanks to (surmise) Steven Taylor's Better Arf, Judy [Hussie-Taylor], 2001? End of Art Catch Up paragraph.

Very nice visit, last two days in Vermont, from the Archive Man.

---

149 Artist Ann Mikolowski and poet Ken Mikolowski founded Detroit's Alternative Press in the 1960s.

Steven Clay,[150] runs a bookstore in Manhattan, Granary Books, and brings out books too—two recent ones: a Ted Berrigan biblio (beautifully done) & a history of artist books (also gorgeous). He seems to be running impressed by my paper trail, & may continue being my Bringer Outer. He's skedded his poem *Cyberspace*[151] for next April pub—Trevor Winkfield's two-thirds through the visuals.

7:50 AM, so I can go out for breakfast. CW behaved like a really awful bratty teenager yesterday, re helping me re gig, menial stuff, like wrapping books to send to LA. But he apologized last night. So today may go easier. Ai-yiii—relationship crud! Wet Behind Ears Young versus Still Cranking It Out Old, what a puzzlement.

Mucho Love,
Kenward

BOULDER, CO
OCTOBER 27, 1999

Dear Kenward,

Called in sick yesterday, first time! Spent the whole day in bed, catching up on reading. Don't know when you'll be back from your Trip, but will send a few words while I have a chance. Nothing to tell, alas. Work way too hard, then I go to bed. On weekends I go to Denver to see Ed [Dorn], take some lunch or a dinner. He is truly suffering and Jenny is exhausted. Both very proud, stoic, continue in a state of denial, (which admittedly has kept him well for a long time now.) God, dying is so hard. I mean in the purely practical sense. People have been doing it for centuries but there are no clear cut How Tos or helpful hints for it. (I just wrote a whole anguished page about My feelings. Handy Delete button.) You know how I'm feeling anyway. He has been my friend, brother, mentor for long time. I met him when I was young and frivolous. He taught me things my parents never did. Honesty, loyalty, humility, etc.

Speaking of humility . . . I can just imagine Kenneth Koch's Snit when your face was bigger than his! I once cried at a reading of his,

---

150   Steven Clay, publisher, founded Granary Books in Minneapolis in 1985.

151   Elmslie and Winkfield, *Cyberspace* (Granary Books, 2000).

because he went on and on talking about himself. The room was very small, I couldn't unobtrusively leave. I'm not making this up . . . I was so helpless and miserable I just Cried.

[. . .]

That CW! What a callow youth. He'd better shape up. Good thing you don't have a car, he'd be borrowing it all the time. I'll bet you don't Seriously scold him or tell him you need him to help you. Be Stern! No sweets, no porn until he cleans his room and does his homework!

I don't have my new computer hooked up yet. Apparently on *Rain Taxi* site is piece I wrote on Paul Metcalf.[152] I did have a lovely literary day recently. Lydia Davis[153] (one of my favorite writers) is doing translation of *Swann's Way*, due Jan 1, Asked me, honored me, which translation I liked and why. I like the old one by Montcrieff,[154] had a lovely time illustrating why, finding examples (cadence, simplicity of language etc.)

Critics raved about the elegance of the language in new translation . . . for Proust elegance was simplicity.

Otherwise I'm pretty dull. Your letters make me very happy,

I did have a sort of a fit last week. I felt guilty about taking that Tinker Belle money. I asked Nancy if she would still write to me and I could still be one of the girls but the $ sent to somebody who really needed it. I haven't heard from her, hope I didn't offend. I AM lucky to have job I love at my age.

> *All my love,*
> *Lucia*

BOULDER, CO
DECEMBER 13, 1999

Dear Kenward,

Ed died on Friday, the 10th. Not true that expecting it makes it any easier.

---

152   Paul Metcalf, American poet and writer, 1917–1999.
153   Lydia Davis, American writer and translator, b. 1947. Davis wrote the foreword to Lucia's collection *A Manual for Cleaning Women*.
154   Charles Kenneth Scott Moncrieff, Scottish writer and translator, 1889–1930.

I'm off to school—one last Hellish week.

I'm taking heavy steroid for back pain . . . so there is no pain . . . I'm just crazy & demented. Have to taper down slowly. I could beat Sammy Sosa[155] in Homeruns.

I'll write to you soon.

> *All my love,*
> *Lucia*

[In the following letters, Lucia and Kenward write of her retirement from teaching at the University of Colorado and her reception of a large grant from Z Press. They continue discussing their writing and their writer friends, including the death of Ed Dorn. They reminisce of lovers and husbands, and detail their daily routines and medical procedures.]

BOULDER, CO

JANUARY 2, 2000

Dear Kenward,

I tried to call you today, fortunately got the stodgy and rather disapproving machine, so I hung up. What could I have said? It's silly to SAY, "I'm speechless." I am embarrassed and feel something of a fraud. You already have Been very generous with me. Oh, well, I'll Force myself to calm down and believe that since you wanted to do it, I should just be eternally grateful, accept it graciously and with much plain old jubilation.

I hope I didn't sound desperate or worried to you, about retiring. Truth is I have less (Had less!) than $500 saved, something like $20,000 in retirement fund. I will be paid until December, since I'm teaching until May. Had planned to Think about what to do, and to move in the summer.

I will be able to think so much more easily now. It will mean the "entrance fee" to managed care home, or down payment on senior lo-income housing, whichever seems wiser. Or it may even just give me more time to think! What I'm trying to say is there has never been a time in my life when money was not a welcome gift, but right now it is

---

155   Sammy Sosa, Dominican American professional baseball player, b. 1968.

especially Reassuring, since I want my Golden years to be Stress-Free as possible.

Anyway . . . thank you very much. I had had slow simmer of "Oh god should I have retired?" going on at all times. Didn't realize it until check [from the Z Press Foundation] came. Yes, I should, I'm worn out and in pain and don't want to work. Maybe I'll even write.

I'm still pretty speechless. I will just send this off and go to the bank!

I love you and am very grateful to you, for the money but also for understanding me and comforting me.

> *Beholden in Boulder,*
> *Loosha*

NEW YORK, NY

JANUARY 18, 2000

Dear Loosha—

This morning, I have my first session at Eye & Ear, a hosp, across the isle of Manhattan, a block from the Padgetts; Patty insisted on meeting me there, as I might skitter away, to escape eye measurement, the purpose of the session. There was a time conflict, so Ron, same time, will be at my house, to meet the Treadmill, head on. We're all to have lunch afterwards, and celebrate the opening of Ken's Gym. Which is situated in the very room The Wolf[156] worked in, now somewhat tidied up, except for one end—a storeroom muss of old wall-work collages of mine, cartons of books, this-a-and-that-a.

Last night, I had a movie-date with Mister Yu. We went to see the Julian Schnabel masterpiece about Arenas,[157] the Cuban poet/novelist, one of whose works I read at the Phat Pharm, entitled something like *The Dismemberment of The Purple Skunks*.[158] Go see it, if you haven't. So rare—a movie with such natural emotive force. I can't believe it was actually filmed in Mehico—looks visceral Cuban. Aside from narrative

---

156 Nickname for companion CW.

157 Julian Schnabel, *Before Night Falls*, 2000. Film based on the autobiography of the same name by Reinaldo Arenas, Cuban poet, novelist, and playwright, 1943–1990.

158 Arenas, *The Palace of the White Skunks* (Viking, 1991).

drive, the level of the visuals is astonishing. What a genius this Schnabel must be. Mr. Yu, my new Reality Informant, sez he owns a chain of hotels, mixes Art and Big Money, gorgeous wife (idealized Mama in the film).

On the way to the film, uptown, he told me about Circuits. There are huge BoyBoy Clubs, where hundreds of this odd species go to dance & take Ecstasy, drug of choice, and form sex Daisy Chains—they all perfect their bodies at gyms, and rid themselves of all body hair, as I guess ladies still do, on their legs, and maybe armpits—smooth flesh undulating. Yu invited me to accompany him at some point, but I don't think I'd be admitted, a still corpulent septuagenarian from a different planet. As a spin-off, these affluent young go to exotic places, a Greek Island, four or five hundred strong, the club gang, for the weekend, and party & do sex and Ecstasy, same as back in NYC. Love hearing about nouveau decadence.

Another Computer Tutor (Yu) session Saturday. Next step: get back "on-line." My new laptop now works, though I have to master How To Print, so I can take it to San Fran, come March 1st, for the to-do—Joe's Show premiere. Six poets will read in succession, including me, at a gig. 20 minutes each. [. . .]

Now Loosha, this check-in-the-mail thing[159] was mentioned to me, and I did say that's a great idea, why didn't I think of that, except as we're friends, I perversely get tight about being pushy, because of emotions bubbling down there, so I'm off the hook as Generator, believe me, plus which there's a Z [Press] tradition, set up by a mysterioso Z Board poet, to deal with medical demands (the poet in question had a bad patch a while back, and nowhere to turn to for fiscal help) so that comes into the award, which is also for Four Star Deliverance of Real Stuff on the Page, a fait accompli, but NOT a breathing-down-your-bodice situation, produce, produce. It's a Fete Accompli Cash Cow Medallion.

Must ready myself for my Eye Measurement + Treadmill Celebration with Ron & Pat—we get to go somewhere to have lunch, as a reward.

---

159   Referring to the Z Press Foundation grant Lucia received.

I've slipped as Eater, alas, though still a lot less voracious than I used to be. Very aware of salt now, no butter or cream, smaller portions. Leave food uneaten in restaurants, bring it home. My "sugar," brag brag brag, is now normal—perf is 80—and I keep ringing in 80s, lately, never done that ever. Got out of control last year, up in the 140s quite regularly, 120 being max OK.

I sent one copy of *Blast [from the Past]* out, pre-Fla, to Steven Taylor, as composer-collaber, period. I'll get cracking this week—to be co-dedicatee, and not get the book from the dedicator, that's very slovenly treatment for which I proffer knee-bends and chagrined big grin.

Mucho Love,
Kenward

[In the following letters, Kenward reports from the opening of the John Latouche revue, and of the New York Times *review he says is sure to close it. Kenward describes the ongoing rewrites for the York Theatre production of* Postcards on Parade. *Lucia reacts to the publication of Kenward's* Cyberspace, *a collaboration with artist Trevor Winkfield.]*

BOULDER, CO
MARCH 3, 2000

Dear Kenward,

Called you this morning to chat about *Times* review.[160] Now I don't know the lingo, etc., but it sounded very good to me, especially the part about it being an argument for a full-fledged play. I didn't hear any of the reservations you had voiced about the production. Oh, and Latouche himself sounded so great. I felt like Cher, in *Moonstruck*, after seeing *La Boheme* . . . "I knew she was sick, but I didn't think she was going to DIE!" Not at 41 . . . that's the part I didn't know. As for "royalty," You know how much pleasure, even with the angst, this has given you so that is of no consequence. No way to PAY for your contribution to the production, or to his life, for that matter. I'm delighted that it is running, hope it goes further.

---

160 *New York Times* review of "Taking a Chance on Love."

Really happy about the continuing life and different Guises and venues and lives of *Postcards*.[161] (You are impressed, I hope, that although I still don't know how to get numbers on pages I have figured out the italic part.) I have a feeling *Postcards is going to . . . damn I shouldn't have said anything... now I can't turn off the italics, really get a big-time production one of these days.*

[. . .]

I spent all day at school. So few of us to work so hard on next year's admissions. Truly worn out, came home, tore off my clothes and went to bed, in pain and depression that have been ongoing for long time. Was struck by memory of how I have felt this low before, even before bad health. It's simply because I'm not writing. Well, any month now I will. Meanwhile I got out of bed and decided to write to you. Mostly because all day I've been singing "Yu made me love Yu, didn't want to do it . . ."

Father Haley . . . in Chile, young Jesuit who taught me Catholicism when I was 12 . . . I believed I wanted to convert, bad bad little Lolita I was actually wildly in love with Father Haley. First erection I Saw Happen was in a cassock! In the rectory. He finally told me that he didn't think my faith was true, that I should wait a few years. Meanwhile he told me a lot of other things. I asked him if a kiss was a mortal sin. No he said, it was a venal (venial?) sin. At least a kiss on the mouth was. But, he added, a kiss on the neck is a mortal sin. I, of course, couldn't wait to get a kiss on the neck and I do think neck kisses are much more mortal than other ones, so loved that part of your letter. [. . .]

As for Jeff Clark . . . he is truly a sleazy (in a good way) sensuous writer. I love that little book.

I don't want a romance or a lover. Do wish I had a driver. But would love to have a crush on somebody. I think I handle being old, fat pretty well . . . not really, more on that in a minute. But I would like to wake up with somebody's hand on my bum or to get Nervous when He comes into a room. I long to flutter.

---

161 *Postcards on Parade*. Lucia's reacting to a confirmation that Kenward's musical would be produced at the York Theatre.

Wish I could write about this without sounding kittenish or simply pitiful. You touched on it mentioning the "youth photo" of you with Latouche, so men must feel it also. Not regretting being old. But a particular nostalgia about once having been beautiful. I know it bothers me because I hate it when people say, "You must have been pretty . . ." Hard to explain . . . I swear it isn't vanity. It is that I'm the same, my self is, but I'm very aware of having lost that Power.

Still don't know what exactly I'll be doing, where etc., after job ends in May. I didn't mention that heavenly $ from NY to anyone but Jenny and my sons. I knew they would be pleased. But Some people get jealous, others would want some, etc.

I told Bobbie my retirement salary will be $791. Just told her, and said I'd have to make a lot of changes. Which I will. No big deal. I have been very wealthy and very poor in my life, certainly always managed. My sons were well-dressed and well-fed and I always had flowers and perfume. But Bobbie calls a few days later saying Don't worry, all of us are going to make sure you are all right. I love her dearly, but she's a horrible busy-body. If she writes to you, please ignore her. Reed Bye[162] called to say he has a few women who want Writing Tutors. Another friend said if I have to sell my car she'll do my grocery shopping. Another wants to help me set up a WEB site to teach writing. Etc. etc. My sons have all offered to take care of me. I'd never do that. I appreciate the kindness but I'm a proud person. I can't wait to be unemployed. I have years left on my contract. I can teach at the university part time any time if I want to. I don't want to! I want to LITERALLY retire, maybe write (I whisper that, I want it so badly). Maybe watch the Weather Channel all day.

Please I need to be always able to say to you I'm blue or lonesome or bitch about being broke even, and for you not to think I want you to DO anything. I hope I can always have this freedom with you, and you with me.

[. . .]

Wow. Now I AM tired and I forgot to tell you the main reason I

---

162   Reed Bye, American poet, writer, musician.

wanted to write, which was about Boris, the Russian cab driver. I'll save
that one for God only knows when . . . we have two more weeks of interviewing for new professor. My oldest son Mark and his wife Judy coming
next weekend for a few days. I can't wait. He's a chef. Both are huggers.

Loved my satin red rose Valentine.

All my love,
Loosha

NEW YORK, NY

MARCH 4, 2000

Dear Loosha—

Lay-a-bed, that's what I am. 9:45 AM, sunny out. Mind skittered
about, thinking up a "telling" acrid letter to the *NYTimes* critic that
trashed *Taking A Chance On Love*, though she squinched in a couple
of positive squiggles, but they were smeared by the tarry excrement of
the mal ton of her pseudo-review. Came out yesterday, and there are
some death-in-the-family type calls I should make to those involved in
the creation of the show. One part of the review may have nasty reverbs
that may affect *Postcards on Parade*. Apart from being mentioned in the
review as the guy John "fell in love with," the killer last sentence

1) Informs the reader of a song sung by a guy to a guy, romantically

2) Affirms John would approve of this, wherever he is—

presuming (subtext) it's really weird for a same-sex love ballad to be
sung in a revue, or, bottom line, in real life. As *Postcards* has a same-sex
chunk that looms large, I hope the York's Board doesn't clamp down on
Jimbo, as producer. I met the Pres, and I suspect The Board is as deep-
dyed Wasp as is allowable in our multicultural broth of a mega-power.
Perhaps a Queen Victoria type situation will happen. They won't mention "it" (guy-guy stuff) as—it's unmentionable. Just as the Prime M,
enacting anti-fag legislation, a first, sent Queen V, left out punishment
for Lesbians, as no one dared inform her that Brit Ladies indulge in
such hanky-panky. Guys, bad enough. It's a wonderful farce scene for,
sob, a revue.

The opening was great—very responsive audience, laughs, how great
to hear laughs at wit. The Padgetts whom I went with, loved it, Patty

Collaged envelope from Kenward.

all twinkly-eyed, and Ron, whom I sat next to, kept the laugh-track pollster part of my antennae pretty busy. Very quiet sort of burble, so you have to listen hard. Much too refined a person to haw-haw. They didn't seem to mind the "happy ending" section, where *Lazy Afternoon* is sung on the purported front-porch in Vermont, us guys, John and "me," holding hands, snuggling inoffensively, and singing this gorgeous song like angels.

After the show, a show-folks type party, kiddies-all-wired-up, love love love, who me?, yes you!, then onto the next clinch. The Padgetts were ready to leave, but I got spirited away and met Marge Champion,[163] whom you perhaps saw in the moon pitchas, gliding with her hubby Gower. She's a beauty, in her 70s, must be, just like me, I mean a BEAUTY, whose first dance job was in the [Duke] Ellington musical of John's, called (in Boston try-out) *Twilight Alley*, which I much prefer to its eventual NYC title, *Beggar's Holiday*.[164] We extended septuagenarian tendrils, so I hope I get to see more of her—summer place in southern Vermont. Ron was SO-O-O jealous! He was amazed how outgoing theatre folk are, having been sequestered all his life with poets and lit folk, who do not, ever ever, fall all over each other with innocent delight and appreciation of each other's very existence. Well, that's a woolly exaggeration, but show folks' total lack of tight-assedness is a joy.

Waste of time and energy to get upset at a dumb, bad review. Glad I'm 71, and have had stuff done, and have read really AWFUL pans of my work. And to know that the work, sometimes, survives i.e—*The Grass Harp. Miss Julie*.[165] But the Latouche review is tough, as it makes the survival of the revue beyond its six-week run at the York quite improbable. Other reviews may come out to redress this *Times* dismemberment. But the *Times* has the clout.

Otherwise, all is OK. CW quite sweet about my momentary incursion into the Fast Lane. Two-hour session with *Postcards on Parade* director went fine, some sensible revisions agreed to. I'll dive back in tomorrow, Sunday Day of Rest, and see how it goes. As Marge Champion put it at the opening night party, "Musicals aren't written. They're re-written"— and she reminisced how the cast performed a new song thrown into *Hello, Dolly*[166]—in ribbons, lotsa ribbons—there were still no costumes.

---

163 Marge Champion, American dancer and actress, 1919–2020, was married to American actor, director Gower Champion, 1919–1980.
164 *Beggar's Holiday*, a musical with a book and lyrics by John Latouche and music by Duke Ellington, premiered on Broadway in 1946.
165 *Miss Julie*, Elmslie and Ned Rorem, New York City Opera premiere, 1965.
166 *Hello, Dolly*, Jerry Herman and Michael Stewart, 1964. Directed by Gower Champion.

Yesterday (came at a good time, post-review, in the morning paper) I hit Nancy Land, the fabled Grolier Club, where the Man from Lazard[167] (who is fiscal caretaker of part of my boodle) is in heaven. His lifelong collection of Ruskin[168] is on view, and was commented on in this week's *New Yorker*. Nancy wasn't there, trundling about, stifling sobs, in the hopes of luring you back into the fold. Maybe she was to home, downing nerve pills, wondering what you're doing out there in the mountains, waiting for the daffs to emerge, having more fun than is allowable for perennial Wasp Landers.

Love,
Kenward

BOULDER, CO
[SEQUENCED BY CONTEXT]

Dear Kenward

Sorry can't sit up to type. Home after another Hellish 5-day week. This one with deep snow & scraping off windows, shoveling & none of these smiling people even help . . . just jog on. Heavy [oxygen] tank & broke. Cross patch. Draw the latch & sit by the fire & spin. So glad it is Friday I could weep with joy—& here was your book![169] Beautiful-inspired collaboration. Perfect. Please tell Trevor W. how much I admire his work.

The mood of it is just heaven. I've read through it twice—too tired to do it justice—will wait until I'm on vacation. Spring break next week. But even 2nd reading found more more amazing surprises & twists & beauty. The rhymes heavenly "kickbacks & (sic) Pax" "unmonitored & bunny turd" . . . Lord it is filled with riches. Dazzle & wit & pockets of sadness & flashes of almost Keatsian loveliness: "I order you to "batten down the hatches," "underfoot pure needles crunch . . . it's fall." Wow.

I'll be back to it more thoroughly when I'm not in state of pain & exhaustion.

---

167 Dyke Benjamin of Lazard Asset Management and the Tinker Association.
168 John Ruskin, English writer, philosopher and critic, 1819–1900.
169 Elmslie and Winkfield, *Cyberspace*.

Was glad to get your letter. The blurbs in this week's *Times* do sound good—sorry it's not running longer but hey, it was well-received.

I totally (college student lingo, sorry) understand your initial reaction. Same as mine when book came out. Fear I'd be judged for sex with minor,[170] alcoholism, the story about woman murdering husband,[171] etc. Was in total PANIC. My mother once said something to me, when I was worrying about something or another . . . "You know, people really don't pay that much attention." Certainly not to our sore spots . . .

My grandma said, "Never talk of money or perspiration." She wouldn't have even said "sex." She read the Bible day & night. *Song of Solomon* section cut out so I wouldn't see it. Imagine my delight first time I was in a hotel with a Bible! Especially since they kept talking about a man's loins & I thought that meant penis . . .

Letter will come. I'm glad you got it right about the book: It Is Perfect . . . & that is very very rare.

> *Bravo,*
> *Looshenka*

NEW YORK, NY
APRIL 1, 2000

Dear Loosha—

Happy April Fool's Day! Benign weather these days, as opposed to my status as a Fast Lane Temp. Handling the pressure, so far, without going bonkers. I move faster in my head, slower on stairs, on streets.

[. . .]

I did one naughty thing, a few days ago. There's been so much GET A FAX pressure, when the installer asked me for something to send, to prove it worked, I sent Clayton [Phillips][172] the first page of one of the sections of *Cyberspace*. He took it nicely. He may or may not have gotten the message—see, I not only do rewrites at your behest, I do this.

---

170   Let Me See You Smile."

171   "Carmen."

172   Clayton Phillips, theatre director of *Postcards on Parade* at York Theatre, April 2000.

So ease up, buster. He said the word "poem" deferentially. My age-old dream of connecting with a director who goes with my stuff, wants it to be at its best, looks like, is fulfilled. Rhoda Levine did *Lizzie Borden* perfecto, but I wasn't part of the process—barred from rehearsals, because the composer had a penchant for jabbing prima donnas in the boobs with his forefinger.

What really delights me is: [*Postcards on Parade* is] a bouncy musical comedy with a loss-of-loved-one frame. Clayton, again and again, finds the humor, unleashes it. Broad humor! The suicidee (Kevin) gets thumped on the chest, pops up, suddenly sings. The "loss of loved one" opening monologue has been staged with such exquisite force, I still can't believe my luck as writer. The changes the kid rings up are amazing. I added an IV machine, ventriloquist dummy device. The kid's worked out a whole relationship with the machine, which is his faux Significant Other, angry that it's replaced the lost one, but—it's his only love connection. So he goes tender too. With huge scary pauses. He's caught between "loss" and his impetus to get on with the musical he invented, to distract his loved one (dying) and himself.

The danger inherent in these pauses, of his going under, is excruciating. The breakthrough is—my text encourages this stylistic opulence but I had no way of counting on it. That's what's so extraordinary about the cast and director. What they do comes out of the work itself, and is gorgeously transformative.

Only one song shot down so far, *Seventeen Years of Living Hell*—where Stan and Valerie divvy up their belongings, prior to Splitsville. The cast of four have become very proprietary about their words. They banish anything into outer darkness that doesn't fit their notion of the person they're bringing to life. They're smart. Fair-minded. I'm enjoying the rewrites. I know the turf.

I've seen almost no rehearsals, sequestered at my computer. Yesterday, I finished the biggest remaining "hole"—taking the place of the lost song—using the space to fill out Stan and Valerie, a bit underwritten and amorphous compared to their couple counterpart—Kevin and Tim. It involved a new song entitled *King Kong Stan*, barely finished in cahoots with Steven [Taylor], before he left for Boulder. Though Fabrizio, the exotico boyfriend of the director, Clayton, found a techie, who came over—Fax installed—I still don't have a clue as to how to use it. I'm from another time, so I went uptown to the theatre to hand the scene, newly written, to Clayton, a necessary, to me, personal geste. I wanted to see him read it. OKed it, and I watched the end of Act One.

Knockabout farce. Kevin suiciding, Stan rescues him via mouth-to-mouth resuscitation. Drunk wife Valerie sees the same-sex "kiss," strangulates from homophobia, as Kevin's fantasy continues to unwind. Cheeky Kiki drifts about in a mermaid costume, played by Tim, his boyfriend. It's a hard scene to direct, the interplay of fantasy and reality needs immaculate precision & micro-timing, so the audience sees chaos clearly. The mood of the rehearsal was quite joyous-exhausted. End of the week. The actors seem to go for what they're doing. And Clayton has stopped "bearing down" on me, re the revisions. He's a sweet man, keeps his stress pretty much to himself. He has only five days to stage most of Act II, virgin territory. Not enough time.

Then comes "tech"—which is hell for the performers, costumes, props, lighting, and, worst of all, rather than the rehearsal pianist, the sound of the orchestra, rendered via synthesizer, scary and confusing at first.

This morning, coming up, my last biggish rewrite. Confrontation between Stan & Valerie, so they can separate, friends, but the marriage is ended. And then some little tidy-ups, and I'm done. Until previews, but Clayton's vision of the piece is structurally so sound—he's guided me cannily, shaping up placement. He can't write worth a darn, but he knows exactly what should go where. So I don't see further upheavals in the writing. But you never know.

April 12th—first preview. The preview audiences for *Taking A Chance on Love* were just about brain-dead. Oldsters tuckered out from a long hard day playing Canasta, and listening to their pacers.

One night I played hooky. Tribute to Frank O'Hara, five partici-pants. One was me. Sponsored by Poetry Society of America, ta-da, at the Tibor de Nagy Gallery,[173] which has links to NY School of Poets & NY artists-close-to NY poets.

I read three monologues from O'Hara's play, *The General Returns From One Place To Another*. I love doing awful voices, and I found one a good while back, first time I did The General, Harvard, a few years ago. Rasping, slow-minded, heavy heavy flatulence. I was first, so the audience was 7:15 PM fresh, wine imbibed. Don't know what I did, but the laffs came loud and clear, perfect volleys that started and stopped cleanly. I just hate poetry-reading titters. This was stand-up comedian response, best ever for me. It's gorgeous material. I may have picked up some technique, unwittingly, from watching the *Postcards* cast. Subsume the words in "character"—all the way.

Skipped the fancy-pants dinner afterwards. Headed home with CW, ate fast, next door, comfort food. He's been a pretty good sport lately. He carried my white feather boa, part of my General outfit, without that much complaint. I forgot to reach down and put it on, between Monolog #2 & #3. The response was full without it. Same night: the opening of *The Seagull*, old opera I wrote the words for, five performances, tiny theatre called Raw Space. Plan to see it this coming Monday along with the composer,[174] now an L.A. fleshpoteur.

Felt like filling you in. And wishing you Joyeuse Avril. Hope the Easter break afforded you catch-up time.

Love,
Kenward

BOULDER, CO
APRIL 7, 2000

Dear Kenward,

Fill me in? UP! So much going on with you. Delighted to hear it. Your letter read like a play or script of Hollywood musical, need

---

173 Tibor de Nagy Gallery, New York, opened in 1950.
174 Thomas Pasatieri, American composer, b. 1945. Collaborated with Kenward on operas *The Seagull*, *Washington Square*, and *Three Sisters*.

calendar pages turning. *Postcards! The Sea Gull*, O'Hara, readings.
[. . .]

This will get there just before first preview. Hope it goes well.
Sounds like it already is together. It must be because you sound so
good, and are usually very hard on yourself. I don't know . . . you say
they're really good, but I hate to hear *Seventeen Years of Living Hell* go.
Maybe it seems too spiteful? I love it. Remember when you once sang it
to me over the phone?

What I can't remember is when actual Opening is. Thanks so much
for keeping me posted on this. Kenward, these performance letters, or
pre-and-post performance letters are wonderful, and should be published
as a Something? Of their own. They are beautifully written, very visual
and filled with the excitement of the Performance . . . so they are in a
genre not literary. You're Describing what's going to be LIVE and on
stage but more than that is the undercurrent of Stage THRILL. Lovely.

Alas, I have truly nothing to write of interest. My classes have
gone splendidly but final papers coming in. STACKS. Mondays and
Fridays full until May. I move out end of May. Don't know where yet,
but I'll be staying in Boulder. I do have dear friends here, and Don't
want to burden sons, Can't be Grandma the way I used to be, etc. I
set Bobbie [Louise Hawkins] straight about her Assistance program.
Since then though . . . maybe I wrote this . . . I was very sick one
day, got scared, called her. She was here in minutes, was helpful and
practical, wonderful. Many other good people I hate to leave. Plan to
stare into space, do yoga and mutter for a month or whatever it takes
to start writing again. My self has disappeared. Please forgive my lame
letters until I'm back.

  Love,
  Loosha

[In the following letters, Kenward writes of the York Theatre preview perfor-
mances of Postcards on Parade, *as well as sharing a conversation overheard*
at intermission dismissing the show. Lucia writes of plans to buy a trailer in
Boulder to live in after she retires from teaching.]

NEW YORK, NY

APRIL 28, 2000

Dear Loosha—

Thanks so much for the birthday nosegay, gay-eye, whatever. Delicate, vulnerable, and gorgeous. Meant so much, delivered all the way from you, in snowy (?) Boulder. Once more, thanks heaps.

My birthday was a hoot. I'd invited Harold and Pauline [Camp] of Vermont, you'd better believe it, to come to the double publication celebration (*Nite Soil* & *Cyberspace*[175]) & also the show, way, way back when it was, potentially, a seeable show. Which it never turned into. It struggled through five or six previews, theatre less than half full, or more than half empty, depending if you're a pessimist or not . . . and expired, by mutual agreement between Jimbo, the producer/set designer and me. I was so relieved, as its audiences, comprised largely of retro-needy oldsters, went into deep revulsion, as a whole. There was one hilarious encounter, as I fled the show after Act One, when walker-outers had the option of rushing for the exit, en masse.

The Direktor, under panic pressure, turned mean & hadn't given my Rewrite of the Day even a cursory glance . . . and I was plumb tuckered out, so there I was, with the sprightliest of the oldster departees, at the revolving door of the Citicorp Bldg,[176] in the lower depths of which the York Theatre is located.

1st Oldster: *Postcards* from HELL . . .

2nd Oldster: Who could've written a thing like that?

3rd Oldster: Well, somebody must of.

4th Oldster: Moment I heard that car alarm at the start, I knew I should of just left then and there . . .

5th Oldster: (to me) Didn't care for it either?

And doggone if I didn't wimp out.

Me: The theatre was so warm . . .

---

175 *Nite Soil* is a collection of forty-one collaged postcards by Kenward published as a set by Granary Books in 2000, in addition to the Granary Books 2000 publication of *Cyberspace*.

176 The York Theatre is located inside the Citicorp Building in East Midtown Manhattan.

Instead of: I am Kenward Elmslie and I wrote the words of this musical.

After two days of cat-cuddling, zombie depths, I'm OK again. I've had to face up to the dreary daily round realization—CW is not good for me right now, need time to pull myself together, solo. He's impatient with weakness, and my old-age slowness. Which is why I can't take walks with him—he chafes at the bit.

I'll be Oky-Doky in Vermont, familiar restorative healing turf. I'm used to solitude up there.

So, off he goes to Amsterdam May 2nd, for three months, not two, as he'd planned. His Amsterdam significant other, A, is HIV pos. I asked CW to take a test, for his own sake (not mine, as we've always been companionate—he is sexually drawn to blackies—as he calls them—not old guys with big bellies).

Great sweetness, remarkable intelligence, and growing savvy about words, but something's broken there, abuse as child, by his dad—so reach-out from me is a toss into empty air, most often, or worse, threatening. And I'm no Fix-It Specialist when it comes to human innards. He can be relaxed and charming, and coheres with others, superficial contact. But bad baggage has built up with me, mutual withdrawal at anything innardsy. So I give up—can't win 'em all. Feel a bit cheerful this morning, three months on my own coming up. Actually by 7:30 AM, I'll be at a Coffee Shop to meet with Chuck, the actor who knew Joe, who loves the musical, and with Jimbo, the York producer, and see what they want to do to resuscitate this bodybagged musical.

Show a bust, relationship a bust, but . . . had a good pub launch yesterday where Ron Padgett is ex-boss—Teachers and Writers.[177] Nice space, kept busy signing the book almost two hours, just sat in a chair, load off my feet, signing and gabbing. Relaxing.

Birthday party was at Chanterelles, a marvelous restaurant where Joe used to take me, on Birthdays, so that was a tradition upheld. Nice Gang of Nine, including The Padgetts, Steven Taylor's ex (Lee Ann

---

177   Teachers and Writers Collaborative, NYC, founded 1967. Ron Padgett was publications director.

Brown) & Jimbo [Morgan], the show's producer/set designer (feel brotherly towards him)—show debacle doesn't becloud that—and Steven Clay and his wife (Granary Books), and Trevor Winkfield, *Cyberspace* chum, CW, me. Good feast. Closed the place—1:30 AM.

Have to pack up by the 1st.[178] So disoriented anyway, might as well do moving. Rattling around alone in a house has been my fate before, including with Joe [Brainard], who came to Vt. June 1st, left mid-Sept, no more, no less. I always came earlier, stayed longer. I'll see how I can handle the prospect of a solo daily round on a non-temporary perm basis.

Worked like a fiend on collages yesterday, and the day before, for an extra-special A-Z edition of *Nite Soil*. Mr. Granary thinks he can sell them for a ridiculously high sum, but in my kiddo days, Cokes cost a nickel, so did Juicyfruit and Dentyne and the Staten Island Ferry—so what do I know.

So, must sign off. Didn't understand last line of your last letter, ended up filled out questionnaire wrongly. Anyway, it's a tradition, so here a check, to celebrate you, on my 71st.

Love,
Kenward

BOULDER, CO
MAY 3, 2000

Dear Kenward,

A sad and confusing mix-up. After receiving the sad news about the demise of *POSTCARDS* I got a letter yesterday full of enthusiasm and plans and re-writes. Sounded as if you were, in fact, starting over with new director, etc. But then realized that this was way before the 70th birthday party. It was a letter written in early April that had only just made its way to the Rockies.

Well, I am sorry about it. But one thing I had never understood until the End. YOU weren't to star in it. I could have foreseen this result. YOU are that show and without you, well, I can't imagine. I also had serious doubts when they 86'd "Seventeen Years of Hell."

---

178 For annual summer move to Vermont.

DO console yourself with so much good work done this year. The *Lizzie [Borden* opera production] was wonderful, *The Grass Harp* a success. *CYBERSPACE* is exquisite, etc.

But it must feel lousy, nevertheless. Painful dialogue with oldsters in the revolving door. (I would have kept them spinning and spinning like *Little Black Sambo*[179]) (Computer says L.B.S. Wrong, mm . . . is IT p.c. as well as being a grammatical fascist?) You should have told them who you were and have been proud to say it. Peasants.

Oh, I'm so dumb. Especially about $. I thought I was sending you a huge bunch of sweet peas, my favorite flower. Later realized you probably got about eight blossoms. "Vulnerable" was a kind way to put that they were not too fresh. Glad they got there at least and that Harold and Pauline were there too.

I'm still facing another 2 weeks of exhausting school. Reception for [my retirement] on Friday, which will be hard, since I do hate to leave. I'm missing Ed [Dorn] a lot. All kinds of $ troubles which you Totally bailed me out of. Medicare says I have too much money. I couldn't pay off car because expenses etc. used up half of last Kenward blessing. Now can, whew. Retirement will pay exactly for my Trailer. Once paid for they can't hold my house or car Against me as extra income, so they will pay me a monthly sum. I'll bet you can't figure all this out Either. Just know that your gift was truly needed and how grateful I am. All kinds of weird things came up. Car insurance, car transmission, car registration, Home Insurance, continued medical insurance, movers, home inspectors, wiring repair. Plus the dumb problem of ALL my summer clothes, stored in basement, completely ruined by broken pipes. I'm wearing dresses that I had down-graded to nightgowns. They are perfectly nice, and nobody Knows that they had been nightgowns.

Well I'm sorry you're alone, but am glad you are so clear about CW. He is damaged and not able to care for you, tenderly, as you need to be. I think now that you see that he couldn't accept love either that you'll be in a way less alone than in that knotty Relationship.

---

179   Helen Bannerman, *The Story of Little Black Sambo* (Grant Richards, 1899).

Your birthday party sounded so fine. I feel I know and love the Padgetts by now and Trevor Winkfield I think must be great. Lee Ann and I have only been together a few times, but Really hit it off. I love her humor and heart.

Thanks, dear friend. What a tradition you started. May you live to be a hundred!

> *All my love,*
> *Loosha*

BOULDER, CO
MAY 4, 2000

Dear Kenward,

Don't know if this is a letter of compassion or self-pity . . .

Because you are such a Dynamic and strong Being, your wit and creativity generate electricity and movement, Your heart is so full of people and your spirit so engaged in the world, you seem very strong to me. You Are a strength for me, so I don't ever see you as being or feeling alone. When you spoke about moving alone I thought you were missing (Joe, always) and C.W.

How I could not have realized that you are feeling very much as I am right now. I am so confused and uncertain. The whole retirement, insurance, (disability denied me), buying A TRAILER? And boxes. After school I only have air enough and strength enough to pick up 3 or 4 boxes. Then I can only, on another day, pack 2 or 3. (And I'm the one to discard most of my things to Fit in my singlewide manufactured home.) I know people would help me, and they are going to help me to move. I did get upset about Bobbie and her project but she was only being realistic.

I don't know what I would have done without your help. Truly. I may have just thrown it all in. You have made it possible for me to move, have medical insurance and not be panic stricken. I was too proud (Bobbie says a control freak) to accept alms from Boulderites. I feel your generosity and love is so unconditional that I can accept it with gratitude and much relief. I wouldn't have asked for it, but now can't see what I would have done without it.

But the alone part . . .

It's not that I need physical help. Well, sometimes I do, but I can't ask. I'm working on this. I know that if I really NEED anything there are dear friends here who would help me. Like Bobbie, when I fainted.

I want to check the world and the day out with somebody.

I want to be able to look up from reading the paper and ask, "What do you think about the Cuban kid?" Or, oh god a million things a day, decisions and confusions. Minor ones, really. Is that bird a finch?

I want a companionable silence.

Well, I packed my Trollope this morning, and thought of you packing up for the country. We're neither of us fit for this aloneness situation because we both love to talk.

Love,
Loosha

PART II | 2000–2001

Letters from Valmont Road, Boulder, CO
Letters from Calais, VT, and New York, NY

[In the following letters, Lucia describes her new home and neighbors, and recalls a visit from her son and grandson. Kenward gives updates from his summer in Vermont where he's compiling work for a new poetry collection.]

Dear Kenward,

It was good to hear your voice. I truly don't like the telephone, and when my new-fangled phone died I didn't call you still again. I hadn't known you were involved again with new and improved *Postcards*, was worried that you had gone to NY because of health problems. Glad to hear that you are fine. The new *Postcards* sounds promising and fun.

I'm still exhausted unpacking, but I like my new place more each day. And night. There are peepers and crickets and mosquitos here, just like in the country. Many ditches and streams run through it. Trains run through it too, mostly in the middle of the night. Many residents say this is the only bad part about living here. I love trains, the sound makes me happy and I go right back to sleep, dream of dear Anna [Karenina].

Doesn't bother me either that back of my place is on 30th, a busy street. The air conditioner masks the noise . . . I turn it off because That noise gets to me. This evening I went outside to sit under huge cottonwood in my yard. Three black stretch limousines passed by. What could that be? A funeral? A sweepstakes winner? They had a hard time making the turn at the corner. My Mexican neighbor's sons all come for dinner so there were about five pick-ups that made it a tight squeeze. The man and woman are my age, and are from Juarez, so we've had great talks about El Paso and Juarez, present day and in the 40s. The trolley, the El Minuto café, etc. He was using an electric saw a few days ago and I asked if he would lop off the top of an oak bookcase . . . too tall for my place. He not only sawed it off but carefully put the top board on, gluing and sanding it. They are all barbequing and playing (not loudly) Mexican music.

I feel very at home here. I have truly hated Boulder yuppiness and new age-ness, bad art and bookstores.

Later: I unpacked a few more boxes and came into my bedroom. Whoa, out the window, up and down 30th it looked like Christo[1] had been here. Orange mesh draped all along both sides of the street for as far as I could see. Then metal constructions started to grow up, with platforms and ladders. Sort of the Pompidou museum right outside my window. I don't have TV now. No cable, would have to get saucers and etc. Too busy to read the local paper . . . so didn't remember the Bolder Boulder Memorial Day race, Huge race. 1000's and thousands, Famous Africans and Mexican Indians, plus all able-bodied Boulderites. Wheelchairs too.

I filled my [oxygen] tank and went out to see what was up. They were the TV crew and race officials. They'll be right outside MY window at 5 AM to set up. The starting gun will go off at 7:30!

I take this as a good omen. Surely I'm in the right place at the right time, since 5 AM is when I get up anyway. Imagine. Thousands of people at the start of the run, only fifteen feet from my bed! It is so awful it makes me happy. Too many people at once has kept me from ever once watching the yearly activity. But it is very different when you are Participating in the event.

Next night: Too tired to write, and long letter must be tiring to read. The race was fantastic. Delightful. Gun shots went off every 20 minutes, with new bunches. Over 40,000 people. I watched, between unpacking, for Hours. Lovely sense of many people enjoying something together. Like opera or baseball.

> *Love,*
> *Lucia*

CALAIS, VT
JUNE 28, 2000

Dear Loosha—

The stabile home fotos are DEE-lish, so comfy, you-all-the-way, love-seats everywhichaway, art on the floor, which is where I leave it, sometimes. Very home-minded today, as there's a Lady Party in the

---

1 Christo Vladimirov Javacheff, Bulgarian installation artist, 1935–2020.

house. Pauline Camp, huge bod, erratic flesh flow, unsunned tallowy skin tone, prizefighter cauliflower nose, squinchy eyes, enormous mishapen ears, mouth down-turned down-trodden—quite a beauty in a survivalist way, to my eyes. An Original, she's doing summer clean-up volunteerism with Patty Padgett, who is barefoot, much to Pauline's recurrent amazement and not-so-hidden shock. Harold, Pauline's hubby, and I, have formed a bewildered, helpless male cabal, in the thrall of this empowerment old-fashioned "real" women are supreme at—Cleaning Up Menfolk Muss.

I've been in a reading-reading-reading mode, a pattern of adolescence, when all I did just about was read, solo occupation that replenished me, offered luscious and reliable escape, and, though narrative was the hook, I did respond to the twists of language. My favorite rerun this summer so far has been *A Handful of Dust*.[2]

I grew to loathe [Stendhal's] *The Red & The Black*. Fell for a Colette shortie, *The Other One*—standard Frenchie trio, wife, mistress, drippy boulevard playwright-hubby philanderer they both care for and decide to share. They're so fond of each other, jealousy isn't a problem. I got jealous at the theatre world details, dress rehearsal, the performers, the routine I feel exiled from.

So adroit. Plus a [Marguerite] Yourcenar historical fiction novella, spare and gorgeous. Between novels, I dip into you to see how your stuff holds up, which it does, all the way—that Gothic Romance slays me, how it refracts out into politics, power plays. Beautiful and natural, nothing forced or gussied up, doomed feudal grandeur dealt with simply via virginal eyes.

Yesterday, raced through a Graham Greene potboiler I wearied of— suspense, yes, but not nearly as gripping as his true-life safari through the unmapped interior of Liberia, so terrific made me lust for more Greene.

Switchover to Harold, who has plunked himself down by my desk, rattles on whatever I'm doing at the processor.

HAROLD: "So I picked up a new belt, only charged me four

---

2   Evelyn Waugh, *A Handful of Dust* (Chapman and Hall, 1934).

dollars, now I'm going to eat dinner. Down to the last set now—then we'll have some sharp blades. Got rid of the rubbish. This spring I got rid of it. I have a rubbish man comes right to the door, all the stuff the girls throwed away from the storage. He'll get rid of it, he won't mind, got one of those big crushers, pushes it right up, then when it's full, gets rid of it. We'll go eat some dinner, then this afternoon get the rest of the mowing done down there. The peonies are really growing, three bunches of lupinia. You never know, never know what'll happen, but it's been a good year for flowers."

Me, again.

Glad flecks of happy dust have fallen on you off that great Swizzle Stick in The Sky. Hope the flecks continue steadily, now you're resettled. Congrats from your boondocks pen-beau—and a Happy Fourth!

[. . .]

Time to see what the Ladies are up to in the house.

Love,
Kenward

BOULDER, CO
JULY 24, 2000

Dear Kenward,

David and the boys left last night after a truly wonderful visit. I need to Say how grateful and happy I am. Any mother whose children love her is blessed, an alcoholic mother is in a state of grace. I know I was a "good" mother, loving and responsible, before I drank, and when I drank I never physically or verbally hurt my sons, but certainly scared them, made them embarrassed and ashamed and worried . . . could have killed them driving and burning down house etc. Took many years of reconstruction, more for me to believe they really forgave me than for them to do so. David especially . . . who, once when I was going to kill myself, with Antabuse and gin, left, saying "Go for it. It's the most decent thing to do."

He and the boys, Nico and Truman, were so loving to me. We had fun, laughed, goofed off, explored, talked and talked, swam, played miniature golf etc.

Fortunately I was very ill a few weeks ago . . . maybe I wrote . . .
lung infection and fever so was still feeling effects of heavy prednisone-
steroids. No Pain, no fatigue! I was able to keep up (on walker) walking
the mall, trails past a million prairie dogs. Got a hole-in-two playing
miniature golf! We found a skateboard ramp for Nico behind a Baptist
Church. Sign said: "GOD TOLD US TO BUILD THE APOCA-
LYPSE! SKATEBOARD PARK. WEAR YOUR HELMET."

We swam every day. David barbequed (He is a chef). We ate lots
of chocolate sundaes and junk food, watched baseball and Kung Fu
movies. They loved my neighbors, the Luceros next door, spoke Spanish
with them, and David smoked dope and drank Coronas. The boys met
Joe, the Dakota Indian who lives down the street, and threw basketballs
in his hoop. They played ball with the little boy next door, son of the
retarded buck-toothed mother, daughter of Judith who says all these
Indians and Mexicans are dope dealers. Really . . .

Yesterday the steroid was wearing off so when they went swimming
I opted for a nap. Before they left David spoke to me so sweetly. How
happy he was to see me swimming and stronger, here with good friends
like Jenny and Ivan and Bobbie[3] . . . and in great trailer, among good,
real people, safe and sound. Big tears in our eyes and sweet hugs before
they went off to swim. I went to sleep, woke up to "Ma! Ma! Grandma!
You ok?"

The air-conditioner had shorted out, wires caught on fire. The room
was filled with smoke. I was fast asleep. Big to do, much to do. Fire put
out, room aired out. Whew. No electricians to be found on a Sunday.
One who said he could come on Overtime today for $100 extra which
I can pay thanks to you, meanwhile no lights or air-conditioner. VERY
HOT Night. Read Martin Amis by candlelight. Hope battery holds up
to print this. Duh. The printer is electric. Hope they fix it today and I
can mail this tomorrow.

Fortunately the kids ate and drank Everything in refrigerator except
capers and horseradish.

Anyway we all calmed down and David said, "Well, Ma, I'm glad

3   Jenny Dorn, Ivan Suvanjieff, Bobbie Louise Hawkins.

that you are Relatively safe." They were dressing for the trip when four police cars in high siren and at full speed came zooming down our little dirt road. Six cops got out, guns drawn. They put Indian Joe in hand-cuffs and into back seat. Then all six, with guns pointed, ran past my living room to the Luceros' house next door.

This was the moment that I'll remember all my life. My dear Nico, my soul-mate and I are Completely attuned: We simultaneously burst into song. "Bad Boy! Bad Boy! Whatcha gonna do when they bust yo ass? BadBoy! BadBoy!" The theme song to "COPS," a tawdry TV show that shows videos of real, ugly police in towns like Lubbock, Texas or Carlsbad, New Mexico, the criminals all with wavery faces.

They didn't take anyone from the Lucero house, were looking for someone else. After they left, Nico and I laughed and hugged each other, so pleased by our identical response, which his father said was "Sicko! Have you guys no compassion?"

Other good news is that I have a story in my head. All I've got is Where it will take place. On the Santa Isabel Grace Line ship between New York and Valparaiso. 30 days, 30 chapters.[4] Details swimming around. This is the part of writing that I enjoy the most. Details appear like laundry in dryer window, fish in aquariums. God, I hope with bet-ter similes when the time comes!

All my love to you,
Loosha

CALAIS, VT
JULY 29, 2000

Dear Loosha—

So glad to hear you had an action-packed visit, and the chance to sing a duet as a miscreant neighbor is carted off to the pokey. Awful quiet, by comparison, up here. My niece and her eccentric hubby stopped by a while back, for a two-nighter—a pleasure, as it rid me of my "transient"

---

4   Lucia is beginning her memoir of places she lived, which became *Welcome Home: A Memoir with Selected Photographs and Letters* (Farrar, Straus and Giroux, 2018).

I.D.—a sort of I Don't Live Here ennui. Next week, Steven Clay, the archive go-between/publisher of *Cyberspace* and *Nite Soil*, arrives for two nights, mostly to take a gander at the archives up here, which are due to be dispatched to San Diego,[5] second and final shipment, come October. The first, from NYC basement, got Fed Xed, last week.

I'm rallying, high time, and, to my surprise, had enough new stuff to fill out a 96-pager, entitled, fairly firm cogitation, Blast From The Past.[6] Some stories, I Remember stuff, poems. Some show stuff. The title song Steven & I launched at the Boulder Musee.[7] I even stuck in the Harold monologue from the letter to you, but it didn't have an End, really, so I took it out. No room.

A favor. Can I co-dedicate this book to you. I got worried Loosha is an imposition, so I put Lucia and Pat, Pat being Patty Padgett, who is such a good daily round looker-after, daily walks, and so attuned to inner whirlings. She's so smart, and compassionate, what a combo. And I guess, every close tight marriage needs an outside chum for contrast. If I had my druthers, I'd finger you as Loosha. But let me know first if this is OK. I sent it out to a Mom and Pop kiddo operation in Tejas, Skanky Possum, nice folks. But they publish books without mass, and mine is hefty. So I may show it to my houseguest, Mr. Granary I call him, and see if he'll take it on, and then send a more anorexic manuscript to the Kiddos—stuff that hit the cutting room floor, but it's printable. Just didn't fit in, this go around.

[. . .]

That's terrif news, a story is coming to you, nothing beats organic blasts.

Time to eat health-giving broccoli for lunch. Your ebullient letter perked me up no end. Resilience, ah.

Mucho Love,
Kenward

---

5   Granary Books publisher Steven Clay is helping Kenward collect his papers for archival storage at University of California San Diego.

6   Elmslie, *Blast From The Past* (Skanky Possum Press, 2000). Codedicated to Lucia and Pat Padgett.

7   Boulder Museum of Contemporary Art.

BOULDER, CO
AUGUST 5, 2000

Dear Kenward,

The now married and shorn of hair and all sex-appeal postman took away my letter to you, so here is a late postscript. I may not be writing, but a lovely poem happened to me this morning. I took your letter and others out to the mailbox, turned on the sprinkler. Came inside for coffee, bagel and the paper. (I DID have rapid heart beatings climbing the few steps! I was happy to be able to write that in diary.)[8]

I watched the sun rise pink and apricot outside my window among fine old cottonwoods, maples and fruit trees. Walking in front of them, toward the opening to the street, was the oldest of the Vietnamese women. There are five generations of women, one granpa and one young married son, all in a trailer same size as mine. Even if all the women had their babies in their teens she is still a very old woman, late eighties, nineties. She is the one who grows the roses, burns incense in a brazier to keep the deer away. She wears either an old ornately embroidered yellow dress or a raggedy silk pants suit with frog fastened jacket. White hair in a bun. Tiny, maybe five feet, seventy pounds. There she was in the shabby green suit, gliding by my window, wearing a conical straw hat and thong sandals, carrying a long bamboo pole. I couldn't have Heard her, but her walk was silent, as if she were on a conveyor belt. What made it so dream-like was that I saw her through the mist of the sprinkler . . . sort of a monsoon haze.

It was such a lovely moment that I wanted to put it in heart-machine diary but just wrote, "washed dishes, swept kitchen, scrubbed the tub." Took the EKG machine back to the hospital and came home, utterly exhausted. We are having heat wave and pollution from mountain fires very bad. Even normal people advised to stay inside.

I sat down to catch my breath, and there came the old woman, past my windows, regal as ever. The pole was lying across her

---

8   In a previous letter, Lucia wrote about an EKG heart monitor diary she was filling out, with no excitement or irregularities to include in the diary for the doctor.

shoulders and hanging from either end were two plastic bags from
Albertson's Grocery.

>   *Love,*
>   *Loosha*

[In the following letters, Kenward writes of his Blast from the Past *book
party, a performance/reading with Ishmael Reed, and readjusting to life in
the city. Lucia remembers her own friendship with Reed and her years living in New York. Kenward tells Lucia about a friend, Jimmy Tampubolon,
whom Lucia will meet in person later.]*

NEW YORK, NY

OCTOBER 21, 2000

Dear Loosha—

Rushed packing, papers helter-skelter, burnished daylight in Vermont, E-Z plane-trip this time, Poets House[9] gig largesse, so CW
drove back with the Golden Chains & Flamingo Shirt Van Man[10] &
the two kitties. I'm coming to my senses, a bit—recoveree from Kultur
Shock. Furious blacks yell in the street, working phone booth right in
front of the house, throws me into hallucinatory panic, as I think I'm
in Vermont. Why are these screamers—ghetto m-f imprecations, fulmi-
nating in my slo mo isolate fastness?

Unpacking mostly done, islands of this goes here, that goes there
order already. Wheezing from cold, system confused by warmth,
shirt-sleeves temps. I haven't seen anyone but CW, so far. Tomorrow,
I trek uptown—back to the York Theatre—to see a book-in-hand performance of a musical by Kurt Weill,[11] one of my theatre composer
super-faves—*Johnny Johnson*, Thirties anti-war work with words by Paul
Green,[12] not expecting much there, as his niche was huge out-of-doors

---

9   Poets House was a national literary center and poetry library based in New
York City.

10   Vermont resident Jack Graves.

11   Kurt Julian Weill, German (later American) composer, 1900–1950.

12   Paul Green, American writer, lyricist, 1894–1981. Collaborated with Kurt
Weill on *Johnny Johnson*, 1937. Green's play *The Lost Colony*, 1934.

patriotic history pageants such as *The Lost Colony*, which played for decades, summer tourist trap, in Virginia.

Weather benign down here—micro-climate, reversal, back a month. Four people have commented that I seem to have lost weight, yippee, though the scales don't show it. Fighting a cold does wonders as an appetite depressant.

Prince Jimmy Tampubolon,[13] a chum, took off from Muslim fanaticism in Jakarta (he's Catholic) for Auckland, NZ, but, phone conversation yesterday, couldn't get "work" papers, & is heading back to his homeland. Someday, I hope, I'll get around to writing down His Story—a venture into deep, deep recurrent Kultur Shock, a muss of Dutch power, privileged Empire natives, allowed to learn Dutch, forbidden to the masses the Empire natives rule, independence, inflation, total poverty, shoeless, sleeps among huddled masses in a stadium, foreign diplomat lady gives him his first job, houseboy, we meet up, take a trip to his home village, in Sumatra, where Tampubolon = Royalty, visit his shriveled barefoot Queen aunt and King uncle, in the tiny Kingdom of Tampubolon, no more car, no more perks, living in a hut on stilts, no more afternoons at the racetrack, mahjong in the salon.

Chickens running around their new hovel. Their subjects, villagers, bring them all their eats, a feudal tradition still observed. Jimmy sent me a pair of sneakers (they used to be called) from NZ—gorgeous white—they fit perfectly. The oldies for all those diabetes walks—never took them off, except for black-tie dinners, haven't been to one in decades—were falling apart, so in the nick of. Celebratory Saturday walk imminent.

Haven't done a lick of work—except the gig I returned for, in a spanking new library. West Side, mostly pretty spiffily accoutered kiddo black users, computer-literate, doing their homework. What a city, egalitarian outposts. I liked my co-gigger, Ishmael Reed,[14] big hand-

---

13 Jimmy Tampubolon, friend of Kenward's from Indonesia who will appear in their future letters.

14 Ishmael Scott Reed, American poet, writer, songwriter, editor, and publisher, b. 1938.

some likable beardy black guy, but his gab was rambly and out-of-focus. He's a librettist-poet too, the tie-in. I just hate operas about Jesus, updated, with Mary Mag turned into a crack-user.

I was prepped fully, in focus, went first, sang one song—*Roy Rogers*, one more time, friendly audience. But the show-stealer was a beautiful black lady, gorgeous singer, Ayana Lowe,[15] the bonus for me. Stage Door Kenward. Sang something from his opera, nothing to write home about, blah-blah-blah, but, heavens to Betsy, I could swoon hearing that lady sing the phone book. Claibe Richardson was there, also fell for her, so maybe, if the revue of our songs gets going, Feb. 2002, she can sing Catherine's songs from *The Grass Harp*. Supposed to confer with the Yorkies next week about the "structure" of the revue. Sensibly, no one likes the traditional And Then They Wrote format. I figure I can write little texts, here & there, not poetry exactly, but close—tapping into ways the songs set my juices a-boil.

Glad you're having some pain-free interludes—hope the pent-up words in your noggin keep hitting the page, with rabbit-ridden snow to check out, in-between paragraphs.

Much Love
Kenward

BOULDER, CO
OCTOBER 28, 2000

Dear Kenward,

I think I have highly distorted image of your neighborhood. I remember it from when we lived on thirteenth, corner of Sixth. Would walk with small children in the morning, visit pet shop on Patchen Place (sp?) across from women's prison, buy brioche and cookies at . . . wonderful bakery on corner, head north on Greenwich toward home, passing elegant shops, a tennis court?

But then, in those days, I even camped out with my boys in Central Park! Deep inside the park when you look up at night you can actually see stars. Could. Have you ever been to the Seamen's

---

15   Ayana Lowe, American jazz singer and educator.

Church Institute? In the Battery. Wonderful scrimshaw museum and a chapel where instead of Jesus there is an enormous painting of an open sea.

Oh dear, not only am I forgetting everything and rambling on about the good old days, I've now started in on Regretting. My mother got into this before she died. Once she called and moaned, "I never looted or plundered!" I regret not living still in a rent-controlled apartment in Village. Ground floor. Have just finished *War and Peace* and am regretting never having gone to Russia, seen Chekhov's steppes. It was fun to read the book with the Atlas open to that vast place. Of course Americans and Russians went into space, we share that sense of space and the frontier. It was a good book to read during the World Series. Napoleon and Roger Clemens[16] similarly egomaniacal and stupid. Bobby Valentine[17] coaches the way General Kutosov planned battle . . . (have patience and wait) etc.

Actually spent yesterday reading Dale Smith's new book *AMERI-CAN RAMBLER*.[18] Wonderful book . . . in company of Olsen's CALL ME ISHMAEL and Metcalf's GENOA. One of first books that ever Struck me was Cabeza de Vacas's journals, which this is based upon.

Soon your book will be out, no?

Wish I had known you were going to read with Ishmael [Reed]. He is an old friend. When I first began writing again (after almost 20 years being a single mother, then a single-minded alcoholic) he was very encouraging to me, read my work and published me in *QUILT*. A review of Judy Chicago's *THE DINNER PARTY*, which I trashed . . . It was called *THE BRUNCH*. I had all these darling place settings for Emma Bovary, Anna Karenina, Marilyn Monroe, Sylvia Plath, et al. Enraged feminists wrote me irate letters. I wasn't saying anything bad about the Women who had places at her dinner party (and didn't

16   Roger Clemens, American professional baseball player, then playing for the New York Yankees in the 2000 World Series against the New York Mets.

17   Bobby Valentine, American professional baseball player, coach, and manager, then manager of New York Mets.

18   Dale Smith, *Skanky Possum* publisher and poet. *American Rambler* (Thorpe Springs, 2000).

even Eat.) It was a stupid Show. And who Would eat off a plate with a vulva on it? I am also grateful to Ishmael because when I was in lowest lowest nadir, after Terry had died, my sons had said So Long, I had no job, no money etc . . . Ishmael recommended me for teaching job at the University of California. Teaching creative writing at Extension classes. Fabulous pay. I prepared for months . . . Oh, dear . . . this is so painful to write about. Briefly: I apparently drank a great deal before I got to my first class. All I can remember is the students leaving, one by one.

I recently had a very kind note from him. I used to see him because my apartment on Telegraph was above his dry cleaners. (As usual I used to hang out of the window, checking things out.) He liked to talk to me, I think, because although Black, his world was academia, whereas I worked in emergency rooms and County hospitals, went to County psych wards and jails, taught in prison, en fin, my world was black and poor. I knew all the Medicaid abuses and realities of racism in a very personal way. I loved his early work, like *FLIGHT TO CANADA* and his magazines *Y'BIRD READER* and *QUILT* were very fine. He helped many many young ethnic writers to get started and his help to me was a start in my getting sober and in writing again.

What a lovely mini-novela about Prince Jimmy Tampubolon! Please do it thoroughly. It could be a musical even.

I relocated my CD player to dining room, where I listen to it more often, especially now that I am much better and not in bed all the time. Cooked a paella a few days ago and listened to the wonderful *THE GRASS HARP*. Hope your Ayana Lowe works out.

I have ten pages of new piece. So far so good. Hey, that sounds like one of my titles!

Quandary. I told you that I am receiving again my monthly $100 from the Tinker Belles, along with dear letters from Nancy. This month's check bounced! I hope Nancy didn't run off with all the loot and the house-boy. [. . .]

> *All my love,*
> *loosha*

November 23

Dear Kenward,

Was it wonderful to get into your own bed?

I hope you are resting - (on laurels) I am even drained by the intensity of both of your performances. They were magic - funny, brilliant, definitely sad, BEAUTIFUL - Moving. Nabokov only such lyrical, brilliant a mind who could be funny - but you have compassion.

My students - describing love affairs, are always writing about sleeping in like spoons. I was so happy to read your two sleeping like forks & knives! (enclosed) PAM DIET

This is a silly book. I think the title is what I love most. I have tried to get people to read it & INVARIABLY they have HATED it - so I won't feel sad if you don't like it. There is one scene with a dog that most found particularly offensive, but I thought it was actually quite touching...

For that matter -- How come people get so upset about cultures where dog is eaten? We eat little baby lambs --

I guess I wouldn't eat Cosmo - he'd be in there meowing & meowing to be let out.

I love you,

Lucia

Handwritten letter from Lucia.

Dear Loosha—

Wunnerful, as Lawrence Welk used to say, your ebullient T-Day letter, with food details, who brought what, and good real life boosts happening to you—a plenitude. It was such a hoot, running into Anselm and Jane [Hollo],[19] in my home away from home,[20] where I eat constantly, having pretty much abandoned my stove. A friendly place, comfort food. Decent meatloaf, Ron's lunch today. My current fave: fruit salad, with two red boobs of jello, lotsa cottage cheese.

Spent the morning with Ron & Pat, cartoning CW's considerable acquisitions. Mostly books, some of considerable value, hard to see go to someone who'll be so oblivious to straight-thinking behavior—given to him, it's his, whether he's a bit of a manipulative gimme gimme gimme type youth, or not. Mostly done, with badinage to lighten the workload, us three in the third-floor front, his lair, three windows, two opened enough of a crack, warm out, to lure a cat to the window ledge—fatso Rilke, who cannot be trusted. Saved. R & P will come back Friday, finish up the job, and off the valuables go, Air, UPS, to the Tutor's residence in Amsterdam. The Tutor is his ersatz Dad, 77, professor, lawyer, who, foolish man, thinks of CW as his son, and will stick by him, no matter what he does, which consists of going daily to the tutor's house: substitute for a dayjob. CW's dropping his Goddard studies, so there's no reason for him to return to the US of A, January 3rd—his possessions will be his again. Bless Patty for seeing the longer the treasure divvy takes, the more entangled I'll be in the Wolfie (CW's name over there) Web.

The book party was OK, mainly because of Hoa & Dale,[21] who did everything, conscientious all the way, in fine style. Few poets came.

---

19   Anselm Hollo, Finnish poet and translator, 1934–2013. His second wife, American artist Jane Dalrymple-Hollo.

20   The Den diner.

21   Elmslie, *Blast from the Past: Stories, Poems, Song Lyrics, Remembrances* (Skanky Possum Press, 2000). Hoa Nguyen and Dale Smith founded Skanky Possum press and magazine in 1998.

T-Day week? D & H read first, as I did, briefly, nice laffs. Till I get my life a bit more in some sort of shape, I "get through" stuff as best I can, but my pleasure centers are still a bit battened down. I'm relieved I get to be a totally private person for awhile, work on my [upcoming collaboration] piece for Trevor Winkfield, which, after finding out what "phat" means from Hoa & Dale, I've decided to call Phat Farm. Spa destination looks to be in Miami, once Pritikin (for heart recoverees). But I haven't booked myself in yet.

I hope to skedaddle by Dec. 9th, stay maybe through the New Years, if it's bearable, and come back New Year's Day, as Vivy and Willie [Russe] will visit me here for three days—at first, they volunteered help with the pack-up of CW's treasures, but now, that mission accomplished, just to hang out for a bit.

I have sort of a weird crush on a black lady named Ayana Lowe. She sang an aria (not so hot) with words by your pal Ishmael, at the Libretto Land gig & I guess the hot response was two-sided. She sent me a "review" of the gig from The Amsterdam Blah-Blah, black weekly—mostly about Ish, as makes sense. Anyway, I guess I'll ask her out for dinner or something. She's so "life force"—and lady singers have always driven me nutso, how do they do this miracle so adroitly? She bought a copy of my book, hope it doesn't scare her off. My mantra "NO MORE MUSICALS & BOYS" is extremely porous, but.

I feel so dumb, wasting years with a boy wolf, but as Vivy my niece pointed out, I shouldn't be hard on myself. He's smart, has a way with words, and, initially, within strict bounds, was capable of thoughtful and caring gestures towards me, very rarely, alas. I hope he treats his new same-age Sig O halfway decently. One reason Patty wanted to get the stuff off fast: before the e-Mail-met Sig O finds out about the dark side of CW, the brain-molested young kid who keeps the cycle going, and molests The Other Person. Hey, that's me.

Cheez, flatulent psychobabble. Time to sign off. My favorite relative was Aunt Peggy, author name Margaret Leech of Reveille in Washington fame, Mrs. Ralph Pulitzer, whose daughter, Susan married an art world creep, Sydney Freedberg, who claimed to have been a CIA agent, was a famous disciple of [Bernard] Berenson. Susan committed suicide, happens a lot on the Pulitzer side, Elmslies, no, leaving two kiddos, whom I saw via my Aunt Peggy, in their early teens. Enchanted kiddos. One, maybe two, are surfacing tonight—Kate Freedberg, now a photog, and maybe her bro, Nathaniel, who (thirtyish by now?) is still a Rock 'n' Roller. I'll write you all about this Evening of Waifs.[22]

Mucho Love,
Kenward

BOULDER, CO
JANUARY 9, 2001

Dear Kenward,

Thanks for the great description of your apartment. It is actually very much as I had seen it. I did imagine a tree of heaven! Forgot to put it in letter. Those trees, and ginkos, my favorite in New York. Loved to hear about the Civil War bed and Vivian's picture.[23] Damn, forgot all about the cat box. See, I'm seriously slipping as a writer.

My Uncle John was a fine caner, would have had those chairs in shape in a jiffy.

Your Twelfth Night menu sounds fabulous, especially tarragon sorbet. And healthy too. The Pritikin tips were nothing I didn't know, alas. I'm going to try my best. The five meals seems like a good idea, if only to combat my main problem with diets: The minute I decide to diet, I get ravenously hungry. I have made progress with no-salt, for high blood pressure. Now most food seems too salty.

So far the swimming makes me sore and exhausted, but it is already cheering me up. Feel like I'm Doing something about getting stronger. The pool is built into the side of Mount Sanitas, with two entire tall walls of glass. When I get into (hot!) water the sun is just coming up

---

22   Margaret Kernochan Leech, also known as Margaret Pulitzer, American historian and writer, 1893–1974. Aunt Peggy to Kenward, she married Ralph Pulitzer, 1879–1939. Their daughter, Susan Pulitzer, 1932–1965, married art historian Sydney Joseph Freedberg, 1914–1997. Kenward is writing of two of their children, Kate Freedberg, 1958–2010, and Nathaniel Freedberg. Bernard Berenson, American art historian, 1865–1959.

23   Portrait of Kenward's sister as a child.

through the pines, hitting the red rocks. Only two or three other swimmers get there so early so it's very quiet. Soft splashes.

Hope things went well with the Eye Lady. Wow. Only two weeks into the New Year and you're winding up major restorations and repairs. Have you reclaimed CW's rooms?

Read fine review of THE SPELL by Tom Clark, written by Dale Smith. The book is very good and Tom is due such a respectful tribute. This was in *First Intensity*, as was review of my book, nice, if inaccurate in several spots. She[24] also sent a chapbook of lovely long poem by Theodore Enslin,[25] who had chilling story in the magazine. Wonderful story by Amy Shepherd, who Lee couldn't locate to tell that the story was accepted. Hope she does, or someone does, sounds like a Good young writer.

I have had a deluge of manuscripts from ex-students this last week. Three good manuscripts. One very very bad. Oh dear, and very long. I'm spending Tomorrow afternoon with him, to tell him why. I hate it when this happens . . .

JANUARY 10 5:30 AM

My back hurt so badly I didn't go out to get mail yesterday, so picked it up this morning when I went out for the paper.

Got the check Wow! $5000! THEN I read the Letter. Oh my god.[26]

Ok so you're not a signer or whatever. You must have had something to do with this. I am overwhelmed, hugely grateful, but also very ashamed. I have written NOTHING all year and truly do not deserve it. Of course I will not reject this money. It will mean Indescribably less anxiety about future, emergencies, etc. for FIVE MORE YEARS!

I will try to see it as nothing to do with my so-called work, but as another blessing that your friendship has given me. Well, we'll celebrate when you come this summer. Maybe I'll figure out a train trip to New York. I have to let this all sink in . . . dizzy right now.

---

24   *First Intensity* publisher Lee Chapman.
25   Theodore Enslin, American poet, 1925–2011.
26   Responding to news of a renewable grant from Z Press Foundation.

Damn. Late for the pool. I mean late for watching sun come up in the pool.

Thank you, still again. I worry too because I wonder if you don't know how very grateful I am already, for your kindness and caring.

> All my love,
> Loosha

[In the following letters, Kenward writes of the Joe Brainard Retrospective show in San Francisco and a poetry event honoring Joe.]

NEW YORK, NY

MARCH 6, 2001

DEAR LOOSHA—

Wonderful Welcome Back Home, your letter. The exciting news in it: Mexican Saga. Hope you send me a snippet or two as I get so hongry for more Berliniana to glam.

Trip was fine. Always a stress-provoker, travel. [. . .]

Plane cancelled, late afternoon departure, with the Padgetts, plunked into our hotel, various rooms, same floor. The stay was great. You have such a treat awaiting you. I found it too hard to really "take in" Joe's show,[27] except a bit formally. Well hung. In context clumps. The most celebrated whippet[28] in history had his own patch of wall. So Ron and Patty and I, instead of oohing and ahing, sat on a bench, mid-exhibit, and recalled what a great earth creature W. (Whip-poorwill, the whippet) was. The whiplash motion of him streaking through Vermont fields, his streamlined lunges visible over the grass. And how he'd race around the house, before the Joe L studio was added, just kept going, if encouraged by Ron, or anyone. One Joe standout—the constructions are in big clear glass structures, not sealed off in any way, so the viewer can fall under their spell without worrying about impermanence, vulnerability, implosion. They're so

---

27   Kenward traveled to San Francisco to see the *Joe Brainard: A Retrospective* exhibit that debuted at Berkeley Art Museum, 2000.

28   Referring to paintings Brainard did of Kenward's dog, Whippoorwill.

safe, yet one-to-one, one great secret of Joe's works—they need the viewer. They beam back, happy you're there.

Great art is so self-sufficient, one reason it's great, but this time around, the old rules bend. The overall modesty took me by surprise—its lack of overpoweringness. Same deep vein your work has. To exist, to be shared, to turn into a happy memory if thought about—that's it.

The event[29] I was part of went beautifully. A Sunday afternoon. Moderne but not sterile theatre, no balcony. Packed full, people were turned away. Errata-esque intro by an ex-USA-poet-laureate, Robt Haas,[30] Anne W. went first, lickety-split pace. [. . .] Bill Berkson, perfecto. Read Joe's Bolinas jottings, hilarious and touching, delivered so charmingly. What a gent! And how reassuring to see how gracefully it's possible for a poet to survive the overcrowded dance floor, without resorting to grand-standing and jabby elbows. He's a prince, and his latest book *Serenade*[31] is a breakthrough, sure-minded and so easygoing, I guess it'll be another overlooked triumph, oy, what's new.

Barbara Guest[32] fumbled from poem to poem, fragile physicality—the fear of her keeling over right then and there lent a poignant force to her words, which generally skitter by me—I get tired watching the hazy cloud patterns they generate—oh, that's a dog's snout, must be, or is it shriveled up wisteria, seen in a reflecting pool at dusk—but for brief passages, her voice got past my barricades. Dick Gallup,[33] who looks a tad like Groucho Marx, I didn't "get" either, but he was OK, poetry reading Normalcy, which I'm not good at, as receptor. Ron [Padgett] perfecto, reading more hilarious Joe, from a secret—till now—work Joe'd sent him to cheer him up—Patty was preggers, they were pretty broke, in Paris—there were slides for that, and for Barbara, and for Bill, projected from a high-up booth.

---

29 Poetry reading by Joe Brainard's friends to celebrate his work, coinciding with art exhibit opening.

30 Robert Haas, American poet, former U.S. poet laureate, b. 1941.

31 Berkson, *Serenade* (Zoland Books, 2000).

32 Barbara Guest, American poet and writer, 1920–2006.

33 Dick Gallup, American poet, 1941–2021.

I'd insisted to the curator on coming last (she'd put me first!!!)—my doggedness surfacing—but it was a fair demand, as the slides were made beautifully by Mr. Yu (perfectionism rampant) & his timings (I sensed) were micro-managed with exactitude. And I let the work—the final section of *Champ Dust*—carry me, with three *Postcards* Songlets inserted here & there, so I could very briefly sing, and also to aerate the work itself, give it light vs shadow, just voice, no accompaniment. And the feelings under the work, of loss, came out, no boo-hoo, but from a sterner, in a way, impersonal level. So I feel happy now, my homage to Joe was worthy of him and the occasion.

I'll wind up this account. It's Tuesday, and we got back safely, the one plane that made it east through blizzardry.

Much Love,
Kenward

Reappropriated "Nancy" comic by Kenward for Lucia.

Dear Kenward,

One of your most beautiful letters ever, the last one about Joe's show in California. You and the Padgetts on the bench. The vivid, vital memories of Joe and the comments about his work . . . its modesty and its inclusion were so fine. I read it several times, remembering that this generosity of spirit is in every great work of art.

Today is anniversary of Charlie Parker's[34] death. Radio has been playing him since I turned it on at six. Have found myself weeping several times. Partly from memories of musician husbands, friends, New York, my youth, our youths, remembering exactly when I heard "Confirmation" or "Now's the Time." But then shut myself up for trying to analyze. It was the music itself that was so intense. Record and after record has been playing all morning, where he dazzles and surprises and shocks at the same time he is opening his heart and soul to us.

I have heard many rave reports of the [Joe Brainard Retrospective] show and the reading from friends in Berkeley and S.F. You and Ron were the stars. Sounds like Bill Berkson too, only my friend [Stephen] Emerson[35] is too mad at him to be objective. Emerson is the man who has every single book you ever published. He was a tall, distinguished looking fellow with a frown, standing next to Bill Berkson but not being introduced to you by Bill. Lord, all of us are crazy. How can a grown man be too shy to introduce himself and tell you he enjoyed your reading? I am so much the same. I probably would not have spoken to you if we hadn't sat together, alone, utterly by chance, at a little table under a tree. Tom Clark hurt that he was not asked to read. I don't understand why Anne Waldman has read 71 times in one year and no one gives Tom Clark the respect he deserves. They hadn't even asked him to read at Ed Dorn's memorial service . . . and he was Ed's best

---

34   Charlie Parker, American jazz musician, band leader and composer, 1920–1955.

35   Stephen Emerson, American writer, b. 1950. Close friend of Lucia's, wrote introduction to her collection, *A Manual for Cleaning Women.*

friend! Jenny fortunately intervened there. I suppose artists and writers have always been this way, amazing we get on at all.

I did go to a dinner party last week, for Tom Raworth,[36] a dear old friend. Lovely evening. Everybody reporting about the Brainard show and the reading, looking forward to this summer. Tom on way to read in S.F., will see the show as well. I heard him and Anselm Hollo talking about your work, with much praise. Anselm said he thought that I heard from you, Tom said to me that when I wrote, to please say hello and best wishes from him.

I didn't go to his reading . . . up two flights of stairs. May not have gone even if it were on first floor. Sitting up so long at the dinner did me in, have been in bed most of the time since.

Everyone but Jenny Dorn appalled when I tell of chucking out my Mexico pages.[37] It was a good decision. If I Labor over something, even if once in awhile it is fun, there is something false and forced to it. I'm very relieved that it is gone.

Pleased to hear that Mr. Yu managed the tapes and slides so well. He sounds terrific. I Know that he is young and probably handsome, but I can't turn off my image of him with an umbrella. I have a Mr Yoo,[38] an ex-grad student, Korean. We email and or/write weekly. He is a fine writer, sharp and witty, has a novel wandering around publishers. One day, soon will soar. I was his advisor during the time the poet Ai,[39] pronounced "I," was here, and the chair did not feel that I should be on Yoo's thesis committee since she was visiting. Well, you can imagine the argument we had . . . full of I's and yous and Ais and Yoos.

Sorry I have no news.

Ai love yoo though,
loosha

---

36   Tom Raworth, Anglo-Irish poet, publisher, and editor, 1938–2017.

37   A novel Lucia was writing that she discarded.

38   Dave Yoo, American novelist, b. 1974. Former student and friend of Lucia's, classmate of mine at University of Colorado 1996–1999.

39   Ai Ogawa (born Florence Anthony), American poet of Japanese, African American, Native American, and Irish descent, 1947–2010. Ai was visiting writer at University of Colorado in 1996–1997.

BOULDER, CO
APRIL 1, 2001

Dear Kenward,

I miss hearing from you. Your letters have become a punctuation
in my days, a good laugh, stop to rest and think and they always
trigger ideas and memories. Didn't realize how much my letters are
a response to your elan until I have tried writing to you cold, not
answering a letter from you. I become at a loss for words. Or maybe
it's not this complicated. More that our correspondence is like a
conversation, and I'm never good at breaking the ice. Although the
weather here is at last wonderful, my crab apple in full bloom. The
blossoms a bluish pink, divine color not seen in any other flower, just
as the blue-red fruit is unique. Red finches are nesting in it. Crows
settling in in the maple tree. Wild group of red-winged blackbirds
blew through from the plains a few days ago, like street gang toughs,
fast and brazen, sexy.

All the other birds stayed put while they ate the deer's corn and took
off in red and black swirl. I think they are my favorite birds. But mostly
when they are in reeds or alfalfa fields, surprising against deep green.
Many ducks showed up too on our many creeks, where children and
the Vietnamese have already been fishing.

I've been Forcing myself to get out and about. Went to a reading
last night by a friend Steve Katz.[40] He read from a new novel, and it
was funny and smart, many meals and love scenes and Italian towns.
One and a half hour of them. Is this Done? I remember the feeling
(the fear of death by paralysis of the neck) as a child in Texan Baptist
churches, in the summer. I longed to cry, to bawl. Then there were
refreshments, hard to get to, and a long line for one wheel of brie and
Carr crackers still in the box and only wine to drink. It was good to
see some of ex-colleagues, all drained and weary after the past semester, and the reading, I think. Strange to see the students . . . even
Younger than they were when I was there only last year.

---

40   Steve Katz, American writer, 1935–2019. Lucia's colleague at CU.

Reading my Tile guy story[41] at a *Sniper Logic* reading on Thursday, which will also be Long, with many readers.

What I want on my tombstone: She's really breathless now.

So maybe won't read, just to shorten the event. A retirement party Saturday, birthday party Sunday. Oh, oh, daunted already. Jenny [Dorn] is coming over today so we can catch up. [Neighbor] Harry and I go to King Soopers tomorrow. Poor Harry fell last week but nobody heard him or looked out of window so he lay there until the mailman came. He wasn't hurt, just couldn't get up. I look out the window more now, often see him looking out of his.

So much for starting conversations about the weather. Woke to total silence this morning. Snow. It has been falling for the past four hours. Branches breaking and cracking onto the roof like sharp lightning bolts. Not a blossom or bird in sight. May 2. Is this done?

Are you in New York or Vermont? Send me a line or two. I miss you.

> *Love,*
> *LOOSHA*

[In the following letters, Kenward has returned to Vermont and is working on a new collaboration with Trevor Winkfield. He's rewriting his musical Lola *and beginning a collaborative website to feature his work, his friends, and his productions with musical and visual artists. Lucia writes of packing for California and goodbye visits with Colorado friends.]*

CALAIS, VT

MAY 13, 2001

Dear Loosha—

Solo Quietude.

Blessed return to country reading. Rushed through a Ripley mystery[42] & Alice James[43] bio sent me by my niece. Vivy's book send-off pattern:

---

41   B.F. and Me." First published *Sniper Logic #9*, 2001, collected in *A Manual for Cleaning Women*.

42   Novel series by Patricia Highsmith, American novelist, 1921–1995.

43   Alice James, American diarist, sister of novelist Henry James and philosopher William James, 1848–1892.

1) Work about manic-depressivity & creative folks

2) Repressed head-sicko women. Whom I tend to identify with, reading about them—me abed, instead of tending to Vermont chores. Plant those seeds, rewrite *Lola*,[44] start on the collab *Phat* with Trevor Winkfield. His black ink illustrations are all done. Over to me.

A "real-life" poem tooled in, so here it is. One Phonemail from Mr. Yu, Berlin, reassuring first contact—complaint of computer virus.

Looks like I've escaped my website for a bit. Call from one of the three kiddo enablers, Andreas [website designer] now of Cologne. *Girl Machine* is being done karaoke style, with a bouncing ball, my song voice, visual—Joe Brainard's dippy art-deco ladies resuscitated from a Sixties put-on, a girlie calendar. Andreas needed assurance re Cut-The-Text. Screen time is voracious versus page time, gobble gobble gobble. Human attention spans hurtle about in space, no speed limit. Crucial to trim.

Harold Camp,[45] 77, with the help of his white-bread-squeeze-the-dough faced son, Newty, hooked up a garden hose, and replaced an underground pump innard, so now there's water for gardening. I've resolved to plant vegs & flowers this year, after conking out last summer—found it torturous to kneel on earth while bugs gnaw, with writing waiting, comfy at my desk. The fenced enclosure right outside my work bldg has been roto-tilled.

Sunday and cool, sun winning out over clouds. The last patch of snow gave up only a few days ago, an anomaly on the front lawn, omen of weather tampering, global dysfunction & millennial cataclysms.

The past week, I've rooted about like an old dog, circling before settling down, tidying up a plethora of old musses. I have a shelf, future projects laid out. A big Fed Ex carton for all my old collages. Joe [Brainard]'s original postcards in a bunch. Waiting to be brought out.

Your letters, treasured, sequestered together. Some bare spaces! Mr. Yu set me up a stereo, which I'll try, later. Songs from *Follies*[46] (seen

44   Kenward's musical written with Claibe Richardson.
45   Vermont native and handyman at Kenward's home.
46   Stephen Sondheim and James Goldman, *Follies*, Broadway premiere 1971.

in NYC, total adoration!) are receding, especially one about a misspent past . . . the road I never took . . . fortunately, I rarely remember the perfecto Sondheim lyrics: prefer to respool the glory of each melody solo. Hoping this ecstasy will impel me to revise *Lola* . . .

No cigs, so far, this past week, so I think that evil habit is disposed of.

Hope your fleshly aches are behaving themselves, snoozing in the sun, giving you a spring respite. I like to think of you, role model, swimming in the morning, peering out at the Rockies. I haven't trekked down to the pond as yet, or even gone for any walks. Today: a walk uphill, though not, brrrr, a swim. The Padgetts should turn up pretty soon, after Paris dalliances.

A one-act play of mine named *Furtive Edna*[47] is scheduled to be performed at the Poetry Project next week, by two poets. It has one song imbedded in it, and I tracked down a tape of me singing it, and another tape of an orchestration, which I hope will be of help. *The Woolworth Song*,[48] first time up at bat, post-Woolworth. I'll head back to NYC next week for a few days, city duties, and I guess (lucky timing) I'll see the one-night perf. I love to hear my words coming out of other people's moufs—quality preferred, but not obligatory.

Love,
Kenward

Dear Kenward,

It has been snowing for over four hours. No phones and the TV out, just as I was enjoying SOME LIKE IT HOT and before finale of *Sopranos*. Looking out at the (quite lovely) huge feathery snow I saw that the lights are blazing in all the trailers. Nobody else watching TV! So I settled in with *Henry Esmond*[49] and a Cherry Garcia bar. (You and I think

47   Elmslie, "Furtive Edna," in *Album* (Kulchur Press, 1969).
48   Elmslie, "The Woolworth Song," recorded at WBAI, NY, 1978.
49   William Makepeace Thackeray, *The History of Henry Esmond*, 1852.

they are diet bars because they are yogurt but know in our hearts anything so addictive is fattening.) But it reminded me of your fine poem, as usual deceptively light and witty. Lovely last lines: "through killing fields, back to/boyhood. Blue Nile source."

Thanks for the Brainard article. Wonderful Madonna.[50] Can't wait to see the show, and you and Mr. Yu too.

I hope the performance of *Furtive Edna* went well and that you had a good time. I can't find your website. Maybe I got the wrong 22 letters? Just kidding. I'll keep trying though.

I dug up some dandelions and other weeds. Major Work! Very proud of my labor . . . turned out I had spent about twenty minutes. Alas, haven't been swimming in a long time. Back is lousy and the wet weather no help. Had a colostomy last week that was particularly unpleasant because my spine is all entwined in intestines, or vice versa. It took them a long time, with much pushing and pulling.

Because of taking coumadin I bruise easily. My stomach and buttocks are covered with handprints! My stomach looks like an African hut! If I weren't so embarrassed about being so fat I'd love to show it to somebody. Sort of masochist art piece. Great color, black turning to yellow and purple in that lovely way. Polyps removed at least. It was so painful I was wide-awake and nicely looped on Demerol, was able to watch the procedure on monitor.

It was like the *MATRIX* or some TV/video game, especially the scenes with my dark vertebrae menacing and then the bright polyps, lassoed deftly by Keanu Reeves. Actually by a weird doctor. Before it began the nurse asked if I knew him. I said no and she said, "Don't gasp when you see him." (Which didn't add to my peace of mind) (piece of mind?) He looked to be about fourteen and was very small, sort of, well, ass-high to a caterpillar. I didn't gasp, but it was hard not to laugh when I saw he was even with the operating table and my derriere. His only other occupational choice would have been jockey.

Ivan and Dawn had their wedding reception Saturday. Informal and low-key. Very very sweet celebration. She is a wonderful woman.

---

50   Referring to a Joe Brainard collage.

Strong, honest, no-nonsense, loving. "Gets" all of Ivan's goodness and ignores his insecurities, which are gradually disappearing, due to her and to PEACEJAM work. He complains about it, but is very proud of what they are doing.

Harry is broken hearted. Judith[51] wants him to buy her a lawn-mower now. He doesn't have the money so he said no. First time in four years she didn't have him to Sunday dinner. She finally got a job, cook at a child-care center. She's the only unlikable person around.

Glad your Harold and Newty helping you out. Have you planted yet?

Sending you *Sniper*[52] with my poor little story in it. Also a translation, which would be more intelligible if they had italicized the names of Indian tribes, but still gives idea of Marcos.

Hope Padgetts have arrived and that you and Patti are walking. It's Monday morning and now I have ultrasound of breast lumps. They always find breast lumps then I have ultrasound then biopsy and all is ok, but going through it all a nuisance and Long walk to X-ray. Will send this off on the way with much love.

I had told Ivan I hadn't heard from you in a long time. He added to my fear of offending by saying that I shouldn't have told you the joke about the Siamese twins. Can't remember telling him I did, but we both have offended other people with that joke. This p.c. business has gone too far. Now we can't even joke about Siamese twins? Or their sex-life? (The real-life twins had a pretty amazing sex life, actually.) One of my favorite lines in literature is E.M. Forster's . . . well, I have forgotten it, but it is something like "as joyous as dwarves clapping." "little people clapping?" "A friendliness, as of dwarfs shaking hands, was in the air."[53]

Love,

LOOSHA

---

51 Boulder, CO, neighbors.

52 *Sniper Logic # 9*, 2001, with Lucia's story "B.F. and Me."

53 This last quote is the correct one, from E. M. Forster's *A Passage to India*, 1924.

Dear Loosha—

Very cold this morning, too cold for Harold to mow: four inches of snow on Mount Mansfield.

Only now it's Monday, June 4th. Ron will stride uphill, any second, 9AM date for a walk, subbing for Patty. Last night, I lured him to dinner & Tony Award TV. I'm slower and less intuitive at cooking, which annoys me, and makes me want to stick to Eating Out. Good simple salad, but a main course muss—a turkey breast in a yellow hairnet & fixings in plastic did not turn out well. Cranberry jelly rescued it somewhat. Decent fiddlehead ferns, a local find this time of year. It grows in the wild, easily, and tastes like muted asparagus.

The best Tony production number was saved for last—sex-crazed old ladies wielding their strollers, molesting Nathan Lane, co-star of the Broadway musical mega-hit, *The Producers*. Funny-ha-ha! Nathan, who won for Best Perf in a Musical, dragged his comely co-star co-Tony-nominee, Matthew Broderick, along, as if they were co-winners. Nicely done. Ron had never watched The Tonys, which I have, for years. Always makes me miss co-watcher Joe [Brainard]. Explained to Ron the derivation of Tony—named after a Denver theatre personage, Antoinette Perry,[54] whose very classy daughter was a chum of John Latouche's. Amid the *Ballad of Baby Doe* hoopla, we stayed with her, the daughter, in a cabin in the Rockies, highlands flat as a prairie, but thousands and thousands of feet above sea level. The moon & stars did seem unnaturally close.

Short walk with Ron. The staying power of my pins has declined from nonattention. Watching *ER* (late night TV)—the sped-up horrifics of hospital interventions, stress max—is a marvelous spur to self-care. Must of dreamt this—someone saying I was "retired," which I took umbrage at, in the dream. Writer guilt.

Finished a Hank James biggie, *The Princess Casamassima*, which

---

54   Mary Antoinette "Tony" Perry, American actress, director and cofounder of the American Theatre Wing, 1888–1946.

startled me with its cast of hazy revolutionaries, and its contoured man-darin depiction of London slumdom. One chapter ends: follow that hansom. Veering into an action tale! Also returned to Faulkner—*The Town*. Way way back, read much of his fictions, seduced by his dis-cursive circlings, narrative pile-up and mix of literary heft & red-dirt Southernisms.

I've recovered from my Congestion, energy a bit less low-'n'-slow, so today—plants I've sent off for, surrounding my work desk, will make it into the soil. Still haven't opened up my writing vent, though, one night, my noggin was inundated by a Faulkneresque flurry of lingo.

Ron is in constant touch with Patty, now in Rome, staying at a B&B Ursuline convent. But he relishes the chance to gab with me, unaccus-tomed to solodom—and it's a boon for me—What a sweet, innards resourceful, friend.

[. . .]

Chatted with Jean Boulte, who lives on the top-floor [of townhouse in New York], and who can get around, minimally, despite invasive AIDS pains. He went to see my one-act play, *Furtive Edna*, as done at the Poetry Project. Went over well, extra chairs for young folks audi-ence, and Edna's rendition of *The Woolworth Song* provoked a strong response. The director (voice-mail again) has promised me an audio soon, and also a video eventually.

Jim Morgan, boss of the York Theatre, phoned, not "to pressure me"—which means, subtext—pressure—to find out about my *Lola* revisions—I promised to send them off in a few weeks, so he can plan his season, in theory, including it for Feb. 2002.

I feel so "unambitious" right now, sort of a lethargic now-I-do-this-now-I-dothat-so-I-won't-fall-further-behind—but I generally enjoy the act of writing—settling into rewrites (I hope I hope) will perk me up a tad, and rid me of grumpy tendencies. I invited Vivy & Willie to come for a visit this month—even though the house isn't quite "ready"—pictures still not put up.

Ron has given me a memoir about Joe to read, which I'll tackle later today. His book about his dad turned into an awful trial, so I hope this "fits." He has a perfect brief collection of

poems-he-forgot-he-wrote, just out, which I'll hand-deliver to you—
next month? NEXT month!!!!

Love,
Kenward

BOULDER, CO
JUNE 9, 2001

Dear Kenward,

"The moon and stars did seem unnaturally close." How fine that
is. Reminds me of Steven Crane's[55] "indescribably blue sky." Which
worked only by him since he was so good with colors.

Nice to know where TONY came from. I watched TONYs of
course. I LOVE award shows. This year was first time in years that I
had actually Seen any of the Oscar nominations. Love them too and
always have favorites even if I haven't seen them. My sons ask me what
movie to see, they have for years . . . even though I never see any, rather
like the way my mother and Uncle John always had me handicap horses
and dogs at races. I was happy that *The PRODUCERS* was a sweep. I
do wish I had somebody to watch these with. Also miss muttering or
hollering with my sons when I watch baseball . . . will this afternoon
watching Belmont. I'm betting on INVISIBLE INK. My grandson
Nico is for MONARCHOS.

I've been watching more TV now that my writing muse has gone.
Wonderful TMC channel. Saw *GRAND ILLUSION* and last night
wept copiously over *LOVE AFFAIR* with Charles Boyer and Irene
Dunne. Good dialog in those days. Saw another with Jean Harlow that
was brilliant.

I've tried and tried to reread old Henry James, will give him another
go. He was a New Year's resolution a few years back, and it was a fine
year. Somehow like trying to discern what is the particular spice in this
soup sort of pleasure with each sentence. A deeply satisfying pleasure
but only if you give him your total attention.

I have been reading Faulkner off and on lately too. Strange and

---

55   Steven Crane, American poet and writer, 1871–1900.

surprising early book: *MOSQUITOS*. Intellectuals in New Orleans, sort of Martin Amisy! *SANCTUARY, LIGHT IN AUGUST* and *AS I LAY DYING* were the ones I reread with awe. I started to say that his villains are the most sexy in literature, but then there was Milton's Satan, and Heathcliff. Popeye in *Sanctuary* and Christmas in *Light in A.* wonderful characters. I love the darkness of his words. Miles Davis[56] said, "You know those dark Arkansas roads at night? That's how I want to play." Faulkner writes like Miles plays.

New translation. *First Snow on Fuji*. Stories by Kawabata. Just finished this. I love his work. Do you know his writing? SNOW COUNTRY and BEAUTY AND SADNESS. Novels, and PALM OF THE HAND: STORIES, favorites.

Anne Waldman scolded me for never having had her in my home. So I invited her to lunch. Day before I made asparagus soup. Good for us, Kenward. Sauté onions in little oil cook asparagus, non-fat chicken broth or non-fat buttermilk, which is creamier than real cream, blend it into puree, chill. (Do same with carrots and broccoli, put ginger in the carrot soup.)

The dumb computer was making red and green lines like crazy here. I checked and it accused me of having too many nouns. I have never been accused of such a thing before.

Anyway next day I made chicken and saffron rice, raspberry dessert, etc. etc. Spent the entire following day in bed. Just can't do it anymore. We did have a pleasant chat. She seems calmer, sweeter. This slowing down that is so painful for the rest of us is very becoming on her! To her?

People don't retire in Spanish. The word is "jubilar" to jubilate, which is decidedly more positive an attitude. I am, in fact, retired, most of the time.

I've been trying to "get out more" be more sociable and also to swim as much as possible. Went to Peter Michelson's (poet/colleague) to swim yesterday and swimming was heavenly but I over-did it, am in bed today. Went to two parties recently. Forget that idea. [. . .]

---

56   Miles Davis, American jazz musician, bandleader, and composer, 1926–1991.

Do you know your schedule yet? I know you read the 19th. When you know could you let me know when you might come over and whom you would like to invite. Whatever. Cocktails Dinner Breakfast Lunch. I will not personally Work or bake etc., but would like to host something to celebrate your visit. But if too much will be going on, then let me know that too. I am very happy that you are coming.

> *Love,*
> *LOOSHA*

CALAIS, VT

AUGUST 22, 2001

Dear Loosha—

The Padgetts are back! Last night, we hit downtown Montpelier, the one Thai eatery: excellent grub—situated on the one back street, spruced up two-story buildings, down a bit from the police station parking lot, where the Saturday Farmer's Market takes place. Patty has gum problems, pain, so we ordered "mild." Ron had a fine time in Copenhagen, enjoyed glamming beauteous blondes, was squired by two Danish youngster lad poets he grew fond of.

He subbed for his poet Dad, Kenneth Koch, who has left his cancer bubble in Houston, the bad cells having diminished markedly. He's feistier now, kept Ron on the phone, upon Ron's return, critiquing Ron's "Joe" bio book[57] mercilessly, Ron confessed. Pat, watching, couldn't figure out what was going on, Ron's appalled face, response restricted to neutral Uh-Huhs. He realized Kenneth was out of his head, from drugs and bubbledom, and let the fulminations wash over him.

Monday, I had lunch with my diabetes-duo relatives, my nephew Gordon [Weir], and his researcher wife, Susie, who made a major breakthrough, year before last. My sis Vivien [Elmslie] was there— we had a falling-out a while back, as she felt left out of my goal—to publish our mom's teenage journal, a project which is mired, right

---

57   Ron Padgett, *Joe: A Memoir of Joe Brainard* (Coffee House Press, 2004), then in manuscript form.

now—Lee Ann Brown, poet taken on by Wesleyan (like her ex, Steven Taylor), has proved pretty impossible as a bringer-outer.

The lunch was full of catch-up, including a full report of a very grand wedding of my oldest nephew, an ex-auto-biz exec, a widower, who has married a wealthy (as he is) widow. They had quite a shebang in Newport—the bridesmaids were given tiaras, a coach-and-four was the post-wedding vehicle, hundreds showed up, the floral arrangements were spiffy, one shaped like a swan, all very glitterati, much to my sister's delight. Her role was to light a Unity Candle, mid-ceremony, to affirm the fact both families are getting along just fine. She demurred, fearing she'd tremble in the act, masses of eyes glued to each quaver. A little flower girl sabotaged the flow, by slowly, slowly dropping each petal, now here, now there, down the long aisle. Bride and groom were ensconced on thrones for the wedding feast—rich folks, putting on the dog.

Today, misty and cool. It's nice to have a daily morning walk with Patty to look forward to. Wayne Padgett has taken over my website, thank heavens! There was a credit card problem (Mister Yu is a bit casual about credit cards, as he no longer has one of his own). We're out of touch, as, as 21-year-olders do, and could do, he's moved on. A new life! A credit card replacement tooled in yesterday—they were very nice about the mystery purchases in NYC, while I was here, and Mister Yu was there. I dimly recall leaving the card in a drawer in NYC.[58]

I'm not being at all Good About Writing. I have started the work Trevor Winkfield has made drawings for, and I've decided to call it *Snippets*[59]—a memoir ramble of fragments, which is how I remember the past.

Mostly, I've been tidying up that conversation with Mary Kite.[60] *Skanky Possum* will bring it out as a little chapbook,[61] fast, which

---

58 Kenward's break with Mr. Yu coincided with the unauthorized use of Kenward's credit cards.

59 Elmslie and Winkfield, *Snippets* (Tibor de Nagy Editions, 2002). Poetic and visual collaboration that, in earlier letters, Kenward was calling "Phat."

60 Mary Kite, American poet.

61 Elmslie and Kite, *Spilled Beans: A Conversation* (Skanky Possum, 2001).

suits me just fine, with little silhouette drawings by Joe Brainard interspersed: deer head, auto, parachutist.

And I've-finished *The Magic Mountain*,[62] which I got very impatient
at, in places—particularly an endless passage, describing the advent of
a victrola, to amuse the TBers after their fifth meal of the day—a new
evening entertainment. Herr Mann dutifully listed every record played.

Jimbo [Morgan] is supposed to come for a visit, and, happily, has put
off the new, scaled-down *Lola*, which I seem blocked about re-entering.
Lately, a Sondheim melody from *Follies* has been whirring through my
noggin, so maybe that's an omen I'll return to the fold.

That's about it, except a full account of being driven to Groton by
Jack Graves, and back. He spills the beans, marvelous monologue,
which, if I could reproduce it, via tape, would assure my place in the
[John Ashbery] Ashcan School of Narrative. [. . .]

Almost time for my constitutional, 7:55—so, toodle-oo, and I hope
you had bountiful familial pleasures, with more to come.

Love,
Kenward

BOULDER, CO
AUGUST 28, 2001

Dear Kenward—

For some reason I often dream about *The Magic Mountain*, the sky,
clear and cold, on balcony, all bundled up, the dining room with the
door slamming. Am I dreaming about my death or mixing it up with
Pombillo? Ski resort in Chile. Where we were all so young and delir-
iously happy. Wish I would dream about skiing scene in *The Magic
Mountain*, so sublime. Think I've given the old *M.M.* its last reading.

Went through my books other day (when I moved to trailer I got rid
of 1/2, criteria being will I reread). Eliminated 5 boxes yesterday. Amazing how many I have reread . . .

---

62   Thomas Mann, *The Magic Mountain* (Alfred A. Knopf, 1927) (English translation).

I'm always pleased when Padgetts are at the Poet's Corner.[63] Sorry about Kenneth Koch. Difficult to imagine him diminished in any way. Everything about him seemed crisp & well-made, fresh.

Loved your description of Newport wedding.

You are not being good about writing. There is a copious amount of material dying to be written, in prose, by you. Glad to hear about *Snippets*. Very sorry about *Lola*—and confused about credit cards. Is this a new credit card problem? There had been an incident when you had gone to get Mr. Yu out of the pokey—but supposably? (supposedly?) he was doing errand for you? I am very upset by this. Hard to believe it of Mr. Yu. CW so damaged & out & out needy & greedy one wasn't surprised. I'm amazed that you write of this so casually. His affection for you, and respect, very real. Sometimes it must be a pain in the neck to have $. People suspend morality like feeling it's OK to be a Brink's Robber.

[. . .]

So far Heaven for me is Oxycodone, that new time-release pain medication. I sleep all night, never feel high or drugged. Pain free much more of the time.

> *No news. Much love,*
> *Loosha*

NEW YORK, NY

SEPTEMBER 2 AND 4, 2001

Dear Lucia—

Today, End of Summer Panic receding, palliated by Vermont-Is-Back weather, clarity of cool sunny days, details sharpened, not muzzy from heat haze, sky a rich royal blue—Mama Nature elbowing her way into Look! No Hands! Art!, happens up here every year, come September.

Earlyish walk with Patty. Knees stiff, so I needs must use a cane. Our usual (this summer) trajectory, down to the pond, over grass, over the earthwork dam, grassed over, past cabin, up a bit via path in woods, which opens back onto the pond, briefly, one more time, pleasurable

---

63   Poet's Corner is what Kenward called his Calais, VT, home.

164

*Love, Loosha*

different vantage point. Duck families swim about, this time of year. No beaver nose, making its V-wave of froth. Windless, but morning pond mist was scudding ethereally in one direction (south?)—downhill, where the Padgetts live. Patty has stopped taking antibiotics for a recurring gum problem she dreads: pain, swelling. She's tired of cooking, wants Freedom from Stove. Wants to eat out all the time. Same here! A bit grumpy from E of S panic,[64] off the idea of food, I initially resisted (yesterday) Ron's invite to

A)   Come downhill to see a Joe [Brainard] video two sweet giggly French college girls made, interviews with Joe near & dear ones, NYC last winter, plus París Brainardites such as Harry Mathews & Ed White.[65]

B)   Dine at Julio's, a Mehican eatery in downtown Montpelier.

I caved in pretty fast. I'm grappling with a new "health" machine, so I can report to my Vermont doc (a sweet guy, cute too) re. new high blood pressure. The machine (Ron has one) of course discombobulated me, wrapping upper arm correctly, the nasty sound Velcro makes, trying to figure out a diagram of ARM and ARM WRAP, an inch above elbow. So Ron tutored me, and I still had time for an afternoon nap, pre-video. Which was well put together (a graduation requirement in lieu of a written thesis). The camera caught me post-fat-farm, so I looked less jowelly and eye-baggy, was startled at how "expressive"— and constant—my hand-and-arm gestures were. Maybe because I was talking to French girls, so I thought my English needed a physical assist—narrowed eyes to show irony, etc. and as the French are such whizzes at gestural whoop-di-do, I was trying to compensate for not speaking their lingo. The gab seemed OK, and my screen personality didn't repel me, as can happen. Like hearing your own voice recorded—a fakery That's-Not-Me intrusion—Tech Trickery. Boo!

A mystery gap opened up. A collab with Jonathan Williams,[66] Gay

---

footnotes64   End of Summer.
65   Harry Mathews, American poet, writer, 1930–2017. Edmund White III, American writer, b. 1940.
66   Jonathan Williams, American poet, publisher, essayist, and photographer, 1929–2008. He collaborated with Joe Brainard on *gAy BCs* (Finial Press, 1974).

ABCs or sump'n he wrote, big yawn, with gay "porn" drawings by Joe
I'd never seen. Immersed as I've been in decorous novels by Barbara Pym
and E.M. Forster and Thomas Mann, in which Miss Manners still is a
deity of sorts, and the blinds are drawn on what can go on in bed—I
was besieged by am-I-seeing-what-I'm-seeing jolts. Didn't know Joe'd
drawn that. He'd been asked to make drawings for A Gay Sex Manual—
successor to a best-selling Hetero Manual. Which fell through, his
involvement, but what about the manual? Ron has checked, and none is
listed. But I half-remember leafing through it, and putting it aside. No
Joe drawings. Along with great angst about mastering new machines, I
find sex programs extremely intimidating. Put that there, while doing
this? Good grief, what'll they think up next? Ed White—his huge white
video flesh legs looked totally unreal; how can human flesh, on film, be
so deadly white?—was to write the text. Or did.

That's the mystery. The ABC drawings have flown the coop, so far,
but are not a mystery. Ron traced them to the gaga-old publisher of
the Jonathan Williams collab with Joe. The oldster's assistant sold a
hundred copies to Ron, mostly for John Brainard, Joe's bro, who has
stashed Brainardiana where he lives in Connecticut with Caroline,[67] a
food world wheeler & dealer, who helps run the James Beard Foundation. Except, summer development, Joe's bro's moved to Paris, to "find"
himself as artist. Temporarily. Or not? That's another mystery.

SEPTEMBER 4

Well, I've veered off into a reality soap opera jungle. It's morning
again, one day after Labor Day. England has declared WAR, Hitler
having invaded Poland. "My" country at war, 1939, me a ten-year-old
in-my-mind Brit. That's as big as it gets—childhood memories of real
world supra-events that impinge on millennial cool.

Patty & Ron are driving to Burlington International Airport to
pick up their son Wayne, who has taken charge of my website. Mr.
Yu is now in another life—Berlin Artist—and we're not in touch. I'm
not non-judgmental re. credit card scamming. [. . .] Wayne has given

---

67   Caroline Stuart, American cookbook author and food critic, was married to
John Brainard, brother of Joe Brainard.

up going to his Brooklyn gym, focusing on my website totally. He has a laptop, so I'll get to see the additions, this afternoon, on his small screen. Mid-month, my website, ta-da, will launch into outer space, joining millions and millions of other websites. I'm incapable of writing right now, it seems, but maybe I'll re-enter *Lola* this very morning . . . it's so still out, cool, and I have hours to myself, before I drive to the hosp for a knee X-ray—to find out about the stiffness.

TERRIFIC last letter from you . . . especially loved the Little Queen you helped create. Guess that brings you up-to-date. Must clean out my icebox, odd aroma, then *Lola*. And straighten up the kitchen. Then *Lola*.

Love,
Kenward

BOULDER, CO
SEPTEMBER 9, 2001

Dear Kenward,

What an especially delightful letter. The end of Vermont summer days sound so fine, with ducks and pond mist, royal blue skies, Padgetts down the hill. I was pleased to see Joe's paintings of the house. Not at all how I had imagined it (and I'm usually pretty good.) (Not true. In first impressions, etc., I am remarkably wrong most of the time, occasionally Very right.) As a child I always wanted to live in a Heidi-like cabin on the woods, so MY version of your Calais place was a tiny unpainted wooden structure, sort of a hut, really, with a little porch and a rocking chair. How all your visitors fit into my version I never questioned.

The paintings I truly loved were those of Whippoorwill, the tenderness of them.

Loved your account of Joe's sexy video. Embarrassing to admit this, and quite amazing, considering all the things I have lived through, I have never seen a pornographic film of any kind! Southern lady? Latin American influence? Whatever the reason I have ducked on occasions when I could have. Once Terry and I went to see *Behind the Green Door* but they wouldn't let us in because he was a minor. I get very uncomfortable during movie sex scenes. Everybody seems to look at them with such detachment. How can images be erotic and not arousing at the same time? I find them very sexy and, well, distracting. Had the same problem with an unattractive female dental hygienist with huge breasts who kept billowing into me while she was scraping away and saying Spit. Lordy. I felt like asking, "Was that good for you, too?"

One of the funniest love scenes ever is in Terry Southern's *FLASH AND FILIGREE*. Two people having sex in a car is described in precise detail, so complicated a tangle of arms and legs and tongues, elbows and assorted members that it seems like the mating of Indian deities. Exhausting, because everybody is doing so many things at once like nibbling left ear while unfastening a bra and shifting into park and blowing on a neck. When I was five my friend Kentshereve and I watched our neighbors "doing it" on or about the kitchen table. We rolled around on the grass, laughing. It was the funniest thing we had ever seen. Coupling is ridiculous, really. I think it was good "spin" to declare it sinful, makes it not so ludicrous and much more glamorous.

I thought it interesting that Reinaldo Arenas, in *Before Night Falls*, said he rarely had sex in prison, that the lack of surprise or pretense and danger, the joy of decloseting someone made it too boring. Or words to that effect.

Fascinating drama of the disappearing ABC drawings, intrigue even more dramatic when it involves the James Beard Foundation somehow.

Don't forget to tell me when you have a web site, and how to find it.

Wow. Page two and I forgot to say that I'm writing a story, or something. Completely dismissed depression and gloominess. I feel like I'm home, I'm me. Don't know yet if it "works." Don't really care, even if I end up chucking it. Think I'll be able to remind myself that any silence need not be final.

Bob Creeley and Bobbie [Louise Hawkins] and Sidney Goldfarb came to breakfast yesterday. We had a long and delightful visit, much laughter, many memories. (My last two husbands, Newton and Berlin, were editors of Harvard *WAKE* with him, and were best friends for years.) I first knew Bob and Bobbie in 1956, love them both dearly. He gave a good reading on Friday, prose. Bobbie is preparing for one-woman show of monologues in October. Six performances at BMOCA.

They are witty, mordant, crisp . . . best she's done in years. She knows it too and is radiant, looks about 45.

Glad to hear you decided to reenter *Lola*. I Know this is good idea. Hope your knee is better. I'm in bad shape, bad back pain, but it is because I went out to dinner several times last week, then the reading, then breakfast. I HAD been much better, which gave me the strength to do all those things. So I'll start all over: do yoga and deep breathing daily, stay in bed and write on my story all next week.

Glad to hear you have your home blood pressure kit. Velcro is awful isn't it. I have a particular resentment toward it. During one of my post-alcoholic crashes and periods of unemployment, desperate to find a job, I took the exam for substitute teaching in the Berkeley public schools. The Exam took ALL day and was very hard. Multiple choice in most areas, with an essay for the writing part. Well I made an A in Math, History, Reading, etc. but in the essay I got an F, so wasn't hired to teach. The Essay question had been, "Write about one of the most important inventions occurring in your lifetime."

OK. I wrote about Velcro. It was a Perfectly written essay. I stated my basic premise clearly and in excellent prose I substantiated all my claims. I had interesting minor details such as the fact that Velcro has exactly the same design as the stomachs of caterpillars, and it sticks in the same way a caterpillar hangs on to branches. I believe that Velcro is undermining the very fabric of American life. Alas I can't remember the many reasons I gave but one was the use of Velcro closures on kid's shoes. Previously a rite of passage in American childhood and perhaps in fact one of few occasions when fathers bonded with their children was when they taught them to tie their shoelaces. Children today are abandoned to their own resources, and to the easy way out. The sound of Velcro, resounding all across the nation, affects our youth more than the media. This constant ripping and tearing incites the rampant violence we deal with daily. (Interestingly enough, in Pacific rim nations where there is no Velcro there is a similar dearth of suicide and murder.) Anyway, you get the idea. They were not amused.

> *Sorry, got carried away!*
> *Much love from Loosha La Louche*

[The following letters are written immediately after the September 11, 2001, terrorist attacks in New York City and Washington, DC. Kenward has recently returned to Manhattan. They discuss the state of the country, weapons of mass destruction, and the war on terror, and share personal reactions to news coverage. Lucia writes of her new book project, a memoir about all the places she'd lived. Kenward writes of a poetic tribute to Joe Brainard in New York.]

BOULDER, CO

OCTOBER 1, 2001

Dear Kenward,

A short note, just because it has been too long that we've been out of touch . . . perhaps you feel the same . . . I can't really Talk or write. Nothing seems to make much sense. My friends are all fine; I hope yours are as well. Everything seems frightening and wrong. The cruelty of the event brought back the pain of many other deaths and has made me fearful for friends who are alive, and for myself too at the most basic level.

See why I don't write? This sounds so melodramatic and goofy. I'm fine, going about my business, whatever that is, but how can I write about how I AM? Which is profoundly saddened and shaken. So please write and tell me how You are. Has autumn come? When will you return to the city? Do you feel like staying in Vermont?

I do have big news actually. My son Dan and his new wife have been house hunting in Venice (CA). They found a duplex with a smaller unit, which could be rented to me. In December two other sons are going to come pack me up and move me out to Rialto Street, five blocks from the ocean. Only a few blocks from Beyond Baroque. I can read fortunes on the boardwalk. I read my own, trying to decide whether this was good idea. The final card was nine of spades, which can be read as a new era, a transformation, or death. Well, we'll see.

I'm very moved, forgive the pun. I have been stubbornly independent for so long, this tragedy made me very lonely for my family. Dan sweetly said that they felt lonely for me and wanted me to move there.

I am excited and of course anxious and nervous. I can't bear to think about leaving Jenny and Ivan, and Bobbie et al.

Would love to hear from you. Hope our letters cross. I miss you and love you,

     LOOSHA

NEW YORK, NY

OCTOBER 5, 2001

Dear Loosha—

Last letter to you (Vt) was lost, due to a tiny power failure, lasted just a few seconds—my "surge protector" was disconnected, so ker-flooey went the words.

Back at Greenwich Ave, I've barely budged from my house, except for nonhome-cooked meals a few doors away—1st night at Bruxelles, fancy . . . Kidneys! Six real oysters! An artichoke vinaigrette! Creme brulee! Two glasses of white wine! Yesterday lunch, The Den, prole cheeseburger, clam chowder, wolfed to be in time for Helper, nice French guy, who got this computer up and running, cleaned out the mouse black ball (mystery cat hairs . . . how did they transplant into the outbuilding in Vermont, which the cats haven't visited in ages)? Blissfully easy to maneuver now.

The basement smells weird. Burnt dust. Same outside. Was so worried Jean Boulte (top-floor) had left the planet, as his answering service wasn't functioning. He's so on his last legs, has been for years and years. But he answered his phone this morning, vast relief, gave his account of The Aftermath, candlelit mourners, the young in particular in deep shock. "Regular" TV still not functioning. I'll see him tomorrow, when he Comes Downstairs for a visit: fairly rare. He's so regenerative, such graceful innards, despite his unbelievable sufferings from AIDS. Has no energy to waste feeling bitter or sorry for himself, two of many thought & mood pitfalls I'm not always wily at skirting.

[. . .]

Yesterday morning, the two Joe Gallery Nice Guys[68] came over.

---

68   Andrew Arnot and Eric Brown of Tibor de Nagy Gallery.

How do they stay nice in the Art Gulag—worse than selling second-
hand cars. The money & greed part is so voracious. A Joe [Brainard]
show is coming up pronto: visual for announcement enclosed. They
picked some works from my massive Joe collection—five gorgeous
moviestar collages, small, for display in a vitrine—outed, finally.

Dorothy Lamour! Mae West! Greta Garbo! Tab Hunter, imbedded
in flowers.[69] I think you saw them screened. Plus five drawings from
Sung Sex,[70] two of which I relinquished for them to sell, to help them
out a bit. The drawings are in the book, and I'm not a fanatic when
it comes to owning 'the original' . . . looks, so they said, like Art Biz
might go into an awful slump, like everything—maybe really stark
times ahead. All these NYC emporia, galleries, restaurants, etc etc—run
savvily, catering to very savvy folks . . . what the city is here for, all very
shaken, fearful of the future.

I have two gigs coming up, week after next. With tech help (to be
firmed up)—I've figured out what I should do. Ten minutes of songs
for the Tribute to Joe—with Ron, Bill Berkson, five poets in all, including Frank Bidart—who had a huge passion for Joe. [. . .] As I come
last, three songs Joe favored may give audience ears a break. I'll risk
Who'll Prop Me Up in the Rain though it has three high-note places now
beyond me. End with *Sneaky Pete*. Probably *Middle of Nowhere*, which
you heard Steven [Taylor] & I do. Naropa tape sent me thanks to Mary
Kite's intervention is "archival" according to the Padgetts—i.e. lousy
Naropa tech. Guess I'll spare myself some grief, and not give it a listen.

Second is with glamorous Rob't Redford look-a-like, Bill Berkson,
the following night, at the Poetry Project. I've decided on reading one
work—*Fifties Probe*—my Ashbery Roast cut a tad. The Yorkies gave me
a 'special' CD of the Latouche revue cast saying *Touche's Salon*[71] (they
had a few extra minutes in the studio—such a nice gesture) so, with
[tech] help, I'll start off with that, and cut in "live".

Must of been a bit depressed all summer, did so little writing, not

---

69   Referring to Joe Brainard collages of these figures.

70   Elmslie and Brainard, *Sung Sex* (Kulchur Press, 1989).

71   Poem Kenward wrote about John Latouche's New York City apartment.

much of anything really, let things "go" . . . postcards, collages, gardening. Bad health report up there, so I'll go see my nice Joosh doc here—"thyroid" problem? True? Knee X-ray proved arthritis is kicking in forcefully, but not bad enough to warrant intervention. Yeah, hi-blood pressure. Enough old age 'plainting.

Glad I have work commitments to focus on—the Nice Gallery Guys want my new collab with Trevor Winkfield by the end of the month, so it can be in hand for Trev's show in Feb. Found a work (woke up at 2 AM, riffled) I'd forgotten about, so I may collage that with the driblet I came up with this (last) summer. Its new title is *Snippets*. Prose poem format. Will need shaping up, but mustn't clobber it into prom presentability. Read a lot in Vermont. Some Grace Paley[72]—such a good ear for gab—I thought most forceful. But I'm not sure she's a "keeper"— one of the potencies in your stories—they can be gone back to, and new shadings keep emerging. LOVED Anselm Hollo selected poems!

Hate to foist my minor (so far!) health troubles on your eyes—but we both get to kvetch, right? I think you kvetch much less than you think you do . . .

Trip back a breeze. Jack Graves, the Man with the Van, gave me good update, including his Viagra experience. [. . .]

Almost 5 AM. The kitties are being a bit stand-offish, punishing me for their caged drive south, but there they are, linked at the foot of my bed, as per usual. The one movie I long to see is by the cheenius[73] who is Joe, in the short *I Remember* flick. *Hedwidge and . . . Angry Inch*, something like that. Raves from chums I trust.

Hope your autumn's going OK. Brightest part of the summer was connecting so pleasurably with you. And seeing for myself how terrific you look and are.

Love,
Kenward

---

72   Grace Paley, American short story writer, 1922–2007.
73   John Cameron Mitchell, American actor, playwright, director, b. 1963. Mitchell portrayed Joe Brainard in the 1998 short film by Avi Zev Weider, *I Remember*, based on Brainard's book by that title. Kenward is referring to the film made from Mitchell's musical play, *Hedwig and the Angry Inch*, 2001.

BOULDER, CO

OCTOBER 12, 2001

Dear Kenward,

Your letters mean so much to me. I complained to Ivan last week that it had been ages since I heard from you. He was instantly comforting, told me not to worry, that he was sure you were fine, just busy. No, I'm not Worried about Kenward, I said. I simply need to hear from him!

I was worried a little. Projecting, and, it seems, rightfully. Our physical troubles are quite similar and our moods are too, especially when we're feeling lousy and not writing. I had my worst year yet. Even with the miraculous Oxycontin my back is very bad and getting around much harder. I had to stop taking it because I'm on Coumadin, but for awhile CELEBREX was great for arthritis in knees and hands, etc. Please let me know about thyroid, blood pressure etc. It's pitiful, I know, but I now find these topics interesting, and I want to know how you are.

In Oakland thyroid guy said I had Hashimoto's disease and gave me Synthroid, which was wonder energy drug. In Mexico the Drs threw that out and my Dr. here says thyroid is fine. There is a special test for that condition. Not that I want any New complaints, but I have fond memories of the energy (not speedy-like at all) I had with Synthroid.

I sympathize with arthritis and difficulty getting around. And how to lose weight when it is so hard to move?

What I can't figure out is why taking out my air hose wouldn't serve as an aerobic workout.

I think I told you that at last I'm back at work. Not really since somehow have no Time. It is impossible not to watch the news. Today there is warning of new terrorist act to come any day now. Period. Why was it necessary to tell us this? They say it is to make us more vigilant. Of What?

Still need my Nap 12 to 3, and still collapse into bed at six. Since people found out that I'm moving, I have many visitors and phone calls, which have been nice but also tiring. My story is "set" though,

Will be a long quirky sort of memoir.[74] Fun to do, so when I get settled, or even when things are quiet here I can get back into it easily. Nothing makes me happier than to have a new piece running through my mind.

Great to hear about your two gigs. Wonderful choice of songs. I have heard them all I think. You and Steven doing "Who'll Prop Me Up?" was wonderful, brought tears to my eyes. Wow, how eerily timely it is now. No? "Middle of Nowhere" is great, music a pleasure.

The Poetry Project evening sounds fine too. Love the combination of you and Bill Berkson. *Snippets* in the works too. You are doing quite a bit, you must admit. [. . .]

I loved Anselm's selected poems. Also terrific is his book *Caws and Causeries*. Wonderful essays. I will miss him and Jane[75] so much. Didn't sound like you had received my letter with news that I'm moving to Venice, CA in a month or so, to live in smaller unit of duplex next to son Dan.

I alternate between Desolation about leaving my friends here and wild joy about seeing my family. All mixed up. Today was Thursday, shopping with Harry day. Sweet old guy sniffled all the way home and when he got out he said, "I want you to know it isn't just that you take me to stores and doctors. You're just plain swell."

I never did really like Grace Paley, although her titles are great. She's somehow too smart. I've been enjoying Penelope Fitzgerald.[76] Sort of "B" novels, not smart but sharp, sort of Muriel Sparky.[77]

Reading [George] Meredith's *The Egoist*. Almost chucked it, glad I hung in there. Language and wit delightful. The hero such an ass you have to love him. Super book.

[President George W.] Bush is talking away now about routing out the enemies. Oh, Lord. Sick sick at heart. The first week the American flags flying were very moving. I find them chilling now, symbols of

---

74   *Welcome Home.*

75   Poets and close friends, Anselm and Jane Hollo. Anselm Hollo, *Caws and Causeries* (La Alameda Press, 1999).

76   Penelope Fitzgerald, English poet, writer, biographer, 1916–2000.

77   Muriel Spark, English writer and poet, 1918–2006.

power and aggression. My Mexican nieces say that Latin Americans would be more sympathetic if the USA would make an attempt to evaluate itself, take a look at the actions that have created hatred toward us. Seems like we're displaying the arrogance that is so resented. Bizarre to watch the news about the tragedy and the war interrupted by our luxury ads. F.A.O. Schwartz toy catalogue with $1000 Barbie dolls, etc.

I am very glad to be going to Venice. My other sons have all said that they will help if Dan or I need $. (I will be paying $800 rent) My favorite grandson in Oakland has asked if he can come some weekends to stay with me. His parents say he's typically impossible teenager and think this is great idea. So do I. One reason I've been depressed I think is not feeling like I'm any good to anybody. Can't wait to be a grandmother again. [. . .] I feel like a child going home to a loving family. Bush's speech is taking over my letter. It's true what he is saying, we have all come closer and . . . He says he is amazed that anyone could hate us. He did just say, "I reinerate" but it's no longer cool to make fun of him.

NEXT DAY:

Hope your cats have settled down. Late in her illness my sister still got out of bed to go in to watch Peter Jennings' news and to pet her two cats. Olivia and Violet, mother and daughter. The mother twelve the daughter six, inseparable. Their fur made it hard for her to breathe, lung cancer far advanced, so we decided to send them to be washed. Marcelino (the Seferino of story[78]) put them in a basket and took them to the vets. The vets put them to sleep, then washed them. Good idea, similar to dentists there, who not like here where you get cleaning and come back three or four times for fillings. There they put you under, do everything, and then send you home in the afternoon when you wake up. Well, the cats came home, still asleep, still in the basket. When they woke up they immediately attacked one another, hissing and yowling. They must have not recognized the other because of their new smell, and they each assumed that the other had put her in a box

---

78   Lucia writes about her sister's death in "Del Gozo Al Pozo," first published in *Sniper Logic* No. 4, 1996, collected in *Where I Live Now*.

and taken her away. They fought, well, like cats and dogs, horribly. Had to be fed in different rooms, had to visit my sister separately. NEVER spoke again, after always sleeping curled into each other. After she died each sat outside her door, one on the left, the other on the right, howling, alone, for days.

Ivan and Dawn nominated for Nobel Peace prize![79] I'm not supposed to tell but have to tell you. Imagine how Ivan is feeling. He's already wondering what to wear to Oslo.

It was so good to hear from you.

All my love,
LOOSHA

NEW YORK, NY

OCTOBER 18, 2001

Dear Loosha—

Your Big Move Letter went astray—jolted me considerably to think of you pulling up stakes, when your stakes were so pleasurable for me, as guest, brunch participant, viewer of your surround of nabe kiddos and nibbly deer, and inside, everything resonated so of you: a comfy welcoming surround.

Fast Lane Week, a bit scary, trying to keep up. The really major news is: I now know, for sure, Joe's a Genius. The show at PS #1, somewhere in Long Island City, is a knock-out, spread out perfectly, not jammed into wily clumps (his Whippoorwills) (my whippet) bunched together gracefully (this was in Berkeley), ditto the *Nancy* works[80] and his flowers. The main room—there are three—is quite huge, simple, authoritative but somehow not museumy. High ceiling. Parquet. I hired a car, went with Jean Boulte from upstairs, and with Jean-Claude, Helper #1, computer expert. Ron Padgett was standing guard for all six hours of

---

79   Ivan Suvanjieff and Dawn Engle have been nominated for the Nobel Peace Prize seventeen times for the work of their nonprofit PeaceJam Foundation.

80   From 1963 to 1978, Joe Brainard made more than a hundred artworks appropriating the Nancy character from Ernie Bushmiller's comic strip, begun in 1938 and continuing today. Brainard's selected images were published in *The Nancy Book*, Brainard (Siglio Books, 2008). The flowers are Brainard collages.

the opening, and there were a lot of oldie pals to schmooze briefly with familial reverbs.

Joe's work takes over astonishingly. Ron [Padgett] and I had the same joyous response—this Joe we spent so much of our lifetime with: we didn't fully realize how great an artist he is, a massive realization to adjust to. Not a dark secret—an ecstatic expansion. Of course we loved him and loved his work, treasured it, never took it for granted, how it lit up our daily rounds. Still, it's a major astonishment, to see him yanked up so high, into such a lofty realm so very few artists are at home in, deserve to be at home in, will continue to survive in, despite fads and trends and changing ways of looking at art.

I wrote a really grumpy letter about my Boulder exclusion to Connie,[81] Joe's curator, and last night, we reconnected (she accepted my openness and anger about being "eviscerated" curatorially at BMOCA.)

I urged her to make sure there's a photo record of the show, what hung where, because it'll be dispersed, post-Vegas, and vanish. My vehemence, I think, will galvanize her into seeing that it happens. I also was forthright with Ron about this—he was going to do the camera-click honors himself—PS #1 has a too shoddily disorganized staff to attempt this itself. So hopefully a Pro will tackle this project.

The Tribute to Joe at The New School[82] was fine—three poets read Joe's work (Ron, Bill Berkson, and Frank Bidart, who did very well.) Then Connie talked about Joe's work, fine, from a curator's point of view, I was saved for last—the cherry on the sundae—took me two songs to warm up, but I ended up OK. Last night, at the Poetry Project, Bill Berkson went first—the deadest reading I've ever heard him give. Post double-hernia operation problem? Emphysema too. Just lifeless, why I don't go to many poetry readings: corpse aura. So the audience (compensation) was very friendly to me, my voice was fine, hit the high notes solidly, and the jokes sailed. Felt happy afterwards that I can go full tilt.

[. . .]

---

81   Art curator Constance Lewallen, b. 1939, married poet Bill Berkson in 1998.
82   The New School, private university in New York City.

Well, I hope your new site works out well, and I'm glad you'll have family at hand. And I'm very happy you're back into word work again. I'm not, not yet, but with no more gigs, maybe I can thread my way back into the labyrinth words come to me from.

Also wish you could whisk to NYC to see Joe's Show. Looks like there's one performance of *The Grass Harp* at the Pasadena Playhouse in Feb (book-in-hand) as well as Three Scenes from *City Junket*[83] in SF (book in hand)—part of a poet play evening Kevin Killian has put together . . . plus Joe in Vegas. I'll head west in Feb, and long to connect with you in Venice: not that far away, time-wise. I'll see my nice Joosh doctor next week, and I'll mention the medicines that helped you.

So great, Ivan a possible Nobelist, which I haven't mentioned to a soul.

Love,
Kenward

BOULDER, CO
OCTOBER 28, 2001

Dear Kenward,

Glad that you realized that Joe really was a genius, not only in your eyes. I had seen mostly his *Nancy* paintings and other pop art. Had mostly admired the wit and fun of him. But seeing the show I was Amazed by the richness and diversity of his work. Also had not realized how ahead of his time he was, how many things he did before others picked up on them. The religious pieces are exquisite, wonderful. I loved what he said about them, that if people thought he was mocking religion he would not want to show them. I saw his show several times. I think most people who see his work feel like I do. The pleasure is not simply an aesthetic one, not matter how visually Fine they are . . . the spirit of them separately and together has a deeply spiritual and joyous Intent. Several times I read where he loved to please but there is more

---

83   Elmslie, *City Junket* (Adventures in Poetry, 1972; republished by Bamberger Books, 1987).

than that quality. His loving comes through in every painting. Because of his paintings and of course because of what you have told me I feel very close to him. Wish we were lying around in your place reading Barbara Pym. So wish I had known him. Really wish I could see the show at PS#1.

Delighted to hear about the successes of the tribute and the Poetry Project. You're still going strong, no? I hope I see you in February.

[. . .]

Huge event. Went to party at Jenny [Dorn]'s last night. Old lover was there. Sportswriter from Boston, married unhappily. Still wildly attractive. I was upset, that he should see me now, so fat and sick and old. But he still liked me! Called this morning to urge me to come up for dinner and to sleep over. We had great ongoing torrid romance for years. Wish I could have gone. I am too worn out after last night. DID cheer me up though.

Oh, the move. I'm Very mixed up. The Venice house fell through. Now they are looking at one in Santa Monica. The cottage for me is one big room, a hot plate and toaster oven. Sounds awful, altho Dan says I'll love it. I love my little trailer and hate to leave. It is light and pretty and I have washer and dryer, deer and rabbits . . . Great kitchen, tons of wall space so I can change paintings around all the time. I asked Dan if my books would fit. He said probably not but that I can store them in boxes in his garage. Oh pain and misery. I can just see myself digging through boxes at ten p.m., looking for something to read.

I know I want to live with them. They are warm and loving. Sincerely Want to take care of me. I'm afraid I will need care, my back and breathing are worse all the time. The world is such a scary and ugly mess I need to be with my family, miss them now more than ever. Have CT scan and ultrasound next week, Jane Hollo pushing me in wheelchair. It will be good to have strong sons to do this. I did tell you that my oldest son, with the alcohol and psychological problems, assorted recent institutionalizations, has decided to move to Venice also. At first I was heartsick. But he and I have been writing emails daily, almost daily phone calls. I've been very frank and tough with him about getting himself together and we are on good honest footing now. I'm happy now that he'll be there. Dynamic, loving, lovable man.

So hate to leave friends here. Jenny, Ivan, Bobbie, the Hollos, Steve Katz, etc. Cried all the way home from Denver last night.

Bobbie gave four performances of monologues at BMoCA. Big success so she is cheered up, looks wonderful.

Ivan wrote a new song. He's happy. He's "relieved, really" about not getting the Nobel. It's tough at the top.

Well, guess I am happy too. Feel very lucky and loved. I've got a good start on story or maybe a novella. Packing takes up the few hours "up" each day, but I've got it in my head, will get back to it once I am settled. That's another anxiety producing problem. Don't know when I will move . . . when they "close" or if my trailer sells I have to move even if there is no place. Mail worries me . . . no address yet. No doctor yet. Wow, I will miss my wonderful doctor. I must have moved 200 times in my life[84] . . . Usually love to move, and love to decorate new places. This time I am totally anxious, terrified of the trip itself. Well, of course, anxious about the entire World right now. Did you read the *New Yorker* article about civil war theory? Latest thing to scare me. Anytime I read paper or watch news I am very glad to be going Home.

While I was packing I dipped into the box of your letters. Ask Ron what he thinks about publishing them. They are truly some of your best best writing, each one a gem.

> *All my love,*
> *Loosha*

---

84   Lucia's memoir, *Welcome Home*, comprises writing of the various homes she lived in throughout her life.

PART III | 2001-2003

Letters from Croyden Avenue, Los Angeles, CA
Letters from Calais, VT, and New York, NY

*[In the following letters, Lucia has moved to Los Angeles, and she famil-
iarizes Kenward with her new surroundings. She's close to her sons and
grandsons, reuniting with friends in California, breathing easier at sea level, and continuing to work on her memoir. Kenward is finishing* Snippets,
*a collaboration with Trevor Winkfield. Lucia writes of the death of poet
Fielding Dawson and of her own health battles and treatments.]*

LOS ANGELES, CA

DECEMBER 10, 2001

Dear Kenward—

Won't have a printer until my boxes come . . . between 18th &
23 . . . (since so little they are part of larger load . . .) Will actually
move in on 25th. My little house looks like drawings I always made as a
kid of Dream House (no chimney)—know this was right move. [. . .]

Went to boardwalk for breakfast today. Parked. Used my walker to
get close enough to Feel the spray! Smell the water! Great day . . . clear
clean skies. Everybody thinks it's cold! So no one on beach except all
these people doing Celebrex, Tai Chi exercises.

I went into Rasta shirt & incense stall—bought some myrrh and guy
didn't have change, for a ten—asked me to watch the store! So cool—I
sold 25 frangipani sticks for a dollar, put them in bag, but people had to
wait until he came back with the change.

Waiter in sidewalk cafe let me in emergency exit so I wouldn't have
to walk all the way around. Central casting sent him—John Cusack-
cute with wisecracking ongoing rap. I asked him what the race was
(100s of people in blue shirts racing past). He said they were giving out
free samples of Nutrasweet. Best part, certainly not the coffee, was that
the bus boy was one-handed! Deft as all get out. Scraped dishes with his
stump!

Small World Book Store—new and used. Had you & me & new
Alice Munro! Much more but I was worn out by then.

I like all the people here. Feel at home walking, sitting, etc. as I
never ever once did in Boulder. Many old people here (unlike Boulder). All kinds of pretty and nutty people here & best part is that the
normal ones and the nutty ones all greet other people, like in Mexico,

Photo of Lucia taken on the drive from Colorado to California in 2001. Written on back: "Foto of me at the Mirage Hotel where there were white tigers in the lobby. Two men do something with them in a performance, but we missed that."

again not like Boulder where they are listening to inner voice or meditation tape.

[. . .]

I'm still writing. Stuck on boat chapter but it's a technical POV problem . . . still have my story so am deeply happy and at home.

I know you're still in the same place, but where I used to get your mail has changed. And writing to you changed. So it's as if you're more distant & I Miss you.

Sort of a new problem: Not new but apparent now that I'm living with others. I'm decidedly batty. Maybe not Alzheimer's but slow & confused & gaga . . . Can't figure out TV, microwave, telephones, computer, and well, most assorted simple tasks. Feel like a fool and or dodderer. Plus I talk too much.

> *I love you,*
> *Loosha*

NEW YORK, NY
DECEMBER 13, 2001

Dear Loosha—

What a vision! A one-armed dishwasher—stump aplomb. I'm tempted to pull up stakes, head out your way, go California in a big way. Proximity to the Pacific does affect human beans, that's for sure. Tan. Blond. Tan Blonds. Organic flakiness—with such an endless expanse so close, thudding away, certain preoccupations and pseudo-necessities kinda drop away. Which brings to mind the year I went to San Diego with Joe—the UC where his & my archives are tucked away.[85] A collector/donor, Robert Butts, whose parents ran a most profitable liquor store, gave the Joes he'd collected assiduously through the years to UC, which put together a celebration to honor this acquisition—including an assemblage of poets flown in for a whoop-di-do reading. Joe and I were given a UC penthouse, for, I assume, four-star visiting dignitaries.

This particular visiting dignitary wasn't averse to peeping through Venetian blinds at a flat rooftop with most fascinating visual exotica: hundreds of young bodies, chockablock sardine-can placement, tanning, immobile. Made me want to reread *Lolita*. Of course Joe's Show was just miserably hung, school cafeteria style, the dark side of California sensibility (cafeterias)—but the reading was fun—Anne Waldman

---

85   The collected papers of Joe Brainard and Kenward Elmslie are stored in the University of California–San Diego Library's Special Collections & Archives.

before she tipped into total self-aggrandizement. Bill Berkson, Ron. And those immobile roof bods to ogle, hour after hour.

So glad California is treating you right. I've fantasized about moving there, SF, LA—I'm prey to a recurrent yen for the West Coast. Seattle, that was serious, until political correctitude swamped *Postcards on Parade*. Daylight's so wondrous, up there, and young men's eyes refract energized blue.

Ambiance, long as you're near the Pacific, is easy-going, full of permission to turn into a character, daft but grounded, like the personae in slice-of-life plays by William Saroyan[86] (boy, is he forgotten!)—goofy, benignly affirmative human nature.

Been real lowdown, now up, whew. Up still comes to the rescue. The Knee Problem had me in a stir, as I somehow thought I had to have the op right away. Get It Over. Then, one recent morning, *NY Times*, I read about three people who died from knee operations. Which seemed to let me off the hook.

Yesterday, the corrected proofs of *Snippets* slipped into my door-slot, three more small errata, but justified both right and left this time, looks gorgeous. Out in January, heaven not to have to wait around for a year. Writing it in a cornered-by-deadline flurry goes against my work ethic, goody-goody brainwash in that Waspy elitist boarding school[87] I went to. Work Hard, or it doesn't count. I've had works slip out of my head fast and easy (the Suicide Monologue in *Postcards on Parade*) but I worry about cheating, being caught cheating, found out as a bad person who doesn't bother with dedication-to-writing eighteen hours a day every day. It's a bit irksome, actually. *Snippets* looked at on the page, holds up. It just does. All these years, I've been putting myself through the wringer, when I needn't have? Of course. The Page always helps words hold up, gives them a sacrosanct aura of inevitability. Anyway, that's done.

I'm extremely non-confrontational, but I got fed up, the other day, with the York Theatre & its boss, Jimbo. The way he runs it, it's just too

---

86   William Saroyan, Armenian-American writer and playwright, 1908–1981.
87   The St. Mark's School in Southborough, MA.

Disorg for an Org. So I've pulled away, wrote him so, plainly. Claibe, sweet Tejan-voiced composer of *Lola*, is delighted I yanked our musical from possible production there. Claibe has an agent, lucky for him, a go-getter, who'll tout the revised, down-sized script I started revamping last week—upon completion. Claibe faces chemo . . . started in his prostate.

[. . .]

I think this is enough Real Life for one letter. The Supper I made was delicious, and sensible. Carrots and onions cooked in chicken broth. A baked potato. Cut-up canteloupe marinated in grapefruit juice for dessert, which I polished off solo. And so to bed, after a couple of swigs of vodka and grapefruit juice. Good grief. It's 7:32, light out, and time for a modest breakfast, in-house, of cholesterol-lowering oatmeal, CREAM, hahahhaha, and java. And then—on to a svelte *Lola*.

Love,
Kenward

LOS ANGELES, CA
JANUARY 7, 2002

Dear Kenward,

I learned so much, about you, musicals, poetry etc, in that jam-packed little book *SPILLED BEANS*. Loved it. You were clear, witty and warm as always. I liked her questions. Loved it when she said your poems were "little theatres." "They are observational." Great word because the reader does visually See so much going on. Not simply the tempo but the fast scenery changes, the surprise juxtapositions, jazz riffs continually happening give each poem an energy that is definitely Physical. In addition of course to the many voices which also make them theatre. Nice, the conversation and book.

Finally saw the specialist today. I have been acutely anxious these months about this tumor in my lung.[88] Gory scenarios. What can be my last words? No wait! THESE are my last words! No, better . . . Honest. THESE are my last words!

---

88   This is the first mention of Lucia's lung cancer diagnosis.

I love both my doctors. The one today is Pavel Patel, Indian, handsome broody fellow. Loving man. He is a healer, for sure. Patients adore him. The waiting room was like some place in Calcutta. Many old old very ill people of every nationality. Chairs full, many of us old folks on our walkers, in wheelchairs. (It looked like the TV show called *Battle Bots*, about robots fighting.) Dozens of kids on the floor, attendants on the floor, babies crawling around. Everybody waited so long that teenagers went out for snacks, passed around Cheetos, M and Ms, licorice. One elderly white woman in lovely gray suit, hat, nice pin and perfect spectator pumps. Her attendant had painted her Long fingernails black with stars on them!

[. . .]

(Later Monday night) Sad to hear that Fielding Dawson[89] died. Dear Fielding. I first met him in Provincetown in 1959 where he had a show of watercolors. Vain and handsome, very F. Scott in seersucker suit and a tan. We have been friends and enemies ever since. I wouldn't speak to him for years because of nasty article he wrote about Tom Clark's book on [poet Charles] Olson. Finally buried the hatchet, then he wrote awful one about Ed [Dorn] and treated George and Martha King[90] badly so got mad at him again until we made up a few years ago. Had a recent tiff about him using and editing a letter I wrote for a blurb for book I hadn't read. The Nice things I had said were about his prison stories which were Wonderful. (He taught at Attica) Oh, why am I blabbing on? I'm sad that he's dead. Was able to share sweet things he had said about Susan[91] in recent letter, when I talked to her earlier tonight.

Ivan just called, feeling sad too about Fielding. Everybody I spoke to tonight is sorry they fought with him. Well, he was simply a big pain in the neck, so his death seems like a relative has died. He wrote some fine stories and was a big part of our lives. By "our" I suppose I mean all of

---

89   Fielding Dawson, American writer and artist, 1930–2002.
90   Martha King, American writer, b. 1934.
91   Susan Maldovan, editor, wife of Fielding Dawson.

us connected somehow with Black Mountain.[92] I'll miss him, and I'm sad, and too it is still another death. Amazing how deaths are always a surprise, especially as we get older and they occur so often.

Ivan loves his new house in the country. If there is a siren, fire or police, it starts the coyotes howling! They live next to preserve for bald (golden?) eagles, are right in their flight paths.

I am ashamed about my complaints about my new Family. It's working great, actually. Dan fixed me up a shower: a bench, great spray attached to flexible hose. Wonderful way to take a shower. Used to be torture because I couldn't stand up for long.

Each of them continues to do thoughtful things. I do too. It is a felicitous exchange now and we have good balance of privacy and visits.

Played my CD of *THE GRASS HARP*

> *Love,*
> *Loosha*

[In the following letters, Lucia and Kenward write about Kenward's visit to California for a Grass Harp *production and tribute to Joe Brainard. Lucia remembers a poorly attended reading of hers where people called out their least favorite stories to be read aloud. Kenward writes of plans to interview and film friends, including Lucia, for video sections on his website, and Lucia responds to having been interviewed. Lucia shares details behind her story "Andado," one of Kenward's favorites, and tells him of meeting the filmmakers who created* Y tu mamá también. *Kenward talks about visiting Edna Ferber with his Aunt Peggy, Margaret Leech. He's also met a new young helper, this one from Australia, whom Kenward and Lucia refer to as Mr. Oz, Mr. Wogga Wogga, or Mr. WW.]*

LOS ANGELES, CA

FEBRUARY 12, 2002

Dear Kenward,

Very embarrassing. The only news I have to report is your visit. I'm

---

92   People who were associated with the experimental Black Mountain College in North Carolina.

so sorry I couldn't go to *THE GRASS HARP* . . . I could have told you all about it. I can't express how much my son Mark and I both enjoyed your reading, slides, comments. He had to be up very early and didn't come to meet you . . . but he knows your work and loves it. (Two of my sons are readers, other two Zero interest.) He was Furious at Mark Salerno,[93] for many reasons, his perfect taste in clothes and his so intelligent questions, but mostly because he did not arrange a better venue and a larger audience for such a fine performance. I think it was pretty tacky myself, but have learned that that goes with being Our kind of writer. Once Leslie Scalopino[94] and I read for Five people! One was her boyfriend and the other four were my sons. WE still enjoyed the reading, and became great friends.

Considering that it was a class the response at your reading was quite good. I love *Snippets*, and *Nite Soil*[95] is a gorgeous collection. I sit and sift through the cards over and over.

My BEST reading was on a freezing rainy night in a hot San Francisco bookstore. Maybe 15 people in the audience. I decided to read stories that were my Worst stories and/or that people had said they hated. What was fun about that reading was how involved the audience got. "No, Lucia . . . the Texan Christmas was worse than that one." "No way . . . Mama and Dad was Really bad." "Read 'Rainy Day' . . . I can't stand that one."

I hope you have rested and recovered from traveling. Look forward to hearing how you liked Las Vegas. I wish I had been with you. Just like I know we would have had fun at the Fat farm together.

I'm sorry I'm 10 years too old and too sick. If I weren't I'd insist that I come live with you, be your assistant, chef, exercise guru and general Factotum . . . Factota? Just the Factotum, maam. We'd have a hoot.

I need to explore more . . . I go to the store on short trips and down to the ocean to sit, that's about it and since I don't get lost anymore and

---

93   Mark Salerno, American poet and founding editor of *Arshile* literary journal, b. 1956.

94   Leslie Scalapino, American poet, playwright, essayist, and editor, 1944–2010.

95   *Nite Soil* is Kenward's collection of forty-one collaged postcards as published by Granary Books in 2000.

end up at the airport it's not very exciting. Still I like this laid-back L.A. People love to talk here, in lines, elevators. So far only sociological Fact I have garnered is that whereas in Boulder people were given to using the expression "wife-beater undershirt" as often as possible, in L.A. they constantly refer to "plumber-butt jeans." Dan had to explain to me that when plumbers squat at your sink you can see the crack. Mercy.

Mark Salerno is coming to tea, so I'll wait and tell you about it. I thought he was nice, so will see how valid my Mark's objections are.

I hope this doesn't sound too stereotypically homophobic, but it does seem that if Lesbians had any fashion sense they would Adore the hair-do and the divine tie worn by the lady judge at the War trials.

SPECIFIC DETAIL! Of course that was one of Chekhov's main rules and so much why he is the best. Things like in "The Duel," when they were all gathered in the forest you knew it was almost dawn when he could see the doctor's cane. You are prince of perfect telling words.

Well, Mark Salerno has come and gone. I had hoped to talk about L.A. writers . . . friends of mine like Amy Gerstler, Benjamin Weissman.[96] Books maybe, you and your work . . . whatever. You have been only other Visitor. He was nice and brought me a box of Lady Godiva chocolates for Valentine's day. We did talk about you and your work, which he does truly like and respect.

Mostly though . . . now Here is a specific detail: Anyone who uses this ghastly expression gets a thumbs down from me . . . he wanted to "pick my brain" about who are THE people to know in Colorado, since he is going there to read. I realized that he didn't want to hear about who are the people I love in Colorado, but who is hot in the literary scene, which has never been my scene. It was a pleasant visit but I'll bet $50 that the next time I hear from him it will be to ask for a blurb.

He dropped a lovely specific detail when he left. Not a matchbook from a strip club or a coke spoon, but a little plastic container with tiny toothpaste and toothbrush, wet. Somehow this made me like him better. He's trying so hard to look good, smell good, get an MFA so he'll

---

96   Amy Gerstler, American poet, b. 1956. Benjamin Weissman, American artist and author, b. 1957.

look good on paper, meet the right people, drop the right names . . .
He has no idea that he's really a nice guy. I gave him one of my books
and asked him to mail me one of his. Maybe he is a terrific writer.

I am proof of another Chekhov theory. It is possible to write about
Nothing! I'll stop here. Hope a letter is coming from you soon.

Love,
LOOSHA

NEW YORK, NY
FEBRUARY 18, 2002

Dear Loosha—

Last night, Mr. Wogga Wogga[97] cooked and hosted for a York
Aussie invasion, must have been eight guys, one woman, Charlotte
[Moore], boss of an off-Bdwy org like the York, Irish Rep,[98] whom
I liked a lot, got to talk with a bit. Theatre talk, very intense, "now"
goings on—writers, ones I know anyway, don't carry on like that, with
a sense of important immediacy. A gifted raconteuse, Lady Charlotte
told about her experience seeing Elaine Stritch,[99] the one-woman show
that's the hottest ticket in town. Elaine's opening line (approximation)
is—"As the prostitute said, 'It's not the work, it's the stairs.'" [. . .]

Today, Patty comes over for treadmilling, but my back is "out," so
I'll just watch. Calming down from the trip. Lucked in, both other
gigs—good-sized audience in a resplendent assemblagerie, so many rows,
a stage, the works. U San Francisco, in what had been a Catholic institution of learning, pietas and Blessed Virgins lurching in the hallways.
Mr. WW startled how my voice opened up. Next—Kevin Killian's Poets
Theatre, *City Junket* scenes preceded by two horrific boring avant-garde
musses. *City Junket* cast fine—the packed-in but small-in-number audience came out of resentment at the first two items. Dialogue spun. And,
same as after *The Grass Harp*, vectors of gratitude zung my way from the

---

97   Mr. Oz, Mr. Wogga Wogga, Mr. WW, another of Kenward's helpers of
sorts, who comes in and out of Kenward's life for a few years.
98   The Irish Repertory Theatre was founded by Ciarán O'Reilly and Charlotte
Moore in New York City in 1988.
99   Stritch starred in Kenward's *The Grass Harp* musical, 1966.

eyes of the performers. They had such fun doing it, same as in Pasadena. Heaven on Earth reward, to be on the receiving end of these heartfelt vectors. Final gig at Mills faculty lounge, very warm intime listeners, Mac [McGinnes][100] present, and the mysterioso Jeff Clark and his new mama mia madonna, Carmen—whose mother left her native Peru for the States, lured by the movie version of *West Side Story*!

Last night in SF, wound up at the casa of my Great Nephew, William Weir and his wife, Margaret—she's studied creeyative writing—three amazing kids tootled around. Willum, as she calls him, did Sound Tech at the faculty lounge gig. He's left his commercial film job, ads, to make a movie about windsurfing—his passion. I've decided to ask him to take on a job for me—West Coast "interviews" for my website. I hope I can inveigle Jeff Clark & Carmen to drive down to Venice, to interview you, filmed by Great Nephew Bill Weir. They look so gorgeous together, Jeff & Carmen, and it struck me, Bill & Margaret & kiddos are a rarity among my relatives—they're together and seem to Love Life. I think you'd feel comfy with them all. Carmen heads her own private writing group in SF. Would this be posseeeble?

Maybe read the Chile Deflowering Gothic Tale[101] (which, as you know, I think the world of, particularly)—its grandeur and nuance-in-your-voice just must be made viewable/hearable . . . IF You reading it ALL would be too mammoth a screen length, then screen the text with voice-over of you reading it. With maybe "the frame" visual (you, reading it) & the journey itself seen text-on-page with your voice as audio. Plus a chat about your daily round, whatever, how you got to Chile, and to California now, how we correspond, in many ways. If you want to read a fragment of a letter from me, one you particularly like, that would be fine with me.

[. . .]

Think about it, and let me know. Shouldn't be stressful, you can

---

100   Mac McGinnes, American actor, director. Directed Kenward's Pasadena and New York City productions of play "City Junket."
101   "Andado: A Gothic Romance," Berlin's short story first published in *Safe and Sound* (Poltroon Press, 1988).

shape its contours—but if you feel it's not something you want to engage in, that's fine. Allen G once berated me for not caring about posterity. And I don't, in a way. I guess, bottom line, it'd give me enormous pleasure knowing I could hear the Gothic Tale in your voice, which is a voice, as I know you know, of great and immediate presence & also see you read it.

It's now Monday, sunny out, time for another date with Patty on the treadmill. Back is better, so no excuse. Yesterday afternoon, went with the P's to see *Iris*.[102] A must-see.

Dear factota, glad I've seen your hideaway so I know you're safe, with feet-on-the ground sonmanship a few feet away to rely on.

Much Love,
Kenward

LOS ANGELES, CA
FEBRUARY 27, 2002

Dear Kenward,

I'm impressed by how you keep things cooking. And you SHOULD be thinking of posterity. I would like to see your letters published. You are one of my favorite prose writers, and there are so many lovely lyrical passages in all of them, besides some very funny parts and historically fascinating information. With that interview in mind, I'll try (in a week or so. I'm going through bad spot now) to find one or two of yours and maybe an answering one of mine, which I could read, someone else read yours.

I hope you have read letters between George Sand and Flaubert. Their letters best thing each of them wrote. I Cherish the 1st volume of Flaubert's letters. If you haven't read them, please do.

I love reading letters and diaries. Delacroix, Darwin, Dawn Powell. Even James Joyce's which are so disgusting, and Faulkner's which speak only of money.

Of course I would like to meet the Muirs and do, whatever.

I'm glad you like my sweet love story. The man in that story

---

102 *Iris*, directed by Richard Eyre, 2001. Film based on life of English writer Iris Murdoch.

(ANDADO) and I remained good friends for many many years. He was Ambassador to the US, and I saw him several times when I lived in New York. He was exiled to Paris during the revolution. He died soon after he went back to Chile, after Allende's fall, was given a State funeral, presided on by his priest son, the one from the story. The story is long . . . about thirty pages. I'll try reading it, will see how it holds up. How I hold up. Maybe a portion could be standalone. I love a very short Chilean story *LA VIE EN ROSE*,[103] about the two girls at the lake, with cadets and kisses. Nobody has ever seemed to like it, certainly never commented on this story. It's in *SO LONG*.

Does this happen to you too? With a poem or in my case a story which is a particular favorite but does not seem to touch other people as other of your works do? I have about four of these. Have tried reading them but audience response was still cool.

You didn't mention Las Vegas, so it obviously didn't have the effect upon you that it did upon me.

Have been planting in the border next to my little casita. Ferns and succulents, small palms, brightened by small pink canna lilies. Nice to dig and water. [. . .] Pool heater got fixed so in a few days we'll be in it. I can't wait. My back has been terrible. They have added a medicine for epilepsy to my medications. It is a tremendous help. They say that initial wooziness will go away in a few days. Hope so. Sick of the damn spoon in my mouth. Just kidding.

Pleased to read chapter from Tom Clark's biography of Ed Dorn.[104] It's written as poet's biographies should be, with the life connected to the poems . . . looks to be a fine book.

Reading Trollope, surefire sign I'm ailing. *DOCTOR THORNE*. At least I'm not depressed, that calls for Hardy.

Will write to you soon.

  All my love,
  Lucia

---

103 "La Vie en Rose," Lucia's story first published in *Safe and Sound* (Poltroon Press, 1988), reprinted in *So Long*, 1993, and in *A Manual for Cleaning Women*, 2015.
104 Tom Clark, *Edward Dorn: A World of Difference* (North Atlantic Books, 2002).

Postcard with "Nancy" addition from Kenward.

LOS ANGELES, CA
APRIL 5, 2002

Dear Kenward,

I'm delighted to be the first of the interviewed. Margaret and Sophie[105] arrived around 9:45. They're the perfect team for this project. Sophie sharp, professional, efficient, Margaret gracious and literate, warm. Focuses right in, both do, actually. Margaret knows just what to ask: real questions about the feel and soul of things, not facts or same old where do your stories come from. I like Margaret very much, want to stay friends with her. She is that very rare thing nowadays, and I suppose I am un-PC to say it, but she is well bred. With all this entails, graciousness, values, and solid sense of herself. Mmm . . . I actually think this is true of me, believe it or not.

I thoroughly enjoyed the experience. It lifted my spirits, made me feel like a writer. Most of all, going through your papers, then reading them and talking about what they have meant to me, (and not really doing that properly) see how very much they do mean to me. I talked a lot about how similar our sensibilities are, our rapport, etc., but think I just assumed that people would understand that in addition to the fun and friendship of our correspondence.

I am grateful that each of your letters is a work of art, some more dazzling than others, mailed to me! You are a brilliant poet, but an equally fine prose writer. I am so grateful for these letters. Things like your RUSTLER postcard, all the *Nancys*.[106] I don't think I spoke highly enough about your work actually. Margaret took many [letters] home to scan both sides. She understood how important these cards and letters (please keep them coming, folk) are. She adored all of what you wrote and drew, of course.

One of the letters I read was your description of the stage for *LIZZIE*. Exquisite prose piece.

She Got everything, actually, in my work, yours. I think I have been longing for someone to talk to. Today made me happy.

---

105 Margaret Weir and Sophie Constantinou interviewed Lucia for Kenward's website.

106 Letters that Kenward wrote to Lucia in the invented character of Nancy.

I had so many things to read that at one point she said, How about just picking one at random. I did, and it was witty, delightful, but alas and alack, I'm so sorry, but it WAS funny, it was one where you described her father-in-law! Wickedly amusing. She loved it, however, said you got him perfectly.

I read *MAMA, UNMANAGEABLE, LA VIE EN ROSE, MY JOCKEY.* My best stories too long to keep listener's interest. These seemed to work. Then I went through photo album and talked about things, and answered good questions about my life and work. A long day, I'm worn out, and so are they, I'm sure.

I wanted to get this off though, to thank you for doing it. I'm honored. Your list is super. Please do Joanne Kyger.[107]

I am indebted to you for so many things.

Loosha

NEW YORK, NY

APRIL 9, 2002

Dear Loosha—

Well, for starters, Margaret Weir confessed she loves and adores you— and you-as-writer, and so does her helper. My Great Nephew, I intuit, from talking to him, was bowled over, just stunned by the intensity of the afternoon, which, he, as guy, felt he was a voyeur of—three women, bonding so naturally and fully. He promised to send me a tape of the conversation so I won't feel left out, which I don't, not at all. A bit like seeing something I've written the words for in the theatre, and—if a certain level of intensity is attained—I can forget about being a writer, and lose myself in an actuality that is deeply pleasurable, to the degree it takes me over. Which doesn't always happen. So: I'm looking forward to your solo flight, dips and whirls and loop-the-loops you've brought into play.

This must be a horrible week for you, vanishing into a medical maw—what will it spew out, at you—Delphic imponderables, a blur of options, invasive rituals. I felt so angry at what Joe went through, despite his amazing nurses, who all behaved with tenderness and

---

107   Lucia is suggesting Kyger be interviewed and featured on Kenward's website.

constancy. I wish I didn't feel riled by what you must be undergoing, as if there's someone gaga up there, who can control such turns of human fate, who has mixed up the signals, the plot lines, and not on purpose, which is really dumb: the waste, the waste.

I'm starting to think of Vermont, a natural outcome of spring and benevolent weather, trees starting to leaf out on Jane Street, which I peer out at from my new window, third-floor front, where my desk is. Which reminds me of my favorite aunt, the only real writer in the family—Margaret Leech was her nom de biographie, Aunt Peggy to me. She discovered she could do history rather late in life, wrote three books, one per assassinated president—having started as a novelist, and as one-time Broadway playwright. The play, co-authored, flopped, but Jimmy Stewart was discovered in it; its sole claim to fame. Aunt Peggy liked to sit at a window, in my successive Village houses, and keep track of the street. Which she couldn't do, way uptown, in her high-rise apartment. Once, she took me to meet Edna Ferber,[108] an aggressive no-nonsense crony Aunt Peggy, fairly fearless, was intimidated by. And no wonder. Edna Ferber, disguised by time pile-up as a *Macbeth* witch, flirted outrageously with me, still a young naif back then. Did you ever read *Reveille In Washington*? About D.C. during the Civil War. It was a Book-of-The-Month Club selection during WWII, which I considered a sign of significant worth. I read it non-stop, was so proud I not only knew the author, but was related, not blood, but still.

So you knew and hosted the two kiddos in the terrif Mehican flick—*Tambien . . . Miasma* (misremembered title).[109] They're so terrific. My favorite moment, how (front-seat in car) one pair of limpid kiddo eyes turn blank as the Older Woman describes how her first lover died in a motorcycle accident. Ties into your last letter, how the young just can't figure out the vulnerabilities old age brings.

My recurrent problem is walking with a young male. At a certain

---

108   Edna Ferber, American novelist, short story writer and playwright, 1885–1968.

109   *Y tu mamá también*, Mexican film directed by Alfonso Cuarón and cowritten by him and his brother Carlos, whom Lucia had known.

202

point, he can't stand slowing down to my pace. A halter he needs must shake free of.

[. . .]

Quieter this week, not so much—going out to see musicals with Mr. Wogga Wogga. I went into a doze trance through most of Act One of *By Jupiter*, last show attended, at the York, book in hand, fine cast, well done—a Rodgers & Hart[110] oldie (1943) which ribbed the pants off masculine Amazons (WACS) and a nancy-boy anti-hero, played back then by Ray Bolger. Dullish songs—Lorenz Hart at the end of his booze tether, as lyricist. Next up—*Oklahoma!*

Matt Cowles,[111] my ACLU chum, ecstatic over a TV breakthrough re same-sex parenting, agin' the law in Fla. Bigtime, Rosie O'Donnell, Guv of Fla[112] just inundated by e-mailage. I love reading about priest pedophiles. And seeing angry oldsters on TV, consigning their seducers to Rotting In Hell.

Read a book rave in *NY Times*—and Patty found it—not something I've gone hog-wild about, as yet, but it's deft, Borges-esque, set in 19th Century Tasmania—*Gould's Book of Fish* by Richard Flanagan. Doesn't quite warrant being sent your way, so far . . .

Thinking of you mucho, mucho. Mucho.

Love,
Kenward

LOS ANGELES, CA
APRIL 17, 2002

Dear Kenward,

Wonderful wonderful last letter of yours.

I have recently been receiving many phone calls. A dear friend has told people to call me so I won't feel lonely. Awkward, since I so dislike

---

110 American songwriting team, composer Richard Rodgers, 1902–1979, and lyricist Lorenz Hart, 1895–1943.
111 Matt Coles, civil rights attorney for the ACLU and law professor, close friend of Kenward's.
112 Actress/comedian/host Rosie O'Donnell called then Florida governor Rick Scott an "asshole" on *The View* television show in 2001.

Wednesday 5:20 AM

Dear Loosha --

Yesterday, I stayed in. Quietude, writing you, so if bed gets dull, you can read an endless letter, to lull you back to sleep. Phoning (I tend to clam up easy on Mr. Bell's newfangled machine) you was such a treat. I'm very susceptible to voices these days, and if I were reviewing your voice (I'm very susceptible to reviews these days) I'd critique it thus:

"Loosha is blessed with a Voice that carries resplendently & with great sensitivity. Some faces get in your face. Some voices get in your ear. Hers doesn't. It is expressive, but not ever intrusive. Her touch of Tejas twang evokes the little pings change carriers made, hurtling about under the ceilings of small-town Five & Dimes, or the rush of air into a flat bike tire at the only gas station open on Sunday, on Mary Lou Fisbee Drive, just before the red rock shaped like a top hat, in the middle of the automobile graveyard yet to be fenced in..." --
The Manhattan Daily Phone Voice Review

Zo. You sound OK. I'm glad you don't have to insert prongs & hooks and red rubber extension units down your gullet to crank up your laff burbler.

Talking about intrusive, in the letter, there is one "intrusive" section, that contains sensitive info. The Two Names left off the list to the Joe's Room opener. Otherwise, if you think enclosed missive would entertain your visitors, feel free to share it with your many chums. The upper half of page 4 is the section that is indiscreet. So, at your discretion, depending on the character and probity of your visitor, just remove page 4, tuck it under the mattress or up in the chandelier with your incredible pincers.

Love,
Kenward

Undated letter from Kenward.

the phone. I love being alone but do miss the pleasure of witty and creative conversation. I am not Lonely, but alone with self-centered stupidity inducing preoccupation with illness. Your letters lift me up and out of myself, always.

I was so relieved to hear that My Film Crew liked me as much as I did them. Margaret instantly a dear friend. Lovely woman. I am very excited about the video.

Lordy I am so impressed that you met Edna Ferber. As a child I read all my mother's books, which meant best sellers, like Edna's, so as you were, would have been thrilled to know her in so-called real life.

I also, more obsessively read my mother's other reading, hidden under the mattress. *Tobacco Road, Catcher in the Rye*, a few other famous "dirty books" whose titles I have forgotten. *Forever Amber!* Was very confused because in one of those books a woman was painting her toe-nails, because, as she said, "You never can tell what he's gonna want to do." This Fascinated me. What could it possibly be?

A life-long dilemma, as was Father Haley's telling me that a kiss on the neck was a mortal sin, whereas a kiss on the mouth was a venial sin. I think he's right about that but it took years before I was old enough to research it.

I am seriously considering writing an article called I was a Priest Molester. Poor Father Haley. I'm always telling people how my first viewed erection was in a cassock, and it did look pretty silly in his Jesuit garb. I could quite honestly say now that I was sexually abused by a nun, Sister Cecilia, and by Father Haley . . . but the truth is closer to what I'm sure is how it happens often. (If all these priest abuses DID in fact happen . . . I taught high school kids enough to know how common a fantasy this is that ends up wrecking adult lives.) In my case having been actually molested by adults since I was four, I think I tended to behave in a seductive manner with ALL adults. Only now, looking back do I see this . . . I'd lean against Sister C., pat her, read over her shoulder . . . behaved with her as I had been taught grown-ups liked. But when the cloak-room scene happened I knocked her down and was expelled. Never accused her out loud and I think that was because I knew even then that I had a part in it.

As for Father Haley, poor handsome fellow! A Jesuit in his early twenties, taught at a boys' school in Santiago, played poker with other priests and my mother. I asked him to give me lessons in Catholicism as I wanted to convert. I went every Thursday after school to the vestry at St. George's. 12 years old. I ACTIVELY tried to make him adore me. He was truly a wonderful priest and person. He tried diligently to stick to the program. He taught me about the church and basic catechism, but gave me nice assignments, like do four helpful things a day without anybody else knowing about them, go to Mass at a different church in Santiago, every morning at 6 A.M. I learned so much about the city. I did this for months, saw hundreds of churches and neighborhoods. Again no one was to know about this. Amazing how hard it is to be good if no one is going to know about it!

He got permission for me to go to Mass in a French convent, where nuns never went out into the world. The chapel was small, stone, very simple and very dark, since it was so early in winter and raining. Candles were the only light. The nuns sang so beautifully that I still get chills remembering that morning. Their voices were high, like children's and were full with joy.

I did work sincerely with Father Haley, but flirted in a shameful manner. Dear man, at last he very kindly told me that it was too soon for me to think about converting. I should wait a few years, then come back to see him. I recall him resisting a good-bye abrazo (little Lolita wept all the while) as he pushed me firmly out the door. Several years later I was at a beach resort, Algarrobo, and heard that there was a Jesuit priest, Father Haley, in a near-by village, working with the peons, the only priest for a vast area. I went by horseback to visit him. He was such a fine man . . . holy, for sure. It was beautiful to see how the people there loved him and respected him, how completely accepting they were of the fact that the (lovely young) woman who kept house for him was his wife really and for sure he was the father of her two blue-eyed red-haired Irish babies.

Sorry . . . all I meant to say is that I feel so badly for these priests.

Many teenagers too are accused of molestation these days doing things we all did and thought we were playing doctor.

Glad to hear that you're faithfully going to the gym. I'm still swimming every day and getting stronger and stronger. Although back pain is awful and assorted cancer ailments quietly increasing I'm healthier than I've been in years!

Later same day: Back from the good doctor Patel. Long talk. He makes you feel like he has all the time in the world just to talk to you. He convinced me to go ahead with radiation, countered all of my arguments. I'm doing it because he thinks it is good for me to do it. He's going to get me a copy of my skeleton.

All this talk about "early detection." This was found in October. Now I have an appointment Tuesday with the radiologist, so probably in May we'll get started!

Time for a nap.

> *Much love,*
>
> *Loosha*

p.s. I cannot possibly say how relieved and grateful I was to hear the offer of medical help from Z Press. The move, high rent, taxes, my idiotic $ neuroses has me stuck in case of emergencies.

CALAIS, VT

MAY II, 2002

Dear Loosha—

Easy move into the woods, this time around. Sunday exodus—The Man With The Van[113] arrived by noon, as scheduled, and Mr. Wogga Wogga and I made it to Calais sevenish, in fading dusk. Still not totally unpacked. Such a pleasure to be back in my outbuilding, computer working, printer too, big desk space, stuff that needs to be filed away still on the floor. Mr. WW a huge help, very organized: clear focus.

Chilly morning, gray sky, leaves emerging, some bare trees still. Ron and Pat Padgett beat us by a day—two suppers downhill, one here—roast chicken impregnated with tarragon. I've hung the pictures in the big room, so it's up to snuff. The piano room, my bedroom, Joe's studio still with muss piles. Spent hours and hours in Montpelier,

---

113   Jack Graves.

choosing frames and matting for a whole slew of Joe works. Took hours and hours, painstaking but invigorating to examine his work closely, between frame decisions. At The Drawing Board,[114] they know Joe's work, by now, oohs and ahs. Tasks so much easier up here. Chores not so stressful, as folks are friendly, accustomed to all the time in the world. And it's true—time expands up here. Country time focus versus city multi-choices, battling unchanneled input implacably on max surge.

Hard for me to read in NYC. Up here, I stay put, reading in bed, squirreling away hours. *Home Again*,[115] a birthday present from my niece, Vivy—another copy tucked away somewhere. Redevoured, astonishment unimpaired. Ron's new Coffee House book fresh out—devoured too. *You Never Know*.[116] Smashing, sequencing architectural. Enhances the poems, which feed off each other. Substrata narrative present. Plain language, pared down to essence of daily round, deftly grounded, with lunges into mind and dream expansion—fantastic "craziness."

Hilarious account, after dinner last night, of Ron going to the movies with a poet pal, Larry Fagin,[117] to a Randolph Scott festival, he of the lantern jaw and no dialogue to have to try to act. Post-fest, at Lincoln Center, he went for a hot dog to his favorite Sabret stand, encountered a blind lady, who asked for help. She took his proffered arm, and Ron enjoyed the ceremonial nicety—becoming a couple from chivalrous times. They chatted, and he learned she was an opera singer. She knew of the hot dog cart, so that's where they went, gabbing away, somehow joined by Larry Fagin, flummoxed to find Ron inexplicably encoupled with a beautiful lady with eyes of milk.

Ron asked what my writing projects are, right now. Good question. Wayne Padgett, website maestro, has put together a bunch of photos, and wants me to write about them. So I guess that comes first. Then

---

114 The Drawing Board is an art shop in Montpelier, Vermont.
115 Kenward mistitles Lucia's book *Homesick*.
116 Ron Padgett, *You Never Know* (Coffee House Press, 2002).
117 Larry Fagin, American poet, editor, publisher, and teacher, 1937–2017.

I'm thinking of a book I read ages ago, *Spoerri* (?) *Typography of Chance* (?)[118] which lists objects in a room, and describes how they came to be present—a form of autobio I could gravitate to, I think. I'm finicky about leaving certain objects behind when I head here (two darky rag dolls I gave Joe—they sit on separate chairs; desk talismans—a tiny silver Buddha, etc. etc.) . . . The Sailor In Blue (porcelain) is back on the mantle, coupled with The Cookie Jar Lady with the Waffled Tummy.

The trip to Connecticut a lark. *The Grass Harp* opening ebulliently sung, dinner with diva (and Mr. WW) beforehand, diva being Brenda Lewis,[119] 81, who was the original Lizzie back in the late Sixties, her last op'ry hurrah. She has perfectly coiffed white hair, hasn't puffed up, good face bones, smart as a whip, two marriages, one acrimonious divorce, kids, who are curious about her stardom past, but can't relate Old Her to it. Husband #2 invented automatic tollbooth gismo, developed Alzheimer's, so she nursed him for years. She was a treat to sit next to.

One song, words written when Joe was failing, for Judge Cool, widower, was finally finally sung, a first, in its entirety—*The Dark Night of My Soul*, beautifully set by Claibe Richardson, and beautifully sung. As happens, this Judge Cool was picked for his vocal skill—I couldn't stand his speaking voice. Well performed as a whole, small orchestral combo, orchestrations reduced for combo by my current song musik guru—David Harris, who came through for this production—musically impeccable, better than Pasadena. Acting? No. But my revisions held up. A solid work, at last. Brenda and Mr. WW (I in the middle) both responded very strongly to the new Judge Cool song.

Wayne Padgett, Mr. WW and I descended on Brenda at 11 the next morning—website gab. Despite two memory loss fits (escapee names)—she gave good autobio, how she went from job to job without worrying about her voice, did stand-up comedy, pride swallowed, to feed her two babes, stony broke after her first marriage, not a shred of

---

118   Daniel Spoerri, *An Anecdoted Topography of Chance* (Something Else Press, 1966).

119   Brenda Lewis, American operatic soprano, musical theatre actress, opera director, educator, 1921–2017. Starred in Kenward's opera *Lizzie Borden*.

self-pity or vindictiveness at being victimized along the way. Hilarious show-biz contretemps, chaotic try-outs, auditioning for Irving Berlin, being chosen to take the Ethel Merman part (based on Perle Mesta) in *Call Me Madam*[120] . . . she crossed over from op'ry to Broadway before that was done . . . Wayne was a super questioner, composed and unintimidated—not easy. A bonus, too, to get out of NYC, a sneak preview of Vermont.

[. . .]

Hope your medical interventions aren't a non-stop nightmare. Salud, again, for writing *Home Again*.

Much love,
Kenward

LOS ANGELES, CA
MAY 15, 2002

Dear Kenward,

Wonderful your first letter from Calais. You are in better "space" and spirit than you have been in a long time. Your creativity and zest rustle the paper as I read the letter. Can feel good things to come, a great summer for you. Tarragon chicken a good start and I think wherever the Padgetts are all will be well. By all I mean you, what good friends they are to you.

I'm getting Ron's book tomorrow, via Coffee House I hope, or good bookstore lady in Venice.

Delightful story of Ron and the blind opera singer. Eyes of milk.

I once had job reading to a blind man. Took it for little pay . . . not out of kindness of my heart but sheer curiosity. I imagined this moving relationship developing between us through our sharing of literature, blah blah. I read law texts to him, hour after hour, over and over. He was smelly, whiney, petty, sarcastic, demanding. I did tons of things for him, (housework, cooking, and errands) that he ordered me to do but

---

120   *Call Me Madam* was a 1950 Tony Award–winning musical by Irving Berlin, Russel Crouse, and Howard Lindsay. Ethel Merman, American actress, 1908–1984. Perle Mesta, American socialite, 1889–1975.

also many things I thought he might like. Nothing pleased him. But that wasn't so difficult to take. Hard part was how much I missed, the rare times something WAS nice or funny, smiling into his eyes. Do you realize how often, as we speak, we smile into other people's eyes? Not "smile" even, as our mouths don't need to be smiling . . . it is simply a warm connection between two humans' eyes. It drove me nuts to look up from an (unintended) funny sentence at him and not only not connect, but he'd be picking his nose or be fast asleep.

I'm afraid my experiences working with deaf-mute people were not so heart-warming either, although it was great once, looking down from a second story window to see a deaf-mute couple signing with their hands on the floor of the car. Other deaf-mute friends were outside of the car. It took me awhile to realize that the couple was WHISPER-ING!

What a good friend Ron is too to ask you about your writing projects. It helps me too, since you are such an inspiration to me Kenward. Not only your letters, which are truly my greatest pleasure, almost only one now in fact, but also they always help me want to get out of my serious slump. I so envy your continued Zest.

Good idea to take photographs and write about them. I loved more that response of yours to incredible photograph of the soldier and the pretty boy, both lost in thought.

Wonderful too the list of objects in a room. Objects themselves. But then we can jump start ourselves with anything really . . . Idea is to let ourselves fly into the world of them. Like Chekhov when someone said they had nothing to write about . . . he picked up an ashtray and said take this, start with it, write about it. The story will come.

My book now, where each chapter is a room or a house where I have lived, few people, no dialogue, minimum of telling the story. Most of the story is told thru place and objects. It is a Terrific idea and fun to do.[121]

But I'm in big trouble. Not because I'm sick. I was in trouble before. I keep avoiding the notebook or computer.

---

[121] Writing her memoir, which will be published as *Welcome Home.*

I've lost confidence or even any sense of myself as a writer. The video day was cheering, but I felt a complete fraud, hating what I read. I love your compliments, but feel they come because you are my friend. NOT fishing for compliment! They won't help. Outside validation would not help at all. I am in low low spirits. Not depression. I'm always in a good mood even when I'm sad!

I feel I was lousy mother, selfish person and simplistic, dumb writer. Please have pity. No Compliments will help, just have compassion for how lousy I'm feeling. Have got to get out of this state.

Hasn't helped that Black Sparrow has folded. He sold rights to Bukowski, Fante and Bowles to ECCO,[122] rest of us now out of print. I tried to order some from Amazon but no dice. "No longer available."

My niece Monica and her husbland (wow, that was a Freudian slip!) were here. She stayed all week, he for three days. Lord they were wonderful days. She left yesterday. I think she is the most beautiful person in the world. Physically gorgeous still at 35 (was Armani model, brilliant, she has won many Mexican oscars, Milan, Cannes etc awards for art direction in film.) She and I grew very close while caring for my sister while she died. I lived there just over a year.

Oh we had such a lovely visit!. We went all over . . . first time I had been to Hollywood and Rodeo Drive, Melrose, downtown, Japantown, Beverly Hills. Great visit to the train station . . . many fine memories for me. Great videos and restaurants. And so graciously orchestrated by them to let me nap, to get me in and out and home to bed with never making me feel an invalid, but always getting rested up.

How to describe the GRACE of these Mexicans? Their warmth connected to practical good sense. I saw more and did more, was tired less than in any time since I've been here. After he left on Sunday, Monica went with me to early AM radiation treatments.

Now these treatments aren't that big a deal and I don't need anybody

---

122 When publisher John Martin retired and closed Black Sparrow Press in 2002, he sold the publishing rights to Charles Bukowski, John Fante, and Paul Bowles to HarperCollins/ECCO.

to go. They only last a few minutes, I'm fine to drive. Holy Christ it was so wonderful that she went with me, and walked down that long hall, held my hand while they touched up the big crosses over the tattoos on my chest and arms. She disarmed every awful person there. Literally de-fused them. She acted like a minesweeper . . . she disarmed the mean radiologist and the bossy technician. So regal, with the most deep and velvety voice . . . what did she do or say? It was more how she treated Me I think . . . Whatever it was they smiled at her and said good morning today to me! [. . .]

Only bad part was she stole my Cat. Heartless little floozy just moved over to Monica's lap, slept with her all night, wouldn't leave her side.

We swam and talked and slept, ate takeout Thai and Japanese, talked and talked and hugged day and night. I must have wept three hours after she left, kept finding presents she had left me. She phoned last night to tell me to go to sleep since I have to be up at 5. (Four more weeks of this radiation)

She made me very very happy. She says I did the same for her, but don't see how. I have been very very lonely, had no idea until I wasn't.

[. . .] Hope to catch the mailman, Sorry to write so long.

What book is HOME AGAIN? HOMESICK? WHERE I LIVE NOW? Strange because HOME AGAIN or WELCOME HOME were working titles for this new book. Or is it somebody else's book you are talking about?

I'm reading Louise Erdrich's excellent new book.[123] All her books together are awesome. Good.

[. . .]

Glad you're home in Calais.

> *I love you,*
> *Loosha*

---

[123] Louise Erdrich, *The Last Report on the Miracles at Little No Horse* (Harper-Collins, 2001).

Dear Loosha—

Cloudy, cool. 1 PM. Spent part of the morning abed, re-reading you. A refreshment. Like Vermont cool spring air. Distracted, mea culpa, lately, by page-turn type schlock, and cable TV movies, despite intrusive ad interruptions. Giant deflative, seeing Liz, Rock and James Dean age into sci-fi blue-hairs, blandishment of racial tolerance at the end: close-up of two babies, one mixed-blood—*the Heirs. American Gigolo* a hoot. Best: *Pollock.* Came in in the middle. There it was, later same night, playing again on HBO. Like the old days, when movie palaces had double-features, provided air-conditioning, travelogues, Disney, Nostradamus and news—one didn't have to wait in the lobby for the show to begin. Except in Europe. Always a secret treat, to stay to watch a movie past where one came in. I used to go to Weight Watchers with Ruth Kligman, Pollock's girlfriend in the Death Car. She also dated de Kooning,[124] whom I once glimpsed at her loft. A truly beautiful man. Good casting—her screen self was quite like her, not that huge a stretch, as Ruth thought she was a moviestar in real life, did Hollywood make-up and hair—aggressive sexiness. The Weight Watchers ladies hated her. She complained about being asked out every night—how to diet in expensive restaurants, Park Ave palazzos: her problem de luxe.

[. . .]

Haven't written a dadblamed thing, so far. Poor Bill Corbett! News of the demise of Black Sparrow [Press], which is beginning to spread in widening circles, will hit him hard. He's edited two massive volumes of Jimmy Schuyler letters[125] they were supposed to publish, though he had nothing in "writing." Jimmy's letters are much sprightlier than his diary.

I'm having trouble springing *The Grass Harp* from its current

---

124   American artists Ruth Kligman, 1930–2010, and Jackson Pollock, 1912–1956. Willem de Kooning, Dutch-American artist, 1904–1997.

125   William (Bill) Corbett's edited letters of James Schuyler would be published instead as *Just the Thing: Selected Letters of James Schuyler* (Turtle Point Press, 2009).

jailhouse—Samuel French,[126] who controls its amateur rights in perpetuity—what an ugly word. A theatre lawyer will take on The Case. The Rodgers & Hammerstein Org, which safeguard all the R&H classics, want to take it on, which, in theory, adding to its cult classic prestige, would help it get more productions. [. . .]

Time for a mid-afternoon snack. My legs are adjusting to uneven ground, but I've been very lazy about walking. Still haven't ventured to Joe's stone uphill, or the pond downhill. Haven't planted a thing. My outbuilding floor still a confusion of old-hat stuff that needs to be sorted through.

One sweet result of my *Grass Harp* date with Brenda Lewis, the original Lizzie. Wayne scrupulously sent her audio website interview, which she played for her family. Now they're impressed! Her kids and grandkids always thought of her as their Mom, Gramma, period. Now she's 81, they realize she's a Diva.

Love,
Kenward

LOS ANGELES, CA
JUNE 8, 2002

Dear Kenward,

Just wrote quite a nice letter to you—Whammo! It disappeared. Computer won't even turn on. Hate it when that happens . . . Will try to write a legible note at least. Still going to radiation—every day—it will go on until first week in July—exhausting—can't even read—have slipped in and out of TV, like dreams—did find *Pollock*—by accident! Not in any guide that secret HBO station, and a few others. It was good. Loved hearing you tell about Ruth Kligman.

Nice thinking of you and me—going about our days so similarly really. Your waffle at the Coffee Corner, my pancake at the Inglewood IHOP. Wonderful new twist & mystery in my IHOP Romance. I did go back again & my handsome stranger wasn't there. In the parking lot though, as I was leaving, I noticed two police cars way in back of the

---

126 Samuel French is a publisher and licensor of plays and musicals.

lot. And close to my car was the mystery handsome stranger's pickup truck—nice rusty red truck with good bicycle on the back. Definitely his car. There was a young black man sitting in it, reading a paper . . . Not him. A son? Brother? I got my tank in and hose connected, and was backing out when the man in pickup made a call on his cell phone, then he hung up, got out, and hurried to back of lot to one of the police cars. One of the cops handed him something and he went back to the truck.

Hmm! I drove along Manchester toward my house. On my right was a big old building that took up a whole block. LA Police Academy—Training School.

So maybe my guy isn't a lonely widower but a trainee in LAPD? Or maybe they saw my connection to the Russian limo drivers and they are tracking me? Yesterday the truck was there but nobody in it. I'll keep you posted.

Did you watch Elaine Stritch receive a Tony? I slept through it and was sorry to have missed it. Sorry too that they cut off her speech.

Waiting now to watch the Belmont Race. Happy for Triple Crown. Only once, with grandson Nico, have I had anyone join me in watching the Kentucky Derby—or the Belmont. True the race itself only lasts about 5 minutes, but whole world of it is so lovely. I'm for Essence of Dubai—we'll see. War Emblem could be Triple Crown winner. Everybody all upset because nobody likes the trainer and the owner is an Arabian sheik. I think I already told you about handicapping races for my mother, my Uncle John, when I was little, 5–6. Even I fell in love with *National Velvet*—Liz Taylor at 11 or 12. I regret not having been a jockey—or scuba diver on [Jacques-Yves] Cousteau's team.

In the early '80s, when my father just got Parkinson's, I took bus from Oakland to San Clemente. Sat in back so I could smoke and drink: had a ½ pint of Jim Beam. So did my seat mate, a black jockey 6 feet tall, 125 pounds. Skinniest man I ever saw, and his name was Sleaze. He was of mixed color with rusty red hair, very negroid features but pink skin with many freckles—green eyes. Strange looking fellow, exotic. I would have loved to have seen him arms and legs akimbo on a horse! He was heading for racetrack in Santa Ana. We took the red eye, which would have us in LA for breakfast.

Back to Sleaze. We hit it off. He said he was a writer too, that he had a novel called "Citizen's Arrest." I asked him typical question, "What's it about?" He said he hadn't written it. All he had was that title. (It is a good one.)

He was getting off at Anaheim. Asked me to get off with him and go to Disneyland . . . Now why didn't I go? I so regret this! Sleaze.

Oh no, today is almost over—back to treatments (2 ½ weeks to go).

What a shame about Bill Corbett and the Schuyler books. I loved very much his diaries. Maybe you knew a social/different person . . .

> *Much love,*
> *Loosha*

[In the following letters, Kenward writes of the death of his friend, poet Kenneth Koch, and of the terminal diagnosis of composer Claibe Richardson. Lucia tells Kenward of her own illness and finishing radiation treatment. She writes of spending time with her grandsons and her sons, particularly worrying about her son Mark.]

CALAIS, VT
JULY 7, 2002

Dear Loosha—

Topsy-Turvy Time. [. . .]

A fact which jolts me out of my Vermont laid-back daily round, thud. Thud. First Harold [Camp] The Mad Mower. His Prostrate Cancer has spread. He's been given Not Long. And Kenneth. Doesn't make sense, death. Death and Koch.[127] For one thing, he was too fervent and dedicated a hypochondriac to ever allow himself to die, thereby stopping a welter of brilliant ploys, on the tennis court, at the bridge table, wherever—enablement tactics to insure him eternal victory and sympathy and even love.

He was my poet mentor, post-Latouche, lured me into trusting

---

127 Kenward is responding here to Kenneth Koch's death, July 6, 2002.

poetry enough to take it on, on the page. For a while, I succeeded
Jimmy Schuyler, incapacitated by loonybin incarceration,[128] as his
closest poet chum, who invariably happened to be queer. [Kenneth]
was married to a devout Quaker, a Smith graduate, who knew how to
fly planes solo. He must have been an impossible hubby, both as non-
stop josher and skirt-chaser with Kosher overhangs. Imitating him, still
afraid I'd wind up in the loonybin myself if I didn't do "something,"
I asked him for a shrink to go to & went into analysis, for years and
years. Sometimes we shared our off-the-couch summer month of freedom. One year, we went to see Mayan ruins, the year Marilyn died.
Another summer, we shared a house in the Hamptons. We were both
cases of arrested emotional development re pretty girls (him) and cute
boys (me)—constant teenager-style reach-out and pining and eying and
drooling and romanticising. He was great fun, awful as his knack for
self-aggrandizement could be—for a bit, Ron replaced Kenneth as my
Tennis Friend. Ron, shaken by this loss, but manifesting a controlled
sadness, recalled how hard Kenneth plumped for Ashbery, did his dam-
dest to put J.A. on the map. One year, according to Ron, the year Joe
and I had a sort of a fancy book party at the Gotham Book Mart for
our first collab (Black Sparrow)—*The Champ*—a big editor showed up,
and, brainwashed by Kenneth, met J.A. and asked him right then and
there for a book—*Rivers and Mountains*,[129] J.A.'s first "uptown" poetry
collection.

[. . .]

Time to head from outbuilding to house. After three heat torture
days, decent temps have returned. I'm taking an anti-depressant, to
lift me out of whatever I'm in. I hope your medical interventions have
come to a halt . . . and you don't have to contend with long corridors—
and respite, as stay-at-home, is feasible . . .

Love,
Kenward

---

128   James Schuyler had the first of many mental breakdowns in 1951.
129   John Ashbery, *Rivers and Mountains* (Holt, Rinehart and Winston, 1966).

LOS ANGELES, CA
JULY 20, 2002

Dear Kenward,

Your last letter is simply tremendous. I thought of you when Kenneth Koch died . . . before actually, when about a month ago what seemed a farewell poem, lovely, by him appeared in the *New Yorker.* (There is another in this issue.) What a beautiful tribute to him is in your letter, witty and alive, like he was. I had never been that impressed by his work until I saw him in person, when he charmed and exited and mesmerized the whole room. Your review of Company, with wonderful show biz asides, was also a treat.

Look. I've said this before but you have ignored me. Your letters have such history in them, valuable information about musicals, poetry, writers. They are not simply marvelous prose, rich with characters, warmth and humor, they are fascinating chronicles. They should be published. I have not at all been hinting for a collection of OUR letters. That would be 2,000 pages. In mine I share with you pleasures and pains of daily life, but do not have the literary and historical IMPORTANCE that a well-edited collection of yours would have.

Your letters remind me of Flaubert's . . . they are where your prose, which is poetry, shines and takes off. They would be enjoyable if only because of the exquisite New York and Calais daily life chronicles, but you have written so much about opera and musicals, other lyricists and poets and painters. Please, show this, and them to Ron. Surely you have copies in your computer so that he can see samples. If he would know of who might publish them, some assistant could sort and choose from my vast collection or from your copies.

This was brought home to me when I showed Mark your letter and his response was that you should have a column, that there were two fantastic essays in the letter. Let me know how you feel about this. I will put together six or seven stellar examples, if you like.

Even though you are sad, you sound great. I'm glad to hear you are on anti-depressant. We need all the help we can get in these times. It seems you have had an especially hard year of people dying, ones you cared for. I'm so sorry about Harold.

I was about to ask Dr. for medication, so sick and down. But just being off of radiation and not being in bad back pain has buoyed me no end. So has hearing from [publisher David] Godine [who bought Black Sparrow Press]. I was blue, thinking my books were out of print. Working every morning now on my book. It's in a rough spot now . . . so I'm writing, deleting, writing, deleting. Talking to myself. Oh I love suffering about words and sentences.

You know what I really really miss? The typewriter bell.

My second son Jeff has moved here too! I was about to say he was my favorite, but I say that about each of them, same as with Anna Karenina and Moby Dick. He is living with Mark in Venice (truly an odd couple). [. . .]

I was the initial catalyst, especially when the C word came up, but everybody is now, supporting everybody else. We're turning into a cornier, stronger family. Wonderful, actually. Dan and I have been driving around L.A., from Beverly Hills to skid row. I love this city. I am feeling better than I have in a long time. Swimming has been help for my back.

Ivan just called with this joke about a man who is very depressed, tells his doctor that he feels like two old curtains. "Pull yourself together!" the Dr. says.

Please talk to Ron about your letters.

All my love,

Your L.A. LOOSHA

CALAIS, VT

SEPTEMBER 18, 2002

Dearest Loosha—

Discombobulated this morning, partly by hearing Claibe [Richardson]'s fatalistic acceptance of his own death. Weather super-Vt—blue sky, non-Jakarta air, crisp & dry—anti-depressant, but, Claibe is battling the Big C—catheter implanted, which before he resisted.

Exuberance about *The Grass Harp*. It's made it out of publisher slumdom, up to a high class nabe—the Rodgers & Hammerstein Org. Yesterday, I read an old *New Yorker* article about Richard Rodgers: personally a monster. Success turned him into an unreachable monument, and he deliberately cheated his first lyricist, the late great Lorenz Hart out of royalties, leaving Hart's bro & relatives dirt-poor.

Pro fans of the work at R&H are fine-toothcombing the score, weeding out errata, making sure that the spoken song cues are accurate, and that the revisions of revisions, some made for the Connecticut production last May, are all in place. What may be Claibe's Last Hurrah is a concert, October 25th, at Carnegie Hall, Skitch Henderson[130] the maestro, NY Phil Pops—first half, two orchestral works, including Claibe's *Grass Harp Suite* (which I know I've written you about before), second half one of the few Bdwy stars still a-glitter, Faith Prince, solo—her songs won't include any Claibe, drat. Sold Out already, so I've phoned Caroline Brainard for help. She invited me to *The Producers*—a hot ticket—and apparently has connections with Box Office Union biggies. Arcane circles within circles. I've invited her, Ron & Pat, and my ACLU lover-of-musicals—Matt Coles. Hate the idea of being Locked Out, due to my slowmanship.

I invited The Padgetts out, last night, to the fantabulous Chinese food palace, Single Pebble. They both looked spiffy, and we ate so heartily, we had to skip dessert. Ron always takes us for a meandering post-prandial scenic drive, heading home. Dark already, so we passed houses and fields, already shadowy. Sleepy, but I turned to HBO, my new enveloping addiction. Watched the same *The Sopranos* segment for the fourth time. Memories of seeing Broadway musicals, again and again and again, relishing favorite moments, clocking variations in audience response. [. . .]

That's the wrap. Bobbie Louise [Hawkins] phoned—great NYC gig at Joe's Pub, part of the Joe Papp Public Theatre show-biz empire downtown. Classy, waiters move discreetly mid-perf. My librettist pal, Arnold Weinstein,[131] had a show of his songs there, expertly performed. I'll still be here, alas.

Work block. Today's the day for a breakthrough, mebbe. Stuff for

---

130   Lyle Russell Cedric "Skitch" Henderson, pianist, conductor, and composer, 1918–2005.

131   Arnold Weinstein, American poet, playwright, and librettist, 1927–2005.

the website—memory snippets to accompany old photos, collages to provide visuals for some songs from an abandoned musical about Oscar Wilde, music by Steven Taylor.

Ron has finished his Dad book[132] proofing, and his editor is co-operating re some design snafus. Old tradition, I re-re-read a Barbara Pym—last novel, put together post-mortem by her assistant, *Academic Question.* Perfect antidote to HBO, wild lingo, sex, total opening up of all aspects of reality that used to be kept off-screen. Amazing, this culture change. Still restricted to low lifers. Particularly *Oz*—prison life. As it's about prison, anything goes. Same enabling release factor as *The Sopranos*—Mafia. Legitimizes the screen freedom. Middle Class values unchallenged. Maybe next—a CEO exposé, based on Milliken, junk bond chicanery. Corporate Greed & Dirty Tricks. Enron. Waiting to happen on Cable.

Skirting Iraq speechifying. Banality = Evil.

Housekeeper just drove up, dressed in white. My Problem Legs better today, for some reason. Patty found me a terrific masseuse, lay on her table for an hour and a half, one day last week, and went into a swoon. She played radio Mozart, a relief—no New Age minimalism. Only a month left, up here. The leaves are just starting to turn—yet to come, the sound they make falling. Blissful silence, right now. And my balky printer is working.

> *Love,*
> *Kenward*

LOS ANGELES, CA

SEPTEMBER 19, 2002

Dear Kenward,

When is it officially autumn there? (when do you return to New York?)

It has been great going through the seasons here . . . still have a fall of sorts to come. Having no memory has been a plus. I planted so much

---

132   Padgett, *Oklahoma Tough: My Father, King of the Tulsa Bootleggers* (University of Oklahoma Press, 2003).

in early spring, then forgot . . . surprised by mass of gladiolas then purple, red, coral, shaggy white chrysanthemums. Now the canna lilies are
growing, stately and tropical. Deep colors Coral, red, burnt orange. Huge
grassy bush outside my door turned out to be pampas grass which is now
in flume (apt typo) festive and rather silly, actually. The ladies in Proust
had urns filled with pampas grass, so I cut some in his honor. They also
had masses of "hortense" which I never found a translation for, market
woman in Paris told me they were rhododendrum, sort of ordinary, but I
can see them now in huge bouquets. It was lovely how many bouquets of
parma violets were left on his tomb in Paris.

Lovely lying in garden when no one is here. No one in whole
neighborhood, at home either. Driving down the streets is sort of like
a bizarre science fiction story. All of these Guatemalans with masks on
and their leave blowers, Tiny Muong men on their hands and knees,
clipping edges, Mexicans mowing, Philipino pool guys, Latina maids
taking out garbage. White UPS men, gay mostly. Why is that?

Inside though I don't really hear the blowers and mowers. I told you,
I think, that our mockingbird includes a cell phone ring in his reper-
toire? Best of all is to stay still enough for the three hummingbirds to
come to the fuchsia. The slight sound of their wings, like applause from
a vast distance, as delicious as their colors.

Amazing that we don't hear the planes. We are so close to the airport. Some very physical explanation for where the sound goes. But it
is eerie to see the planes, landing gear down, only inches above the wall
and looming Large as they sail by relentlessly day and night.

It will be very scary when they stop. Anything possible now that our
idiot president is determined to defy the whole bloody world. He even
walks like a thug now.

I am reading Joanne Kyger's new selected, from Penguin.[133] Lovely
soothing silent poems.

All is fine here. Between Mark and IRS I had money problem, asked
for Z press check early, which I think is not done and caused a big nuisance. Sorry for that, turned out ok without it.

---

133   Joanne Kyger, *As Ever: Selected Poems* (Penguin Books, 2002).

Good news is that radiation halted tumor growth. People think I should be more elated than I am about this . . . Truth is I never paid attention to the Cancer situation. I'm just sorry it came up, and REALLY sorry I told anyone. My back and lungs as much a pain in the neck as they were before all the hullabaloo.

Mark is in a rehab, three months, up in the mountains, bless his heart. This may seem like end of the world to him, but we all think it will be really good for him. He sounded good when I spoke with him yesterday. Oh, heartbreaking, Kenward, to see what a mess he has made. So good and loving and gifted.

Still fine how his brothers are "there for him" and each other, me. Jeff and I spend a lot of time together now, which is great. He's smart, funny.

No, alas, no pov or pox or abracadabra can help my book. It's a memoir.[134] The original idea did let me keep some distance and my "self" out of it. That's not possible. Not possible now either is to Look at all the bad choices and thoughtlessness my self did in chapter after chapter to come. Haven't the courage. So I have big old mess, sort of like packing up a whole house to move, then changing my mind. What do I do with everything now, and do I really want Any of it.

Sorry to go on so long. My literary career is in Shambles. That's all I needed to say, and shambles is such a good word that it even cheers me up. I'm not even in a huff anymore!

> *I love you,*
> *LOOSH*

[In the following letters, Kenward and Lucia write about her progressing memoir and a performance of Kenward's with Lou Reed and Sonic Youth, among others, for a Naropa/Poetry Project benefit, as well as outings to the theatre and an upcoming production of his opera The Seagull. *Lucia writes of reconnecting with a former student and enjoying getting out to readings and movies.]*

---

134   *Welcome Home.*

Dear Loosha—

Happy to be back in NYC: reassuring hubbub of car alarms, the subway under the house—but no furious phone booth vents from the sidewalk out front—it's been removed, leaving a broken cement patch: very third world look, reminds me of Washington D.C. & Buenos Aries (misp), cities in distress.

Last night, I hooked up with Steven Taylor, sang four songs as part of an Archive Benefit for Naropa & The Poetry Project. Started off with a new oldie, *White Attic*—very gentle, wispy childhood nostalgia— which Steven, bless him, made a guitar accompaniment for, writing it all down, using mystery words like "augmented seventh." Very strong response so I knew we'd be OK. Next, also with live guitar, *Middle of Nowhere*, faux CW from *Postcards on Parade*. Then, two works to ghetto blaster tape: *Sneaky Pete*, a poem song I made up that I love risking, despite its perilous high notes. Wowed the folks, always surprises me, as the words are tough, including a mention of Papa-Doc only specialists in Haitian history would be likely to grasp. We wound up with a vocal duet, *Girl Machine*, an old reliable, set as reggae by Steven. Got a little lost, but it didn't matter, as, via instant ESP, we barreled through the small goofs. Such fun to hear a HUGE audience respond so vociferously.

The church was packed, Lou Reed[135] being the star draw, along with Sonic Youth[136] (?), three guys, three guitars, whom I brushed against after my 15-minute stint, happy to be heading home. I missed Anne Waldman, hair black as a raven's wing, now an NYC resident for 8 months. The audience included a van load of Naropa kiddies. There were some stunner youths to ogle, which I attribute to this invasion—usually poetry buffs don't provide much in the way of eye candy—hapless victims who arouse serious eye lust.

---

135   Lou Reed, American musician, singer, songwriter and poet, member of the Velvet Underground rock band, 1942–2013.

136   Sonic Youth, American rock band.

My voice came back out of mothballs, and I hit the high notes broadside, scary, as, if fatigued, they're out of reach now, and I sink into a sick bleat. Steven stayed at my place, ideal guest, very considerate about my old age vicissitudes—knees worse, and it's a strain to walk far. Didn't notice this in Vt, as I kept my moves circumscribed.

Today, I get to stay in, and savor the all-blue sky from my third-floor vantage point, where I work, desk spang against an enormous tread-mill, and a new acquisition Mr. Oz found—an architect's huge slanted drawing board of wood, for collaging. House still has patches of disar-ray I'll slowly investigate. Tomorrow night, I head for Carnegie Hall, to hear Claibe's *Grass Harp Suite*, as conducted by octogenarian Skitch Henderson. Caroline Brainard, who somehow procured a ticket to this SRO event, will be my date. Then quietude for November, except I may watch rehearsals of *The Seagull*, as done by the Manhattan School of Music, the same gang that did *Miss Julie* a few years ago.

So scary, your riveting account of the lifers with self-made dark glasses! I hope you expand it as one of the "places" you're tackling.

That's the news. Trip back was easy, via van—Ron & Pat helped me get my stuff in cartons and cartons and cartons. Brought the Oscar Wildeiana books back, in the hope I'll shape up, work on something abandoned.[137] I've been to see two musicals, thanks to Matt Coles, the ACLU Gay & Lez head lawyer—my go-see-shows chum. The first is a massive hit, and deserves to be—*Hairspray*. Gorgeous. Doo-wop glo-rified. The second I just loathed—*Amour*, Frenchie, music by Michel Legrand. About a man who finds he can walk through walls. Cutesy—and so old-fashioned in a presumptuous way: whore with cleavage, office scenes where, at a long table, regimented work is enacted, expressionist simultaneity. I'm rereading *The Sex Offender* by Matthew Stadler.[138] My cup o'expresso—invented setting, Kafka meets Dennis Cooper.

Steven Taylor full of a mysterious corporation George Bush & Saudi

---

137   Kenward had been working on a musical about Oscar Wilde with com-poser Steven Taylor.

138   Matthew Stadler, *The Sex Offender* (HarperCollins, 1994).

Arabians & ex-premiers all over have a piece of. Paranoia about power-brokers not paranoia I fear.

Ron will be in your nabe soon—Otis [College of Art & Design]. Don't miss him. He has the deft Oklahoma timing Joe Brainard was maestro of, heirs to Will Rogers, one of whose phrases my dad used to repeat as an essential mantra—"I never met a man I didn't like." Well, he never had to look at W [Bush] & his ilk on the boob tube.

Love,
Kenward

LOS ANGELES, CA
OCTOBER 29, 2002

Dear Kenward,

Wonderful to envision you and Steven at the Naropa fest. The two of you are an inspired combination. Could not you do a proper New York production, to large audience, on your own? I have seen you together a number of times, amazed each time with the ESP and attunement between you. Favorites like *Sneaky Pete* and the reggae one new every time. (I think these are the ones I'm remembering so well) Wow . . . to be on bill with Lou Reed, one of my all-time faves. [. . .]

Hairspray sounds great. Glad you saw that and *The Grass Harp*, I hope, as well. John Waters[139] is terrific, fascinating. I long ago saw a documentary about him, mostly about his house and obsessions.

Tell me again about Oscar Wildeiana. What are your plans there?

My granpa had an actual phone booth in his office waiting room, where you got in, closed the door and a light came on. It had a wooden plaque that read "I never met a man I didn't like." My father, too, was always quoting it, yet neither one ever had any real friends.

If it was Will Rogers that died in a plane crash in Alaska, then I have about a hundred photographs taken of the wreck by Daddy's Kodak.

Lordy those days seem far away, no? I remember grown men, Texans, weeping when FDR died. Seems like H.V. Kaltenborn[140] was always

---

139 John Waters, American filmmaker, actor, writer, and artist, b. 1946.
140 Hans von (H. V.) Kaltenborn, American radio commentator, 1878–1965.

on the radio. Even as a child, perhaps because my father was overseas, off of Nagasaki on an ammunitions ship . . . I felt an intense shared patriotism with audiences at the Plaza movie theatre when we watched the jerky newsreels, applauded our G.I.'s, booed Hitler dancing on his balcony. Scenes of FDR and Stalin, Churchill, etc. were Reassuring, as I recall. Our country would pull through. Checking in on the news now is absolutely terrifying. Not just the threat of war, but the insanities erupting all around it unnoticed.

In "A Child's Christmas in Wales"[141] there is a scene where a house is on fire, the fireman have come, flames are lapping at the windows and an auntie comes into the room asking "Would anyone care for something to read?" The Snipers scariest because they were Not part of terrorist plot. The Russian theatre tragedy a ghastly metaphor for our governments today. Stay tuned! More to come.

I can't wait to hear Ron. Pray that it is not November 12th. My crazy sister-in-law, the one with the minks and Alzheimer's, coming for four Long days. I dread this visit. Alas, everything is hard for me now. I so love Anselm and Jane [Hollo]. Had lovely visit with them, but we had agreed to 9:30 am for breakfast. They came very late; I got home at 4:30, complete wreck, during and after our lunch.

[. . .]

Thank heavens I was sent an angel. Ben [Jackson[142]]. A 24-year-old Keats. One of the best students I ever had. Young man, beautiful in every way. Found me to ask for letters of recommendation, then when he realized I was close by he asked if I'd edit his poems for him (to send with college application). He and his twin brother are sons of the Laker's basketball coach Phil Jackson. A great coach and an absolutely fine parent.

Ben and I have had such enjoyable talks. Bless his heart he comes at nine and leaves at noon. I have brutally red penciled his work. He has been rewriting and writing away, calling me with revisions, new poems.

---

141   *A Child's Christmas in Wales* by Welsh poet Dylan Thomas was recorded in 1952.

142   Ben Jackson, American poet and teacher.

It has been great to feel like a teacher again. Actually it is nice because he thinks I am wonderful! He told me that he had discovered a great poet: Vicente Huidobro.[143] I had translated and edited his long poem *Altazor* for my M.A. in Spanish Lit, amazed Ben by reciting pages and pages from memory . . . beautifully translated.

His health cheers me. His eagerness cheers me. His physical beauty cheers me. Especially since it is not simply that his body and the features of his face are fine, but the humor in his eyes and his laugh are so simply alive and young. Great tonic. Sent me to my own book! Some of that enthusiasm had to be catching. Up early yesterday and today. The steroid med has helped too. I'm not very weird now but feeling ok, so hope I can get a good momentum going before it wears off.

Sorry to hear that you too are having a hard time getting around. And you have a third floor? I have trouble with one step on my bathroom trips at night.

Found a sweet TV show that I like: British sit-com with Judi Dench,[144] "As Time goes By."

Reading lovely Sarajevo writer Alexander Hemon,[145] collection of stories. He had a fine one in the *New Yorker* several weeks ago, about his Uncle's bees.

Another student sent me great collection called *LA* . . . read super Isherwood[146] on LA last night.

So good to hear you bopping around and enthusiastic. It inspires me. This time of year, when it gets Dark so soon, so do I. Need to head these blues off at the pass pronto. Your letter cheered me yesterday, just in time. Thanks always.

> *Love,*
> LOOSHA

---

143   Vicente García-Huidobro Fernández, Chilean poet, 1893–1948.
144   Dame Judi Dench, English actress, b. 1934.
145   Aleksandar Hemon, Bosnian-American author and critic, b. 1964.
146   Christopher Isherwood, English-American writer and diarist, 1904–1986.

Dear Loosha,

Ahhh, you've found a youthful compadre—a fall tonic, with capabilities sufficient to engage your capabilities, and, a big bonus, provide you with eye candy, a phrase I fleer at, but feel entitled to trot out for a worthy occasion: hook up with a gifted young poet.

It's five after midnight, and I've crawled out of bed, unwatched TV turned to Charlie Rose.[147] TV blare turns into a white sound that puts me out. Replenishing sleepette, after sending out for supper, to a new take-in place, a branch (three doors down) of the Greenwich Ave branch (just across the street) of the food emporium Joe [Brainard] subsisted on, when he lived on Greene Street, in Soho. It stars lively Latino servers, green to city ways, surely with fake papers.

Don't have the patience to cook, these days—even breakfast a maybe. Providential to answer the door, packages! Of food! Still warm! Surprise! Plastic cutlery to throw away. They take credit-card money, too, these amazing institutions. Veg soup + lasagna terrif, so filling I didn't touch the salad. Raced to the Apple Crumble. One of the perks of Eating Alone—Miss Manners is in absentia. One can wolf and skip.

An easy switch, from back bedroom third floor, to front room third floor workspace, dominated by an enormous Treadmill, as yet untrod on. Patty's back today from Vermont, and she's my sole co-treader. An acquisition Mr. Oz procured, also looms, a separate work unit to spread collage materiel on. It's an architect's slanted drawing-of-skyscraper blueprint desk, the size of a nouveau riche front-door in Hollywood. Unused, so far.

Elinor Pironti,[148] an artist, referred by my niece, came over today, 9:30, punctual to help me straighten out the house. Her ladylove lives in the nabe, so it's an easy commute to this once-a-week day job. She's cheerful about going out for latte to the Starbucks down the street, something only a kiddie should do. Now, have stash of copy paper,

---

147 Charlie Rose, American journalist and TV host, b. 1942.

148 Elinor dei Tos Pironti, American artist, worked for Kenward from 2002 to 2007 on his art collection.

pentels that work. Her love of orderliness is a boon. Went unbeliev-
ably fast, the tidy up. Alone, I lose my focus fast, papers papers papers
papers, head for a liedown. A ways to go, but I feel I've moved in. Dis-
orderly House (something sinful, no?) is retreating, down to the dread
Basement. Collages & material, under the Hollywood Door. Photos
too. Scripts, in desk. Letters, there. Paid bills—oh, Lord, forget where
they ended up. And I don't know what on earth I've done with the photos Wayne Padgett gave me to write about.

FOUND—

A) the flyer (for website) of Ruth Ford[149] Joe Brainard touched
up, her face whitened. She's my snooty *Grass Harp* actress chum who
launched the Z Press readings in Calais. Need it for Wayne [Padgett]
for those website foto memories I started tackling in Vt.[150]

B) $150 check, emolument for Poetry Project gig. Furious with
myself—waste not, want not. Turned up, haven't a clue how.

MISSING—

Don't ask. I place "important" stuff in a special place, so I won't lose
it. Then I forget where the special place is.

Today, 1 PM, sez here, Take In Lunch with the director of *The
Seagull*,[151] opera with the mal-de-mer flyer. He has some libretto questions, a good sign—I hope. Later on, but soon, soon, I expect he'll let
me in to watch rehearsals, which I love doing. I've seen five productions
of *The Seagull* through the decades, and it's always worked, held the
stage in frighteningly huge opera houses. Once: a famous moviehouse
mega-palace, in Atlanta, where *Gone With The Wind* premiered. A bit
embarrassing, as the couple of hundred opera buffs attending opening
night had to walk past acres of empty seats to get down front.

So loved Chekhov, I fine tooth-combed the words, so there aren't any
lines I wince at—except "Will o' the wisps." The devil to sing that "s-p-s"
but I couldn't have substituted "Monarch butterflies," now could I? *The*

---

149 Ruth Ford, American actress, 1911–2009. Appeared in production of Kenward's *The Grass Harp*.

150 Kenward is referencing materials being gathered for his website.

151 Elmslie and Pasatieri, *The Seagull (An Opera Libretto . . . Based on the Play
by Anton Chekhov)* (Belwin-Mills Publishing, 1974).

Seagull had a sixth pseudo-production which doesn't count. Right here in NYC. Small basement theatre. Year before last, I think. Some dedicated techno-goof spent months transplanting the orchestral music to a computer, which disgorged the music. A gaggle of showcase singers, trapped on the tiny stage, did their darndest to cohere with their "orchestra." Pasatieri's music sounded as if it had been recorded by a listening device Scotland Yard discarded way back. A floating around sound—in an ocean crevasse, biffed by subterranean currents, brushed against by lobster claws. Awful, though the second act began to shape up in a horrible way.

The Director sounded nice on the phone. Mark Harrison. Name sounds possibly made up to look purty in bright lights. I'm shamefully crush-prone when it comes to showfolk who are involved in something I wrote. Pleasurable intimacy via words, mine all mine, that start on a page & wind up coming out of human mouths, if I'm lucky—so "in character"—sound theirs all theirs, mouths that sometimes seem kissable. No bugaboo of real-life "commitment."

A smoke-and-mirrors netherworld, part real-life flesh, part entrancing being who sings my words, day after day after day. But with directors, no dice, except maybe a couple of times, way back. Such a dangerous situation. All that power to maim my words via a ditzy concept—Madame Arkadina is a drag-queen, Constantine has the hots for Trigorin, they are White Roosian refugees in Chile, surrounded by fields of marijuana they needs must sell to keep afloat, surviving in a ruin of a mansion that used to belong to—U know Who. U've been thar, in palmier days.

Must think poz. Directors aren't all dumb. The smarties know how to make my words take wing. Let the singers face front. IF they have strong pipes, let them grovel about the stage for the inevitable Mad Scene.

Tonight, I go to the York to see *Jumbo* thanks to Jimbo, sole time I'll get to use this assonance in a sentence, legitimately. *Jumbo* is a circus music spectacular. Thirties, Rodgers & Hart. This time around, just book-in-hand, no seals-in-pool.

Tomorrow a matinee, Brooklyn, to see a Robert Wilson[152] version of

---

152   Robert Wilson, American filmmaker, director, and playwright, b. 1941.

Wozzeck,[153] songs with words by Tom Waits,[154] Robert Wilson being the cheenius who (twenty years ago already?) expanded and shrank stage time as it had never been slow-mo'ed or sped up before, sometimes simultaneously.[155]

Left leg acting better on the stairs. Very little walking around outside. Trouble is—gets stiff from hours sitting.

End of catch up. Been re-rereading Ron's *You Never Know*. Temporarily off Ashbery, its bedside table mate. So moody, as reader. Are you?

[. . .]

Claibe [Richardson] phoned—really happy. Loves his website section, via Wayne Padgett. When the SF team come east, for the op'ry, I'll get to see a finished version of what they've done.

Time for a snifter of Laphroag, two flights down, then two up . . . So mild out, haven't a stitch on.

> *Love,*
> *Kenward*

[In the following letters, I enter the picture, as Lucia proposes to Kenward that I might be an appropriate assistant. Kenward details plans for a Manhattan School of Music production of The Seagull *and an "in-mufti" performance of* The Grass Harp.*]*

LOS ANGELES, CA

NOVEMBER 10, 2002

Dear Kenward,

Wow. Thrilling to be able to watch *Seagull* rehearsals. To have written words to this must feel so fine.

I've been trying to say, sort of sing "Will o' the wisps" as I go about my days, the play itself unfolding in my imagination.

---

153   *Wozzeck* is the first opera by the Austrian composer Alban Berg, first performed 1925.

154   Tom Waits, American singer, songwriter, musician, composer, and actor, b. 1949.

155   Referring to Wilson's use of time and sometimes long theatre performances, from seven hours to seven days and seven nights, such as the twenty-four-hour *Overture.*

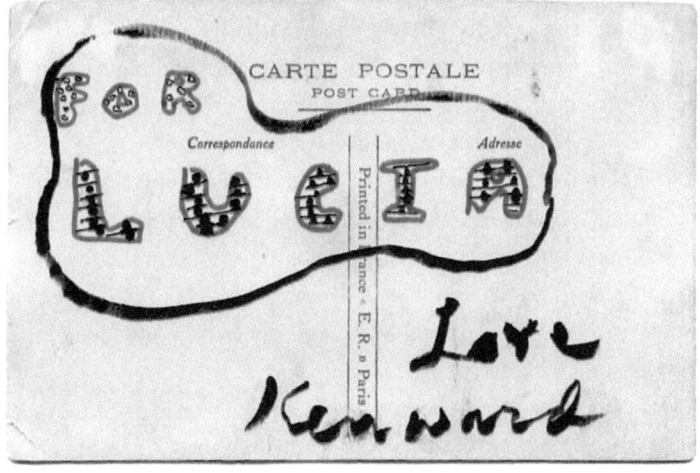

Postcard from Kenward, inspired by Lucia's story "Carmen."

(Pastieri's music:) ". . . as if it had been recorded by a listening device Scotland Yard discarded way back. A floating around sound—in an ocean crevasse, biffed by subterranean currents, brushed against by lobster claws."

Your letters are sparkling now. Crisp is word favored by sports writers lately (my favorite section of the paper) in Spanish it would be chispa or spark, more fire than dazzle. hmm Will of the chispa!

234

You and Chekhov, what a combination. Your language, in lyrics, poetry and I think particularly in your prose, and letters, unequaled in elegance and plain old beauty. I am inarticulate, but have a good ear . . . this observation has Chekhovian objectivity. People don't often realize that C was Funny. He would love Madame Arkadina as a drag queen with hots for Trigorin!

How great to go to rehearsals, especially when you are part of it. My mama had so much, well, chispa, really. She would take me to rehearsals of plays, amateur and professional, just barge us both in, and to days and days in the courthouse. Real TV, for sure, in Texas.

One of my favorite books is Nabokov's on Russian Literature. Predictably, he disses them all except Pushkin and Chekhov, especially poor old Dostoyevsky. He is fine, though, assessing Chekhov. He says C.'s writing is "gray," without any grace or beauty at all. This is true in a way and I think why it is so easy to translate well. Nothing happens in his stories or plays either, N goes on to say: his greatness is spiritual, he captures the (Russian) soul of his characters.

This is true in the simplest of his stories, of yours too. He has no real "minor" characters. Each one is Seen and heard and entirely whole. (This is me talking now.) Agafa (sp) splashing around in the river, too late to deceive her husband. Uncle Vanya, the couple in the Party dancing together in the hall once the guests finally leave. I love, deeply love many of his characters.

I am so impressed that people have heard, will hear (day after day) words that you have written. I know that people read the words we have written . . . what a joy for them to be SUNG.

If I didn't know better I'd think you made up going to *Jumbo* with Jimbo.

Wonderful letter!

I am very cheered. That stupid steroid worked. Its awful side effects gone but benefits have remained, will stay for awhile. It broke the pain cycle so it has been a relief to breathe easy, have no pain and no Vicodin, good sleep, a clear head. Can't express how liberating this is, literally freeing. Whether because of this or the inspiration of your letters, or mornings with Ben [Jackson] talking books . . . I have been writing for days now, two or three hours a day . . .

(Paying attention to pain. If it starts now I stop, stay ahead of it.) Have got us out of Yelapa, great road trip to Guatemala, super time in Chiapas, Lacandon Indians and Chamulas, have us settled in a village in Oaxaca San Felipe de las Aguas. We had a great life then, Buddy and I and our boys. Jeff and I have had good talks lately about those days. He and Mark too remember them as idyllic, adventuresome . . . close to magic realism sometimes. We were struck by lightning on Monte Alban![156]

Just went next door for pancakes made by Dan. His son Cody here for the weekend. Turned in to surprise breakfast for me. A new coffee-maker, candles and hand lotion, paintings and card from Cody. My birthday next week . . . very sweet of them. Cody is a bright likeable kid, 10 years old. [. . .]

Gorgeous splendid bright blue day after a week of rain. The birds are beside themselves. What a terrific expression, Does it mean that they are singing so loud it sounds like there are extra birds beside them? Whatever . . . they are celebrating. Did I tell you that when Hollos were here we saw a flock of lime green parrots? A common event in Venice, but a first for me. Divine surprise. The vulgarity and transience of this place is becoming more evident to me, the anomalies striking and as if scripted, the parrots, the man with his head on backwards, etc. I still like it though.

Are you looking for a secretary/factotum? I have a dear friend, Chip, an ex-student, Aging gay . . . (35!) He thinks it's all over now. (You guys . . . it's like dog years or starting pitchers.) He was editing newspaper in the Virgin Islands, then taught at the university for several years. [. . .] He has been a kind and most loyal friend to me, has stayed closely in touch. He's back in Denver recovering from broken heart with group that became close in one of my classes. He had had a 10-year relationship, ended with taking care of the lover dying from AIDS. Finally

---

156   Referring to places she's lived as she is writing her memoir, *Welcome Home*.

had nerve to fall in love again, oh, poor guy. Anyway, he writes a lot, publishes a lot. The last magazine, *Our Family*, dedicated to porn and it shocked me! But it had this poem of his in it, am sending.

Getting to the point. He loves your work. I have no idea what his plans are but it strikes me that if you needed or wanted somebody he would be good. He used to take care of my cat and plants. He's utterly trustworthy. Has great supportive parents, both teachers. Would not be AFTER anything, would never use you, not into things. Only problem I've had is that he wants praise for his work. He's fine tho . . . will send email saying "That Rocky poem you hated? They Adored it at *Kenyon Review*!"[157] He's especially healthy. Again have no idea whether he wants a job or whether you want anybody. Do know he would love to do anything for you . . . so if you ever do want an assistant he is a thought.

Sending you also one of the boats my nice but snobbish friend has done.

> *I love you,*
> LOOSHA

[In the following letter, I've come to meet Kenward to discuss the job with him. We go to the rehearsal of his opera, The Seagull. *I do some test cooking. It's decided I will return at the start of 2003 and move into his home to work as his assistant.]*

NEW YORK, NY
DECEMBER 3, 2002

Dear Loosha—

Chip has gone out to shop at Balducci's, best Food Mosque & Delice Centrum in NYC. It's five long blocks away, so I haven't gone there in ages—my walking radius has shrunk. So far so good. He's leaving day after tomorrow for the rest of the month, to tidy up for his

---

157 Here's the moment when I became a direct part of the story, and often the correspondence, between Kenward and Lucia. Lucia hated the "Rocky" poem, which wasn't published in *Kenyon Review* but did appear in an anthology, *Bar Stories*, from Alyson Publications.

Dear Kenward —
  Please forgive me
for being bossy about
your Health. I HATE it
when people give me
friendly+helpful (worse)
advice. Naps are
nice — that's all I'll say..
  Do hope you're
well though + love,
                    lucia

Can you see moon
from your apartment?

Kenward Elmslie

New York
New York
10011

Postcard from Lucia.

removal to NYC. We connect at lunch and supper—diet-y, & well put
together. He's cooked for a veg cohort, and eats carefully and lightly
himself, so that's no stretch for him. He once appeared in his shorts, to
ask for a towel, and his body wasn't NUDE DESCENDING A STAIR-
CASE by a long shot, but the effect on my one-eyed vision led to great

splintering alarums—visual delight & excitement. He moves quietly, with animal stealth, and once, I suspect caught me peeing into a glass at the kitchen sink, a ploy to avoid stairs to the nearest facility.

Today, I stay in. Uptown—blocking, enlarging the staging to encompass the stage size, which I don't feel I need watch. Yesterday, *The Seagull* Folks moved into the theatre. Nice size, big balcony. Chip came with me, uptown, as I thought I was on call to work out the tempo & content of the sur titles, which I would have fobbed off onto him—practiced editor as he is. The titlist was down with the flu, so we sat in the front row and watched the "sitzprobe," the first confrontation of singers and orchestra-in-the-pit. Such huge climactic sounds! And soft delicate passages. So much to get accustomed to—large sound and larger space to contend with. The shtudent orch sounds marvelous— salud to Tom P[asatieri] who knows how to orchestrate. It's a good opera, shameless in places, romance throbbing away, Italianate, but not bothersomely so. Very un-2002. The cast sounds marvelous too—most of the words sung with clarity. I got upset by "rolled" rrrs, Frenchy style, by one guy—he promised to forego them.

The set, according to the director, may have cutesy-wootsy Hansel & Gretel trees painted on plastic shields—nothing to be done about that. The costumes are also a mystery still. But the cast is super-duper, and hopefully will transplant the delicacies of their Chekhovian inter-involvements into the theatre, fully, but subtlely. The director has prepared them well.

I've been reading C[hekhov]'s letters. Cholera! A third world primitivo nation. He made himself so useful, fending off the horrors. Versus tiny city clots of volatile culture, extraordinary practitioners, prone to savage each other—turf jealousy, ideological conflicts, personality clashes, official policies. A welcome diversion from the snippets of tunes that haunt me, unbidden. I'm In Love With Constantine is # 1 on the Aria Parade, again, today. #2—Dr. Dorn, confronted by Masha's confession she loves Constantine: "So nervous, all of you, so nervous . . . there's nothing I can do about a magic lake." Last two words, held long, plaintively. Breaks me up, in performance, every time, unbidden tears.

I asked Chip what he made of what he heard—the performers lined up behind music stands—no staging yet. His face lit up, broad beam, eyes sparkly. Honest pleasure. Whew. That's all he'll see of it, drat, just the first half. Second half—tomorrow—second sitzprobe. A bit easier, I expect, the work itself narrowing down for the kill, and the cast surer of themselves in their new habitat.

So sunny out. Leg bothersome. Going through the grocery list with Chip got me out of my initial crosspatch mood, left leg cumbersome and achy. Diminishes. Sweet chat with [niece] Vivy, of Maine, how ninety-year-olds communicate, sort of, at her place of work.

Time to bathe, second floor, only tub big enough for me, while Chip is out shopping. To be cont.

Diet Lunch: a slice of scotch salmon, and a small salad. Sprite. We talked about Coming Out to our respective families (which, actually, I never did) & his horrible relative (a redneck Christian) who wrote Chip & his AIDS-ridden boyfriend that they'd burn in Hell, etc. I told him how, when my older sister, Cynthia, tried to break up my coupledom with John Latouche (somehow she found out from a bank that I was giving him money)—my father told her to mind her own beeswax. Chip reminds me, facially, a bit, of John Latouche[158]—same darkness, skin, hair, and cheek smile lines, natural handsomeness.

Next on my afternoon agenda: haircut, a block away. Chip's having dinner with a lady friend of long standing who works in the fashion world, which entails parties where everyone is dressed to the nines, and looks fabulous. I'll try to prepare, lolling in bed, for the arrival of the Website Trio, day after tomorrow, rehearsal tomorrow, plus an evening gathering at the New School to celebrate Kenneth Koch. Haven't fig-ured out what to read. Tons of poets, so it has to be very short.

Thanks heaps for sending Chip my way. Again, so far so good.

Love,
Kenward

[In the following letters, Kenward reports of the death of close friend and The Grass Harp composer, Claibe Richardson. Kenward writes of breaking into

---

158   Eerily true. The first time I saw a photo of John Latouche, it was like seeing a photo of an older and heavier version of myself.

tears at The Grass Harp *auditions, then walks Lucia through casting, rehears-als, and opening night, Sandy Duncan's 11 o'clock number. Lucia writes of Christmas with her sons and grandsons, of particular ongoing worries about one son, who's been living on the streets while waiting to get into a rehab center.]*

NEW YORK, NY

JANUARY 7, 2003

Dear Loosha—

Today at 11 AM — auditions for The Grass Harp. Chip taxied up with me, sat in the theatre next to me, along with Jimbo, pianist David Harris, and two York [Theatre] helpers. The first Babylove sang so feelingly and superbly, Jimbo and I were plummeted into helpless sobbing, grief for Claibe Richardson, who died on 1/05.

Claibe, according to his partner & devoted looker-after, Richie, was listening, heavily morphined, to The Grass Harp album, specifically Yellow Drum, which is all about courage, the unconquerable courage it takes to face up to life's journey, from city to valley to—death isn't mentioned outright, and I didn't know that's what the song was "about"—life's ultimate journey's end . . . So now I know.

In the musical, the song's source is identified by Dollyheart—she remembers hearing her grandfather sing it, a Civil War march. And it gives Dollyheart & her nephew Collin, and Catherine, the black lady who thinks she's a Choctaw, the courage to leave home, and take up residence in a treehouse. As they sing it, they gather up a few belongings, and as the song ends, (scene change) they're at the treehouse. It's the show's signature what-the-show-is-about song. Audiences sometimes clap in time to its martial rhythm, at curtain calls, when the whole cast lines up to sing it: closure.

Claibe had phoned me to let me know he was going, to escape cancer pain of five years duration, and to avoid the senseless cruelty of further medical intervention. No self-pity, no drama—true gallantry—like Joe Brainard, a good while back, who faced his own death squarely, considerate of those who loved him; he told me of his AIDS only when he knew he'd be going downhill. According to Richie, Claibe, pain-free, listening to the show album, sat up in bed, and began to conduct

Yellow Drum, joyously. And that's how he went. And that's why Jimbo and I, as "Babylove" was singing (she got the part), held each other tight, sobbing. Not easy on the auditionee, but she knew of our loss.

Your life is bumpy enough, as is, right now, so I hate having to let you know about Claibe. But our closeness, in life and our letters, is resilient and forthright, and ought to stay that way even when our bad patches coincide.

It's a help to have Chip to lean on, a bit, in casa, and out. He's handling my grief with great tact.

Love, as always,
Kenward

LOS ANGELES, CA
JANUARY 13, 2003

Dear Kenward,

Thanks again for telling me about the sweetness of Claibe's death. I loved how you spoke about what *Yellow Drum* was about. I think every good story, song, poem is about death. Sometimes if only how it connects us.

It touched me so to think of you and Jimbo embracing at the audition, weeping about Claibe. It seems you have lost many other friends recently, from a close-knit brilliant world that will never happen again. Hope this proves to be a healing and opening year. The San Francisco production, *The Grass Harp*, a wonderful way to start.

The Grass Harp is one of my favorite CDs. I don't listen to music often, hate background music. Have some favorites tho that I will put on and really be into . . . The G.H., Two Chopins, Marvin Gaye, Charlie Parker, several operas and Johnny Cash singing gospel.

I don't think this was done in the US, although I think there were newsreel theatres: In Santiago there were quite a few theatres that showed the same movie several times a day, every day for years and years. *Gone with the Wind, Fantasia,* two Al Jolson movies (not him but someone acting him and lip-syncing his songs), two Fred Astaire movies. My favorite movie ever: *Children of Paradise*. These weren't together, each had its own small, filthy theatre with rickety projector. Audiences loved Fred Astaire's glamour. Everybody in Chile danced beautifully and theatrically then, especially the tango. But what these movies did is create Singers. Everybody sang all the time, all over town. Chileans who did not speak any English at all would be walking down the street singing *Toot Toot Tootsie Goodbye! Toot Toot Tootsie Don't cry!* On busses you would hear *Mammy* or *Night and Day*. In the audience at the movies themselves everybody sang. When I was in Mexico in '92 I saw *Mambo King*, which was terrible, but I loved the way the audience sang along, hollered at the bad guys, etc. In Latin America people really cry at sad movies, men too. I mean sob, blow noses, etc. So much nicer.

Glad this memory came to me. It was much a part of the culture, and humor, of those times. Everyone could recite all parts of *Gone with the Wind*, and did, often. American tourists would ask a cab driver a question and he would speel out the introduction to *Night and Day*, something like "When the beat beat beat of the tom-tom and the winds upon the bay etc etc," then say "No speak English."

Jeff is off to Palm Springs to look for an apartment. It has been wonderful with him here. He's delighted with new job . . . Art Editor of Palm Springs magazine, which doesn't sound all that great, but they are paying him wonderful salary to redesign, recreate the entire magazine. He has such freedom and budget that he can't wait to get started. Dan and I will miss him.

[. . .]

Grandsons keep calling me about cool Christmas presents I gave them . . . oh they are delightful. I gave them a small ramp and a pipe for skateboarding practice . . . They keep getting better.

Oh oh . . . letters are falling. Have you had that problem? I'd better close, with much love to you,

LOOSHA

NEW YORK, NY
JANUARY 18, 2003

Opening Night Report For Loosha[159]
Dear Loosha—

Yesterday, I went up for the run-through, which was supposed to

---

159   Opening night of *The Grass Harp* production at York Theatre, January 17, 2003.

start at 1 PM—I thought I'd be home by four, easy. But there were some rough patches that needed to be attended to first, involving the entire cast of thirteen: The end of Act One was the toughest, starting with the tree-house oldsters, waking up in the morning to find Collin & Maude smooching, which erupts into a quarrel scene, with everyone talking at once, disrupted by Babylove's appearing out of the blue, followed by the Babylove Show, disrupted, in turn, by Verena & Sheriff Amos, the Act One closure being a parade of the arrested (ten) up the side aisle of the theatre, with Babylove, last in the parade, singing *Share My Love & Joy*, fainter and fainter, so as not to cover Verena's dialogue, left, marooned, at the tree-house with Dr. Ritz.

I stayed at the theatre, while Chip fed and cosseted the Padgetts, and two chubby, cheery Weir relations,[160] plus Trevor Winkfield. At the theatre, they all said they'd had a wonderful time. For the show, Jimbo found an extra chair for me, with space to stretch my problematic legs out, at the side of Row A, mid-aisle. I had to move it a bit to make way for entrances and exits, up and down the aisle. My vantage point was to the side, but close, helpful for my good eye.

The theatre was sold-out, largely elderly subscribers. The show started slow. Friendly response, but not all that involved. The break-out came with *Chain of Love*, sung bravura by Dollyheart. Technically, it's a Love Ballad, and I don't know of a Love Ballad in any musical play (different from opera) that stops the show. Not counting *Some Enchanted Evening* as sung by Pinza to Mary Martin in *South Pacific*—I'd better take back that boast. After that, a good ways into Act One, granted, audience involvement-and-love flowed, sometimes cresting, and the show kept on building, solidly, till the final curtain.

Sandy Duncan[161] brought in the Act II Eleven O'Clock Number—*What Do I Do Now He's Gone*. Amazing integrity. Started almost whispered, but fierce. Defiant, close to frantic, big voiced on I'll start

---

160   Jimmy and Rosalind Weir. I had prepared a "pre-theatre spread" for Kenward's guests, and then he called to say he wouldn't make it home to host them. It was the first time I had met the Padgetts, the Weirs, and Trevor Winkfield.

161   Sandy Duncan, American actress, comedian, singer, b. 1946. Starred as Verena in *The Grass Harp*, York Theatre in-mufti production.

again, right here and now. Then dropping back down, terrified by the prospect of solitude, for the final quatrain, which ends—*Nobody home at all*. She did something daring. Held back on the final *at all* till the last few notes of the accompaniment—the waiting for this end, taut tension, preceded by a lengthening silence—then the semi-whispered *at all*—sung artistry doesn't get any better than that.

And that's why the show sailed home-free, despite glitches, lines dropped, lyrics forgotten, confused moves. It should go better today— if the voices hold up: so much stress, extensive rehearsals, carrying scripts, jotting down what to do, dealing with props, how to climb where. No standing ovation, but healthy applause, and some bravoing, which began (confession: helped by me) starting with *Chain of Love*. And Dr. Ritz assured me Friday audiences tend to be draggy—tired from their work week. Saturday audiences are sprightlier.

A few people came up to me to tell me of their love of the work, its part of their life. They remember when they first saw it, first heard the album. One Yorky, shaggy hair, weirdo, told me he worked at a record store, and, when asked for a recommendation, ta-da—*The Grass Harp*. And some purchasers would come back to the store, to thank him. Real life happenstance I don't get to hear about, as poet.

There was a party afterwards in a dinky room, wine & eatments—I talked mostly, schlurp schlurp, to my Jason [Dula], who plays Collin. Sweet trouper. He teaches voice, $50 an hour, to help him through dry periods, "at liberty." Hmm. That'd be a lark! He was apologetic about being, in real life, older than Collin.

Home at one, made it up the stairs. Chip was a trouper—seeing me though a morning attack of computer fury, and a repeated problem— wallet loss (no I.D!)—hidden under something else, right in my desk, where it should be.

Today, lunch with Claibe's Ex, here. I've asked Chip to make a healthy soup, though it's Saturday, when, technically, he's off-the-case. Claibe's Ex has a worse weight problem than I do. Next week the show pressure will be off, back to quietude, and, hopefully, no infringement on Chip's time.

End of report! I think I'll sneak out for waffles, and a giant carrot juice at the Den, a few doors away. Freezing out, but no blizzard, as predicted, Friday night.

Love,
Kenward

Dear Kenward,

The Final Report came today. Wonderful wonderful piece. Like the others it is more than a letter, written like a poem but layered like the best of short stories. Catherine's ad libs, Sandy's timing and wit, your concerns and pleasures, the man in the gents . . . the songs themselves, which have a life of their own. I'm singing them too, like Chip!

So happy about Chip. When the idea first occurred to me I was thinking mostly about his character, intelligence and heart. Forgot that he can cook, would be likely to become a personal trainer. Great that he'll be guiding you toward the gym and pool. Aren't those spider poems good? What I remember of him is his easy cascading laugh (much more, of course).

Back to these letters . . . especially the *Grass Harp* Series. You say you are a "civilian" again. Kenward gauging by these letters you are at the top of your game. Is that the expression? Fit of your fiddle? Your sense of rhythm and natural symmetry never better, language dreamy. And so beautiful that "the ascendant quality" of Claibe's music shone through the performance, your letter. And the letter ending with Orpheus in the Underworld and memories of John Latouche . . . "his beautiful handwriting, slanting down the page, somewhere. . . ." Wonderful touching letter. You are bound to continue writing this year—so far better than ever.

I'm happy for you, also, not just because of this fresh *Grass Harp* success, but because I'm hearing an awareness of how incredibly rich your life has been, how many brilliant artists have been close to you, loved you. Sometimes I think you don't at all realize your true stature. Chekhov's gift was partially due to his humility. You are closer to him than any other writer I know—in every way. Didn't you like letter to his brother?

I'll try to write about your work in some kind of grown-up way, maybe for *RAIN TAXI*. Can't think right now, still.

Oh dear Mark. We have been so mad at him, feeling impatient and clueless. He seemed to be lying all the time, hasn't let anybody see him, the security guard said he found him drunk on the street, etc. Jeff finally got in yesterday. Jeff thinks that melanoma on his navel has metastasized. Still no diagnosis or facts about doctors, prognosis, etc., but he has lost about 30 pounds in a few weeks, is very very weak. Is not drunk, but perhaps a brain tumor disconnects his thinking at random. We are moving him here tomorrow, where he'll sleep in Dan's house. I will be with him during the day until Dan gets home at night.

He was trying to hide this from us, or from himself. Sometimes he would say he had a brain tumor but was so goofy we didn't believe him. He is sweet and clear now after finally saying, "I want to go home."

I am relieved not to be worried about where he is or mad at him for lying. I'll have to know facts or see him myself before I can believe he's dying. Right now I'm just glad he is coming here. I'm following AA rules now: A day at a time. Today is ok.

Thanks again for visual care package. Fun to look through the architect magazine with Jeff . . . we both loved it. He is big fan of Trevor Winkler's work already, loved the new jazzy images.

> *All my love,*
> LOOSHA

NEW YORK, NY

FEBRUARY 7, 2003

Dear Loosha—

Snowy morn, the scrape of shovels on sidewalk, light flurries sideways—the wind from the Hudson must be strong. I'll stay in today—good timing. Last night, I was invited by Jimbo to see a baseball play with "frontal nudity"—*Take Me Out*.[162] All guy cast, beautiful timing,

---

162   *Take Me Out* is a play by American playwright Richard Greenberg, b. 1958. First staged in London in 2002, Broadway premiere 2003. Kenward took me to see it shortly after he saw it with Jim Morgan.

tough dialogue, reality-based, with riffs to now and again lift up its lingo. Sam The Glamour Star and [David] Mamet tap into this US of A performance skill that outdoes the Brits, for all their savvy at character-acting—an unstoppable vitality that matches USA musical theatre at its best.

I don't know beans about baseball. My bro-in-law took me to see the Cleveland Indians, around WWII, and that was that. Beautiful set, no curtain—wall of lockers & above it, score area that flashes huge numbers. A few stools & a metal floor grid, water run-off for the Nude Shower Scene. Nozzles descend, lightly done, no curtain fol-de-rol. And verismo acting (the guys soap and squirt stuff between their toes to avoid athlete's foot)—Invisible Fourth Wall so present, they're, seemingly, absolutely free of any awareness of the audience ogling their privates, the "point" of the scene being their awkwardness with each other. A gay black super-hitter star of their team has outed himself & the easy, towel-snappy camaraderie of the team has been disrupted.

[. . .]

Not a Perfect Play, the morning after, but so brilliantly timed—and energized—comedy riffs had the audience applauding the zingers. Still in previews, but it's so honed from its London birth and downtown Public Theatre run, it should run for ages. I'm tempted to see it again with Chip, if I can pry him away from an everexpanding novella he's eager to end. Wonder if the "writing" will hold up, second time around, despite the smoothie plot turns & riveting actors.

Sniffle sniffle, won't go away. Valentine's Day, I get my New Eye. I do fine with the one, except for footing inexactitude. Have to look down, where I'm going.

Long chat with the Website Honcho, Bill Weir, who'll start finishing up your interview. Most appreciative of added visuals you loaned the team. And so inspired by you! [. . .] Bill mentioned adding music to your sector, made me extremely nervous, WHAT music, Huh, as your voice has its own music.[163] But if it would help, these tracks

---

163   Referring to Lucia's interview for Kenward's website.

might prove simpatico, as intros and seg glue (dividers) that fade gracefully & fast. There's a harmonica solo that might be at home, at home with you.

Much love,
Kenward

LOS ANGELES, CA
FEBRUARY 13, 2003

Dear Kenward,

I can't stand it that your gems aren't being enjoyed by hundreds of people. Wish you had a column or your own theatre review section somewhere. *Take Me Out* was tremendous, especially after the very short intro about your baseball experience, a Cleveland Indian game in WWI with a bro-in-law (Oh I can just see you!)

I read the play section out loud to Mark . . . got into it, very Anne Waldman. He loved it too. As always you bring the stage workings alive . . . sounds like they did that part really well . . . the showers and drain, curtains, set.

When you and Steven [Taylor] sang *Who'll Prop me up in the Rain* once at Naropa I wept shamelessly. Since it is one of the poems that most connects me to you, I think it is perfect for web-site. Adore it. Harmonicas my favorite sound . . . next is the Argentinian ? forget the name of that . . . accordion, so sexy and plaintive. I am very excited about this! Love the fact that you'll be with me, on the same page so to speak!

[. . .]

Mark is doing ok. Going to group therapy three times a week, to AA meetings. Well I THINK he is. In a few weeks he will be going into the facility, which will be a relief, have meanwhile decided to stop worrying about him. What's to worry? He already disappeared, then was dying. The fool is indestructible far as I can tell.

Thanks for your kind words to me, about staying firm etc. I'm ok. Certainly saw what worry etc can do to my health, especially my back. I'm re-establishing peace of mind and all my aplomb. [. . .]

We're having a storm! Wonderful . . . days now of pouring rain. Looks like the swimming pool is going to flood. MMmm. Cat is mad as a wet hen. I'm reading Trollope.

> *Much love to you and to Chip too,*
>
> *Loosha*

[In the following letters, Kenward and Lucia discuss the national political situation, presidential primaries, and Kenward's experiences with John Latouche during a similar period of suspicion and fascism, McCarthy's "Red Channels list" and its effect on Hollywood.]

NEW YORK, NY

MARCH 18, 2003

Dear Loosha—

So glad you're back, cat-licked, safe from hosp air, laden with who-knowswhat, closed off in a labyrinth of medical practices I don't dare try to imagine. Did me a world of good to hear you, felt replenished by your vibrancy of voice and being. As inspiring as a visit to Eire ages ago. I was enchanted by the locals' lilt, the natural music daily round words were lifted by, the remembrance of which perhaps helps me open my ears more fully to you.

I was a guest of the Guinness laird, Lord Moyne,[164] an ex-amour of Ruth Yorck,[165] who took me on a tour of her Europe, one year, to show me many remarkable survivors of her pre-Hitler life. I was her Candide. Lord Moyne was a gentleman poet: Georgian poesy I dismissed it as. One of his ex-wives was the Mitford[166] who went Fascist. We gathered five times a day to eat stolidly at a big table—children and nannies and a proper mannerly sensible wife. One lump or two. I wanted three. So I loved escapes to Dublin, which seemed

---

164 Walter Edward Guinness, 1st Baron Moyne, Anglo-Irish politician and businessman, the English minister of state in the Middle East, 1880–1944.

165 Ruth Landshoff-Yorck, German-American actress and writer, 1904–1966. Close friend of John Latouche and Kenward's.

166 Diana Mitford, English politician and writer, 1910–2003.

Dickensian—gap-toothed smiles, dark alleys, the mystery (and lure) of widespread poverty, which didn't seem to quash the lilt of talk.

I don't fathom current events. So many deep silences. Is Congress even in session? Are they incarcerated on that island near Cuba, where "terrorists" are being sequestered, to muzzle them, while Bush attends his war conference on another island peaceniks & media interrogators can't fly to?

Vermont's Senator [Patrick] Leahy? Our lone ex-hippie independent Representative, Bernie Sanders. And California's Senator [Barbara] Boxer, so outspoken before The Deluge. Brings back scary realities when I moved in with John Latouche, '53.

Three men came every day to create movie cartoon shorts. They couldn't work for corporations (they'd helped create Mr. Magoo for UPA[167]) as they were in Red Channels.[168] John's problem, too. No radio work to keep him going between musicals. Via Gore Vidal,[169] John & I (thrilled to write dialogue John actually found usable) wrote a "pilot" TV script, called *The Devil's Theatre*. The concept was: the Devil would appear each week in a different guise. We went to an actual TV studio, where the assembled cast, Broadway-ites, some with illustrious but non-star names, rehearsed our dialogue. The Director materialized, had a fit when he saw John, booted us out so fast he didn't have time to summon Security. Ironclad corporate rule.

NO Reds. Ignominious, John treated that way. So inexplicable. But my senior year at Harvard ('50)—The John Reed Society[170] was closed down. Classmates were summoned to D.C. to explain themselves,

---

167 Mr. Magoo (J. Quincy Magoo) is a fictional cartoon character created at the United Productions of America animation studio in 1949.

168 *Red Channels: The Report of Communist Influence in Radio and Television* was an anticommunist document published in the United States at the start of the 1950s, a pamphlet-style book naming 151 actors, writers, musicians, broadcast journalists, and others in the context of purported communist manipulation of the entertainment industry.

169 Gore Vidal, American writer, 1925–2012.

170 John Reed Clubs (1929–1935) were an American federation of local organizations targeting Marxist writers, artists, and intellectuals, named after the American journalist and activist John Reed.

according to rumors. And before that, my cousin Adrian, mid-WW II, was purged from the State Dept., along with his—er—boyfriend, part of a massive firing of homosexuals, justified (national security) by the danger of Undesirables (as newspapers dubbed them) being black-mailed by male Mata Hari Commie perverts.

Patty and I treadmilled this morning. Then she brought up four boxes of old financial records from the increasingly orderly basement, to be thrown out. A ritual, when she comes over. Still more to go. She found a Brainard, made for a party in honor of the legendary acting coach, Stella Adler.[171] Heart-shaped stiff paper, bent now, imprinted with dozens of lipsticky kisses by Joe. Slowly, such works are being tended to by Elinor, an artist who comes over once a week to help straighten up the muss. Dusted off, flattened, sealed, framed.

Chip looked gleamy this morning—it's a warmish spring day— winter is over, finally. He made oatmeal for breakfast, reported he'd watched Bush on TV last night. Hard to thrust War Dread and scary, nutso leaders into that mental cavern where dark, shameful doings one can't stop are tucked away.

Love,
Kenward

LOS ANGELES, CA
APRIL 20, 2003

Dear Kenward,

Reading this over I do sound loopy. Don't know if it is prednisone, leg pain, stress, whatever. Could say I'm not myself, but I have forgotten who that was by now. Anyway will continue to connect with you as much as I can. Dear Forster, at end of *A Passage to India*: "only connect." Wish I could remember the most wonderful quote about dwarves clapping.[172]

Dear Kenward, please let me know where you physically Are. Need to imagine you placed in order to write. Where I wish you were would be on an old and elegant ocean liner on the way to Australia.

---

171   Stella Adler, American actress and acting teacher, 1901–1992.
172   "A friendliness, as of dwarfs shaking hands, was in the air."

In my youth there was one such fine English ship that went from England to Valparaiso to somewhere in Australia and back. My girl-friends would only travel on this ship. Captains, chefs, stevedores all Italian and handsome. Alas I had to go on Grace Line, since it shipped ores for my father's company, owned by Guggenheims and Peter Grace. Somehow always met or sent off with roses and champagne or in canasta or chess games on rainy days with Mr.? How can I forget this man's name? He was in our life for years and years, Chile, New York, New Mexico, Mexico, California. He was in the hospital when Jeff was born. (Jeff's father off in Italy with new lady, patroness, villa.) I had been teaching junior high in catholic school. MR KIRBY! So the nuns all came too. He arranged with Italian deli for sweet party with several friends of mine, the nuns who had been so good to me. He ordered dozens and dozens of roses to go with the party that day Jeff was born. He was in his sixties then . . . lived another thirty years as my friend. Benefactor, He never gave me, never loaned me money. His function seemed to be Elegance. The Santa Fe Opera. Flamenco. Dinner at the La Fonda with four Spanish bishops (yes all had read Willa Cather.) Cocktails at the officer's club on Treasure Island . . . incredible view. Dinner at Merle Oberon's[173] mansion in Acapulco.

That really was a digression. Are you in Vermont? Australia? Manhattan? Are your eyes okay? Your knees?

Strange thing is that you sound fine but your keeper is a wreck! Poor Chip. I swear his problems are caused by worrying about you.[174]

Elaine Equi sent me her latest book, The Cloud of Knowable Things.[175] Wonderful book. I have been fan of hers for many years. Remember the L.A. magazines like BARNEY when she and Dennis Cooper, Jerome Sala,[176] et al. were young rascals? It was nice to fall in love with her and Jerome (in person) at Naropa several years ago.

---

173   Merle Oberon, Indian-English actress, 1911–1979.

174   I was suspicious of Mr. Oz and his motives regarding Kenward, especially when they went to Australia together. Kenward would later have his own suspicions of this particular "helper."

175   Elaine Equi, *The Cloud of Knowable Things* (Coffee House Press, 2003).

176   Dennis Cooper, American writer, poet, critic, editor/publisher, b. 1953.

Bon voyage, if you are off to Australia. Will you see your other friend, the royal one?

> *All my love,*
> *LOOSHA*

[There has been a gap in their letters as Kenward traveled to Australia with Mr. Oz. Lucia and Kenward then made plans by telephone to see each other in California. Lucia was hurt that Kenward never arrived at her apartment. Kenward returns to Vermont and, in the following letters, returns to the correspondence as if no error were committed.]

> CALAIS, VT
> JUNE 14, 2003

Dear Loosha

It's 8:50 AM, Vermont time, I think. I'm facing the pond, swollen white water waterfall, its white reflected, slanty, in the pond. The trees have leafed, not surprising, as it is mid-June. I've breakfasted on goat's-milk yoghurt (a Vermont delicacy) & toast, with cut-up jalapeno peppers & garlic & almond oil. Strong coffee.

[. . .]

Slowly I've come out of Middle of Somewhere Jet Lag. Sleep patterns still jumpy, unreliable. Re-Re-Read an old *New Yorker*,[177] beside table, a George Plimpton piece about Capote, and his part-fiction murderer duo, being hung. And a beautiful story, same issue, about two guys, sheep-herders, who become an item, get married to girls, but reconnect. One is gay-bashed, dies. Anne Proulx—have her name a bit wrong. Her guy-guy stuff unabashedly lyrical but not gushy—so firmly grounded.

Today, and for months, I get to stay put. Chip seems genuinely boondocksfriendly . . . whew. I'm used to the Isolation . . . no human sounds, just rain on grass and trees. Undecided how long he'll stay.

---

177 The *New Yorker* magazine's October 13, 1997, issue featured George Plimpton's "Capote's Long Ride" and Annie Proulx's short story "Brokeback Mountain."

One night, his idea, we drove to NJ, the Paper Mill Playhouse to see a high energy production of *Grease*. A showbiz dancer boyfriend of his, Colin, was in it—tough fast dancing. Sweet youth! The problems of The Young, heartthrobs, multiple choice.

Brought home by a book I can't wait to order for you—a photo book by John Gruen: *Young In the Hamptons*[178]—I'm the Cover Youth, large as life, profile, facing a beauty, Jane Wilson, his wife, painter, who is beaming at me. What had I said? My dog Whippoorwill can be seen between us, along with Ruth Yorck's neurotic whippet, Rossignol, who leapt out of the car, one summer—I was driving up to Vt with Ruth. Never found.

I kept yowling, Chip upstairs, napping, at the sight of Us Happy All, young, smiley and tan, ages and ages ago. Larry Rivers, Kenneth Koch, Frank O'Hara, J.A.[179]—etc etc etc.

Chip's up—it's now 2:30 PM. Placement resolved, his carefulness about o'er-reaching overcome—he's working at the Big Table facing the pond. He asked its name. I fell back on a joke Joe Brainard & I shared: Veronica Lake.

The Padgetts will join us for dinner at the Greatest Chinese Food Palazzo in the whole US of A—A Single Pebble. Another Vt. perk. I've begun carrying cartons of paper chaos from house, across road, to outbuilding. Time to crank up as wily Filing Clerk. Slower legs this year. Have counseled myself not to vent fury at my defenseless sinews & joints for "letting me down." Summer Resolve # 1.

Summer Resolve #2: accept mind slowness and name loss, tortuous paths through memory rapids. One persistent block. Have trouble recalling my Dad's (and Step-Mom's) refined name for queers. Fairies was too "common." Not plum pudding. Not nuthatch. Gone again. Ah—fruitcake. Fruitcake!

178　*Young and in the Hamptons: Photographs of the 1950s and 1960s* (Xlibris, 2003), by American critic and photographer John Gruen, 1926–2016. The book featured Kenward on the cover with Gruen's wife, American painter Jane Wilson, 1924–2015.

179　New York School artists and poets, and Kenward's friends, appearing in the photography book: J.A. is John Ashbery.

A pleasure not to feel cut off from you by time & distance vagaries, travelworn gaga-hoodedness, & no print-out possibilities at hand. Do your stuff, HP DeskJet . . .

Have your latest pub, patted tenderly but unread so far, saved for when I'm zoned again, rooted in the moment, & know where I am.

Love,
Kenward

LOS ANGELES, CA
JULY 12, 2003

Dear Kenward,

Wonderful to get your good letter. I have missed hearing from you. Thought I had bored or offended you . . . realize that you have been getting things in order, resting and refreshing.

Please forgive me for the letter I wrote a few days ago. (In yellow or orange envelope.) I am so sorry that I felt it, wrote it, sent it.[180]

I never want you to feel obligated to write to me. I have certainly written less than I used to. Letters are only good when they are felt and spontaneous, as yours always are. I'm so ashamed of myself, oh.

My only excuse is that your letters are so important to me; they sustain me. Dan had been in Bay Area for a week. I hadn't seen a soul except for the pool guy, talked only to the lab tech on the phone. I received only a few letters; had especially not received a letter from you, for a long time, but especially not this particularly lonely week. (wow, what a construction . . . I could wonder if there would be an easier way for one to have expressed this thought!) My solitude was scary, (coincided with your deliberate and pleasurable one in Vermont.) Sounds like you got a lot accomplished as well.

[. . .]

I'm doing well. Off of Prednizone at last, which has relieved paranoia. Back in the pool finally and working in the garden.

Steve Emerson was here for a brief visit. Wonderful to see him. I have got to make serious effort to see people and really have got to get

---

180   See "Vermont Letter to Loosha" (296).

Little Bunny Foo Foo

_He tried so terribly hard to be good.
But sometimes, sometimes he
couldn't help himself.

Cecilia Johnson - Copyright © 2003
www.downtherabbithole.com

July 10, 2003

Dear Kenward —
Please tell me
why you have stopped
writing to me.
It has been
painful. after many
years of several
letters a week then
have been months
of silence.
It has hurt me
badly, What could I
have done?   Loosha

Postcard from Lucia.

back to my writing. Meanwhile I apologize for being needy and whiney. Yukko. [. . .]

> *Love,*
> *Loosha*

Dear Loosha—

Back-To-School Dread is surfacing, unwittingly. Plus War Dread. Sept 1st 1939: my very own kingdom declared war. I kept a scrapbook of the subsequent battles—for awhile. My favorite pin-ups were perfume ads of beauties.

My father, a single widower who decoded secrets at the British Embassy (we'd moved to D.C. from Colorado Springs, so he could participate thus in the war) used to date perfume beauties. The most beautiful, a blonde Dane, was named Ingrid Arvad. A half-a-century (?) later, I came across her name in a bio of JFK. He was just starting out in DC. His dad forbade him to date Ingrid—he'd had her checked into. Was she a spy? Is that why she dated this handsome ex-rancher, who carried his age well? He worried about Loss of Memory & his modestly spreading belly, but otherwise, age left him unscathed. In the Springs, my dad played polo at the country club, which looked hard, racing about, wielding a mallet.

Patty came over, this morning, to invite me to dinner tonight. She looked all recovered from her funeral trip to Tulsa (her sister, Bernie, died of cancer). We smoked a cig each—chatted a bit. She's so relaxing to be with. For her menu, she took the yellow bean harvest from my very limited veg garden. [. . .]

I haven't done a lick of writing, all summer, just feel rather out-of-it. Ron feels the same I-Don't-Care detachment—but that may be due to the hollow feeling after a book comes out (his Dad book). His Joe book,[181] looks like, has been taken by Coffee House, which is still struggling along.

This year, I'm not pushing myself to walk, solo, or with Patty. So glad you're breathing on your own again! Must be so hard to be dependent on a machine for something so personal.[182]

I'm getting worse and worse at coping with machines! Last time I drove back uphill from the Padgetts—I went into a wild panic. I couldn't figure out how to release the child-proof door lock device. Finally, I did something, and fled, free again, back into the night.

Jimbo of the York is supposed to come up here, with his cohort choreographer, to chat about a spring production of a four-person revue of my stuff. He got pretty excited on the phone, thinking of the range of my stuff. For one thing, the artists I've worked with. Joe. Alex Katz. Larry Rivers.[183] That perks me up, their work being seen in a theatre. But I'm still terrified at the prospect of being on stage myself, show after show after show after show, like a pro. Which I'm inexperienced at being. But it's also exciting to get absolutely petrified by a future possibility. Which is all it is, at this point—a possibility.

Thanks for putting up with my laggard behavior, as communicator . . . hate to try to put words on paper unless I'm feeling somewhat non-gaga re my daily round, no excuse for plaints and gripes . . . I'm a lucky septuagenarian, I keep telling myself. If only I didn't have so much trouble remembering names. Just like my Dad. Always draw a blank trying to think of Albert Finney's co-star in *The Dresser*. Tom Courtney! Came to me right away, this time, no struggle! Whew! Put his name in a work—(*Cyberspace*) so I'd know where to look for it, in case I forgot it.

Love,

Kenward

---

181   Ron Padgett's biographies of his father, *Oklahoma Tough* (University of Oklahoma Press, 2003), and of Joe Brainard, *Joe: A Memoir of Joe Brainard* (Coffee House Press, 2004).

182   Kenward is referring to Lucia's oxygen tank, which she is less reliant on at sea level in California than she had been in Colorado.

183   Alex Katz, American artist, b. 1927. Larry Rivers, American artist, 1923–2002. Friends of Kenward's. Artworks by both artists were featured prominently in Kenward's New York home.

[During these few months, their correspondence has slowed down dramatically. Lucia emailed me of being angry with Kenward, both for his slight in California and for his lack of letters. She wrote me in September 2003: "Haven't written to Kenward, or anybody, in a long time, or heard from him. Not something I can force, nor he. Really sad, I think he enjoyed our letters as much as I did." *Their letters and regular correspondence pick up again at the end of October. Kenward was back in New York and planning a musical revue of his works,* LingoLand, *and writes of a Philadelphia production of his opera written with Ned Rorem,* Miss Julie.*]*

LOS ANGELES, CA

OCTOBER 31/NOVEMBER 2, 2003

Dear Kenward,

I'm writing this in the dark! It's trick or treat night and I forgot to buy candy. I've never NOT had treats . . . Do they actually Trick anymore? I only remember one Halloween as a child. I had the measles. Health Lady had hammered a CONTAGION notice on the front door, so kids didn't even come up on the porch.

Next Day. Day of the Dead . . . anniversary of my mother's death.

Sunday: Found a great apartment yesterday. Tiny studio on seventh floor. Very safe, easy parking, etc. Light, bright with wonderful view of Venice beach, the mountains, miles of the city. As the face-lifted botoxed dyed blond realtor said, "If you lean off the balcony and look north you can see the letters of the Hollywood sign!" Wow, I've arrived! Love it. There is super real grocery only ½ block away. Wooden floor, real butcher. Three blocks from the beach! View of the beach from kitchen window! Can watch sun set from my bed!

[. . .]

Many things better here. Easier. Many coffee shops and little cafes in "my neighborhood." Interesting diverse people, mostly my age, sitting at all these sidewalk cafes. I'm very pleased.

Did I say that I have been sick? Bad patch. Breathless from the fire ash air. Scary. Back on high prednisone dose. It will be good for packing at least. And standing, for cooking, etc.

Mark came to visit this morning. I made him lunch! He's doing so well. Best I have seen him in years. Dan joined us for dessert and coffee, laughter. Seemed like old times. Whew.

Much love to you, dear friend,

Your *LOOSHA*

LA Loosha

NEW YORK, NY

FRIDAY, NOVEMBER 7, 2003

Dear Loosha—

5:30 AM. Travel jitters. Today is Philly #1 Trip, Chip at the wheel, to see two performances, different casts, same day, of *Miss Julie*,[184] at the Curtis Institute de Musique. Its premier, back in the Sixties, given by New York City Opera, was my only opera disaster. Helpful, eventually, as it steeled me for subsequent theatre disasters—the dreadful birthings (three) of *The Grass Harp*, the misfire of *Lola*, and my most recent debacle—*Postcards on Parade*, at the York. Plus the Detroit premier of *Washington Square*,[185] which was saved by a diva, Catherine Malfitano,[186] who pulled the audience into the work, somewhat, by her canny pyrotechnics.

Octogenarian Ned Rorem will be there, so, should we meet in the lobby, I'll get to genuflect. He's managed to do Fame, non-stop, and he's wily, about generating homages, as a perk, when he tacks on another five years, another decade. So, the November Birthday Boy has been tootling about, attending concerts of his oeuvres.

My sister Cynthia [Weir]'s youngest-of-three sons, Jimmy, an architect, will be there with Rosalind, his missus, and their son, Chester, who is dangerously handsome and charming, a would-be architect who has been so disillusioned by the inroads of capitalism at its greediest, he's floundering. Rosalind has invited my sis, Vivi [Elmslie], but

---

184   *Miss Julie*, Kenward's opera with music by Ned Rorem, based on the 1888 play by Swedish playwright August Strindberg.

185   Elmslie and Thomas Pasatieri, *Washington Square* (Belwyn-Mills, 1976), based on the 1880 novel by Henry James.

186   Catherine Malfitano, American opera singer and director, b. 1948. Starred in the New York Lyric Opera premiere of *Washington Square*, 1977.

I suspect she'll forego the trip—we're in spasmodic contact, a family vice—great gaps between face-to-face meets.

Vivi lives in Lenox, now, and has abandoned her L.A. houselet. New England suits her better. L.A. (all that driving + flaky population) became too challenging. She has her church choir (Methodist) and relatives in Boston who care for her, especially Gordon [Weir], another Cynthia son, a diabetes titan, who is hyper-active, running the oldest established diabetes organization in the nation. Rosalind undertook the hotel arrangements—so Chip and I will stay at a B&B near Rittenhouse Square, and will dine, between shows, with Fambly. Ned will have his own celebratory dinner, to which I wasn't invited. He hates to share The limelight—curtain call bows, etc.

These days, I keep careening down a swervy fast lane, sleeping lots, napping a bit with Satie curled up on the coverlet, waiting for massage sessions. Start at neck scruff, work fingers back past arching back, along tail sticking straight up. Philly Trip #2, gig arranged by Chester: next week. Must start preparing.

Jimbo came over last night to chat about the revue, now firmly titled *Lingo Land*.[187] He's helping me a lot, battering down my rigidities. I tend to lay stuff out with bald (and boring) clarity, so fearful of audience bewilderment. There's a list now, of Act One and Act Two entries, twenty-six for Act One, twenty-two for Act Two. There'll be a workshop in late Feb, a long, long, long thirty-six hours of intense hurtling from rehearsals to a test performance. Then revisions. Then rehearsals for a month in April, then wham.

The doorbell rang, a few afternoons ago, which I answered, thinking it was Mail For Me. Instead it was Male For Chip, blond, gleamy eyes, a beauty, a real twenty-something beauty, and nice, not stuck on himself, seemingly, or intimidated/dismissive of ancients, such as me. Name: Colin.[188] Heartthrob Colin. He's off, touring in a musical, but, maybe, if another role doesn't pan out, he'll be available for *Lingo Land*.

---

187   Kenward is working with York Theatre director Jim Morgan on a revue of Kenward's musical works. *LingoLand* would premiere February 23, 2005.

188   Colin Cunliffe, American actor/dancer, b. 1981.

He's promised to practice *Floozies*[189]—and audition for Jimbo. I sense he'd be perfect.

Enclosed: list of revue items, pared, but still way too long.

I'm so glad, even though gardenless, you're re-situated. Window boxes? With droopy branches bent & trained to spell out HOLLY-WOOD?

I hope your air surround rids itself of charred filaments. Jimbo wants a Letter to Loosha,[190] as of last night, plus some journal jottings of mine, to break into my I Remembers,[191] which will act as glue between numbers. He's found me a gifted young composer[192] to work with, if his setting of a poem (*Vaudeville for Jean Harlot*) comes out OK. He's Sondheimy, but not slavishly so, and knows how to orchestrate. Maybe some new songs will emerge if we click. He isn't thrown by meandery words, a good omen.

Finally, whew, Prince Jimmy Tampubolon of Lake Toba, Sumatra, isn't arriving next week, as I feared he would. Regulations trouble. So sweet-voiced on the phone, but no room at home, and he'd have been miserable alone in a hotel. Maybe, next summer, for a bit. Risky, but . . .

Chip's up. Gentle cough from downstairs. Time to head out.

Much love,
Kenward

---

189   "Floozies" is a song from Kenward's musical *The Grass Harp*.

190   Kenward incorporated a "Letter to Loosha" section in his Off-Broadway musical revue *LingoLand*, in which he sat onstage at a typewriter and read his letters to Lucia.

191   Based on Joe Brainard's book *I Remember* (Angel Hair Books, 1970). Kenward uses the "I remember" format to write memories of Joe and others, as poems and essays, and in this case as part of the song interludes in his musical revue.

192   Andrew Gerle, American composer. Set Kenward's poem to music for *LingoLand*.

PART IV | 2003–2004

Letters from Washington Blvd., Marina del Rey, CA
Letters from Calais, VT, and New York, NY

[In the following letters, Lucia writes of her move to a new apartment in Marina del Rey near Venice Beach.]

MARINA DEL REY, CA

DECEMBER 11, 2003

Dear Kenward—

Thank you for luscious sleep poem—*Venus Preserved.*[1] Oh ". . . as cold as old holy toes/smoothed by crusader kisses . . ."

Another stunner. I hope you haven't left for the holidays. I know I wrote you with my new address. Hope letter did not go astray . . .

One of my favorite things about France was stone floors, as in Chentre and the Louvre—unbelievable softness of the stones. I couldn't help touching them, smooth as skin, centuries of people, sweet frisson of I'm walking in their footsteps!

Moved in . . . Worn out . . .

Rapunzel in magic tower full moon. Sat. 5 a.m. Erroneous alabaster noon. I didn't know if it was sun or moon, coming up or going down. It was as bright as day—LA was, and then it was night. And then sun came up. I was unaware of these fantastic cycles back in Westchester. Just now, for example, I looked out at vast expanse of city washed in coral. In the color of old technicolor movies—then the gaudy orange sun set onto the Pacific. Now the trembling clouds are crashing into one another in Santa Ana winds of soft pinks and corals . . . Palm trees glittering, thickening yellow, pink light, like sparklers on 4th of July!

Dan has been over several times . . . We spend visits looking out the window, like people watching TV on home movies.

Ducks! Terns and gulls. Crows. No building noise and very little street noise.

Haven't the energy yet to explore neighborhood. Interesting people though, all ages, classes, races.

Did you get a flu shot?

Do write me a note before you go.

---

1   Kenward's poem "Venus Preserved," new as he sent it and dedicated it to Lucia, would be published in *Agenda Melt* (Adventures in Poetry Press, 2004).

Thanks again for poem, for dedicating it to me.

Hope you are well and not blue. Holiday blues have settled in on me.

> *All my love,*
> *Loosha*

MARINA DEL REY, CA

DECEMBER 30, 2003

Dear Kenward,

Chip did a terrible thing. He told me the news about *SIBLING RIVALRY*,[2] but then said it was still a secret that you would want to tell me. But I can't wait to tell YOU! Wonderful news, wonderful timing for this news, on the cusp of a fine New Year.

Congratulations! I have been noting for months now a particular crispness and elan in your poetry and letters. A firm grasp . . . an authority . . . ? Whatever it is, I'm pleased that others see it also.

No, I have no such creative shifts going on. Still there is a Change in that I can't stand it anymore. F . . . that muse. Hellova lot of good she has ever done for me. I'm going in for the old New Year's Resolution. In three more days will try first for a story that might break your heart, well, anybody's heart. Alas I may be too rusty for Grandeur, so will settle for a madcap caper. Actually I'll take anything. A page of vague language poet splatters, What I did on my summer vacation. Menopause and Your Diet.

I may be losing my mind. Phone Company said they would be here between 11 and 5. It is 4. They are supposed to install a separate line for Internet. Have truly missed a working e-mail.

I am so glad that Christmas is over. What a lovely solution[3] you have to it. Although I'm always DYING to talk to you when I know you're not at home. Called you twice!

---

2   Kenward's poem "Sibling Rivalry," published in 2003 in *New American Writing*, was selected for inclusion in anthology *Best American Poetry 2004*.

3   Kenward's solution to holiday blues was to go to a Miami hotel before Christmas and stay until after New Year's Day, ordering room service and writing. He wrote "Sibling Rivalry" on his Miami trip the year before on hotel stationery.

We used to pile the boys into Bonanza and fly to the Yucatan or to
Yelapa. Dave and his family are in Yelapa now. Dan called me from
Cabo San Lucas this morning. He's having terrific holiday, Scuba diving
several times a day. Watching humpback whales!

The divorce and good therapist have made such a difference in Dan.
He is now easy going, bad tempered, spontaneous, lazy, funny, warm,
selfish. Wonderful qualities all. Before he was perfect all the time.

Another storm coming. My window is a black and white screen,
with the huge breakers against sea wall a strobe electric white. An occasional blue/green iridescence of duck necks. Duck's neck? Many ducks
fly over from the lagoons . . . waddle down the lawns, their harems following them like pull toys.

Whoops. It is totally dark! Too cloudy for a change in light or a sunset and too dark for the phone company to show up.

Love to think of you and Chip and the Padgetts welcoming in 2004.
Great news too about Ron's book.

>   *I love you,*
>   *Loosha*

*[In the following letters, Kenward writes of his homosexuality and coming
out as a youth, being bullied by his classmates at boarding school, and the
sanctuary and community he found in theatre. Although comforted and
understood by his father, he tells Lucia of proposing marriage to a female
friend, his fears, and sexual fumblings with other adolescents. He writes of
his surprise birthday party thrown by John Latouche, full of the "fairies"
(and celebrity) that Kenward's sister had warned him about.]*

Dear Loosha

Retreat in a Coconut Grove hotel, over. Back in the tough city. My
computer didn't weather being Fed-Exed, but, second housecall, an
expert from Hong Kong rid it of infuriating kinks. Attempts at writing
you turned into a misadventure so rife with tech futility, my innards
flailed with helpless fury and nostalgia, many decades ago, for my

portable manual Olivetti with carbon paper for copies, small-lettered font, so poetry lines subsequently published always had to be broken into two. So simple to operate. I still haven't retackled Internet, so my website isn't viewable. Grrrr. Must call Wayne Padgett.

Patty and Ron came over to confab about Ron's Joe book for Coffee House—I was supposed to track down a drawing I made of Joe, which Ron wants to include, haven't a clue what I've done with it, but he found it somewhere, internet sleuth that he is.

Days later. Discombobulation Sinking Spell over—6:05 AM, figured out it must be Sunday—no callers, Chip in the Virgin Isles, just [cats] Satie and Rilke for company. Yesterday, the Love Daughter of my teen-age plus Harvard Years Girlie Passion, Dorothy King, phoned up. We never "did it" though I do remember fooling around a bit, on top of Dorothy, on a sofa in the Park Ave apartment I lived in (teen-age years) with my father & step-ma, Jean. I was very skinny and very "nervous," so "nervous," at meals, with my father and Jean, my left hand would start to tremble, lifting my fork, and I had to dissemble, wait till the tremble subsided, momentarily, and then do a quick lift, when they, at opposite ends of the table, weren't looking at me. Marital tension, plus teen-age pre-analysis nutso angst.

Insertion of erection was a frightening mystery, plus how to get rid of girlie underthings. Plus she was a devout Irish-Catholic, and kept trying to convert me via books by French intellectuals such as Jacques Maritain. Her father was a nouveau rich building contractor, bossy, very uncultured, "low class"—with a big mansion in a posh suburban area—Wilton, Connecticut. He went broke when his three daughters were young ladies. Dorothy and I met, the summer I graduated from St. Mark's [boarding school] '46 and, through a theatre lawyer friend of my stepmother's, because of my love of theatre, I was dispatched to Jutland, Northern New Jersey, a woodsy vacation area, to become an apprentice at a summer-stock theatre with a resident cast and an acting school adjunct, run by a Stanislavsky expert, a bona fide Rooshian named Boris Marshalov.

I "sized" scenery flats mostly, bunked with the set designer who was visited, weekends, by gentleman friend from D.C. They did things in bed, on the other side of the room, made sounds, once invited me to join them (panic!). I faced the wall, and pretended whatever was happening, wasn't happening.

I had deep crushes on athletes at St. Marks. Dormitory corridors were bedecked with photos of past teams, which I stared at longing, eying telltale bulges in their uniforms. My nickname was "Homo," and the liberal head of the school (Reverend Brewster) called a meeting to discuss homosexuality, and told us, if we were, to seek therapy. It was a sickness, not a Biblical Evil.

My sister Cynthia, alarmed by a Cleveland Heights ladyfriend, made a special trip to warn me against predatory Older Boys. She praised "fairies"—they were talented at interior decoration. And once, during the war, when her husband was a Navy doctor, they were visiting in NYC, and some fairies invited them in, total strangers, to a party, and they couldn't have been nicer. My love of theatre presented a problem I must confront. The theatre was filled with fairies. Noel Coward![4]

I dummied up. My diary, enpurpled with slush about Carleton Rand, a comely football team-member, and co-editor with me of the school lit mag *The Vindex*, got passed around, unbeknownst to me, lifted from its bureau drawer. I grieved, later, when I heard he was killed in Korea. I had scant actual experience, except for one episode of "frottage" (encoupled body rubbing) on a table in an empty schoolroom my homely seducer led me to, making it quite clear I was a substitute for a girl.

Once, in a corridor, Richard Kobusch, from St. Louis, beauty of beauties, goosed me, moved on, peered back at me, shattered, all smiles. Homosexuality, along with Miscegenation (Lillian Smith's *Strange Fruit*[5]) was a Problem best-selling novels explored, back then—Gore Vidal's *The City And The Pillar* being the break-through book (the guys' sin was punished, by death (?))—an unhappy ending the publisher

4   Sir Noël Coward, English playwright, composer, director, actor, and singer, 1899–1973.

5   Lillian Smith, American writer, 1897–1966.

insisted on.[6] I also read *The Fall of Valor* by Charles Jackson,[7] author of *The Lost Weekend.* Subsequently, I met him—he and his daughter played bridge with my stepmother—they'd met at a Park Avenue AA.

These perverts were called "fairies"—or, with an uppercrust bemused tinge "pansies." "Queers"? "Fags"? Not yet. I once heard a cab-driver use the word "cocksucker" and figured out what it must mean. During the war, my cousin Adrian Moore worked for the State Department and was fired—homosexuals were purged, as security risks, purported prey of Commie spy tempters, who'd blackmail them, and worm classified secrets out of them. Adrian Moore divorced his Texan wife, one son, and lived with a man he'd been involved with from his prep school days. I knew about him, and a Broadway actor, Robin Craven,[8] who had a small part in *My Fair Lady*, was a guest on the Gulliver, my father's yacht—he was amusing company, a bon vivant raconteur who appreciated a taste of high life.

The summer of '50, post-grad, I took courses at Harvard, not knowing what to "do," other than volunteer my services for the Socialist Workers Party. I invited Frank Frost, a college-mate crush to join me in Florida, to attend a roommate's marriage. I crept into Frank's bed, and was rebuffed: "Cut it out!" Long sad solo walks on the beach. When we proceeded on to Palm Beach, my father sensed why I was so disconsolate, and, one night, the three of us dining in the galley, my father began to talk about homosexuality non-pejoratively—how it was part of life, always had been. I was so proud of him!

Once, in a cab, with my sister Cynthia, my stepmother Jean revealed she firmly believed my father was a homosexual. They began to light into my father's faults. I was so furious, I got out of the cab. I did recall, one day at lunch, in front of my stepmother, he began talking about his war years, driving an ambulance in the Sahara, pursuing retreating Germans—how beautiful Arab boys were. And there were photos from his

---

6   Vidal's novel *The City and the Pillar* was first published by E. P. Dutton in 1948 but was revised and republished by Dutton with a different ending in 1965.

7   Charles Jackson, American writer, 1903–1968.

8   Robin Craven, English actor, 1906–1978.

Cambridge University years, a production of *Julius Caesar* (?)—British youths in togas, of breathtaking physical perfection. Including him. He was a rebel, a Socialist politically, angered by the rigidities of the class system and Victorian morality. Oscar Wilde was his hero. When he went to Alberta to make his fortune in oil (no dice!) so he could marry Constance Pulitzer,[9] and not be seen as a lowly fortune-hunter, he went to Toronto to perform for Princess Alexandra in a production of *The Importance of Being Earnest.*

Back to Dorothy King. I was in love with her, platonic, but—so I actually proposed to her, in Boston, when I was at Harvard. She had a tiny part in a Broadway play trying-out—*Jenny Kissed Me*, a quick Broadway flop. I was saddened by her lack of presence as a performer. Her father had put money in the show, guaranteeing her this walk-on role. She turned me down, sensibly—she didn't want to "rob the cradle."

When I turned 25, John Latouche gave me a semi-surprise huge birthday party in his penthouse, where we lived, always with other people, first with his boyfriend, Harry Martin, a would-be artist, whom I supplanted, also with Pat Coleman, a non-produced lesbian playwright, an alcoholic, as John was. And subsequently with Countess Ruth Yorck, who was recovering from a cancer operation, who became my great friend and mentor, my mom substitute, after John died of a heart-attack in the summer of '56, in our Vermont house. He was with Harry Martin, who drove him up there in a big Buick convertible John had bought from Tennessee Williams,[10] whose longterm boyfriend, Frankie Merlow, John absconded with, at one point—for a wild weekend in a gay mecca—Provincetown.

Dorothy King came to that party—John tracked down people from my past, trying to wean me away from my total immersion in his glamorous, celebrity-ridden life—Lena Horne, Carol Channing, Tennessee, etc.[11]

---

9 Kenward's English father, William Gray Elmslie, was originally a tutor for Joseph Pulitzer's sons, but in order to marry Constance Pulitzer, Elmslie returned to England to make his own money.

10 Tennessee Williams, American playwright and screenwriter, 1911–1983.

11 Kenward's poem/song "Touche's Salon" recounts Latouche's apartment and

I saw her very occasionally—I found her a bit batty. She confessed, at one point, she'd had an affair with Jack Kerouac, had become pregnant, and had had an abortion, provoking deep Catholic guilt.

Dorothy died, ages ago, of cancer. Her love-child [. . .] lives in Newport, where she works at a restaurant, is currently house-and-pet sitting in Vermont. Her voice is like Dorothy's—well-spoken, gentle. Eerie blast from the past.

End of Happy New Year memoir, to make up, a tad, I hope, for my Holiday Discombobulation Incommunicado Spate.

Much Love,
Kenward

MARINA DEL REY, CA
JANUARY 20, 2004

Dearest Kenward,

You are SO stubborn. For years now I have been asking you, begging you, to speak to someone, Ron, I hope, about collecting your letters to me. They are a fine work. Proust felt that Flaubert's letters were his masterpiece . . . I think yours are too, equal to your poetry and prose works. They ARE poetry. I would do it but don't have the strength, simply don't, am so sorry. Do you have them in your computer? I am so frustrated about this. I know you will continue to ignore me. Please. Show a copy of your last letter to Ron. Tell him that there are 800 to 1000 more. Rich, brilliant, moving, funny, historical.

Not simply beautiful writing, good gossip, funny stories. They are like Dawn Powell's novels . . . whole worlds come alive.

Deeply moving, the first paragraph about Dorothy King. What a devastating scene, with the parents at either end of the table. Skinny you, holding a fork in your trembling left hand. The painful terror, the "nutso angst." You describe this quietly. Unbearable, lovely.

---

all the celebrity composers, actors, writers who hung out there. Lena Horne, American actress and singer, 1917–2010. Horne starred in Latouche's *Cabin in the Sky*. Carol Channing, American actress, singer, and comedienne, 1921–2019. Channing starred in Latouche's *The Golden Apple*.

Would love to hear more of St. Mark's and Boris Marshalov, although it is amazing how much you tell in two paragraphs about that prep-school world. The Loneliness of it, no-one to talk to about Anything, much less fairies and pansies.

The years you spent in such isolation are what I find so sad . . . learning almost by accident about the "queer" world, which in spite of being sick and Wicked obviously had glamour. Oh, to think of you walking, sad, on the beach.

For some reason I had imagined your father to be very negative and unkind. Wonderful paragraph about him, so Noel Coward and adventuresome. Great that he came through that night, talking about homosexuality.

Alas, he could have talked to you as you grew, eased your fears, given you pride, tenderness. Did this happen? Human parents are worse than bears, the way they just shove us out of the trees. Silence causes so much unhappiness.

Your 25th year could use its own novel for Lord's sake. Your letter a mini-novel, for that matter. What an ending. Dorothy a guilt-ridden Catholic. An affair with Kerouac, a love child who works in a restaurant, is house and pet-sitting in Vermont.

That was my favorite part. After all those fabulous years: famous artists and Buick convertibles, Countesses. Here is this rather dowdy woman in a too tight snow-jacket like the Michelin tire man, following a toy terrier down a Vermont street . . . She has a plastic bag and a pooper scooper, calls shrilly in the cold air. Pepper, slow down!

Who would imagine that you once proposed to her mother?

Thanks so much for this dreamy letter.

Your poem triggered a nice memory for me . . . Riding in back of Greyhound bus from Oakland to San Clemente to visit my parents. Smoking and sharing 100 proof vodka from bottle in a paper bag with a black jockey six feet 6 inches tall! Skinny. Lord he must have looked funny on a horse. Best part about him was his name: Sleaze. We shared a lot about ourselves, got another bottle in Fresno, were asked to keep the noise down, laughed until we cried, behaved badly in the bathroom, in general hit it off great. He was a writer, he said, hadn't written the book yet but the title was CITIZEN'S ARREST.

He was getting off the bus at Anaheim (would be going to Santa Ana racetrack in a few days). He asked me to spend the night with him and to go to DISNEYLAND. I said no. Can imagine myself tearily waving goodbye to him from the bus window. There are so many missed opportunities in my life . . . surely not going to Disneyland with Sleaze was one.

Actually I have almost no missed opportunities. Very lucky life. I think you and I have known remarkable people, worlds, share a dazzle as well as painful childhood times. I misspelled it: "chillhood". [. . .]

Oh oh letter too long again.

All my love,
LOOSHA

NEW YORK, NY
JANUARY 23, 2004

Dear Loosha—

Needs must look at my 2004 black Standard Diary to find out what day it is. Friday. Madame Zapata[12] comes to clean. She is very Law and Order, in a cavalier way—Spanish lingo, plus short chards of transformed English. She leaves the house in apple-pie order.

In a semi-subterranean ancient hut in the backyard (originally to store vegetables?)—there is a washing-machine, introduced by Jimmy Tampubolon, whose stolid passion was clean clothes. And in Indonesia, a washing-machine means high status. Jimmy didn't trust the cleaners in the nabe, and it's true, clothes were lost, joke costumes substituted. Well, the house has been bereft of hot water for days, now—but yesterday, Chip to the rescue, he dealt with the arrival of a new huge heater, uneaten by rust, and the removal of the oldie. He looked worn-out afterwards from the stress of the phoning, the men, standing guard. Not up to cooking, so we ate take-in chili and rice.

His food is impeccably and carefully prepared. He's blocked on two poems, but not in an overt snit, which I'd be likely to be after a bad

---

12   Felicia Zapata, longtime caretaker of Kenward and his New York home.

day at the word processor. I think he's a bit fascinated by the turn my daily round has taken, from isolate, reclusive quietude to the double whammy of Show & Book, and the collaborations that entails. In the wall-less kitchen, he listens, sometimes. He caught me mis-proofing, wrong page correction. What a safeguarder.

Today, Elinor comes to continue her inventory of Art Works and what still needs framing, protection from city granules that seep in, somehow. Her list is approaching 300—many by Joe.[13] Something still needs to be done about my wall collages to protect them. I finish something, it's on its own. OK with poems, not with visuals.

At noon: Jimbo. We are still trudging through the revue, whose title I still have to strain to recall, Lingo Land or Lingoland—which do you prefer? Jimbo, as happens in theatre, is high-wiring between this spring, and next fall: other show schedules to juggle. One other show is a one-woman musical about Florence Foster Jenkins, the rich lady who sang in public so badly, a Carnegie Hall-type audience developed who came to hear and hoot.

My [University of California] San Diego archive dispatched a copy of a lyric, *Culture*, about a lady with art tattooed all over her body, sung once by Lisa Kirk[14] at the Waldorf-Astoria. Lisa Kirk helped put *Kiss Me, Kate* (Cole Porter's best score[15]) on the map, specifically by stopping the show with *I'll Always Be True To You Darling In My Fashion*—gold-digger rationalizations.

What's become of gold-diggers? Off the screen! A kiddo fear of mine, when my weekly allowance was 75 cents: gold-diggers, who, once we were married, would leave me broke and broken-hearted.

Culture proved a keeper. Stayed up one night adding on a button at the end to give it a fuller climax. Made up one couplet that won an inner guffaw:

---

13   Kenward's basement stored his enormous art collection, which Elinor dei Tos Pironti organized and cleaned, rotating the art that was hung on the walls upstairs.

14   Lisa Kirk, American actress and singer, 1925–1990.

15   *Kiss Me, Kate* is a musical written by Bella and Samuel Spewack with music and lyrics by Cole Porter that premiered on Broadway in 1948.

If you catch me mooning—
Then ogle my de Kooning.

And the worst doggerel rhyme I've ever thought of: isma, risma.

I adore Minimalism, ah!
The secret of my charisma.

Which leads into the climax:

Yo, I got culture from my Pointilist head
to the tip of my ity-bitsy
eensy-weensy
Post-Impressionist
Abstract Expressionist
Neo-Surrealist—
Wanna see a list?—
Toe!!!

Double whammy. Decades ago, every so often, I'd have a show and a book to contend with, simultaneously. The book's come through— proofing long long sheets. So fast. I think Trevor Winkfield is the activist behind the book.[16] Got Larry Fagin to take it on, to get me back to working on poetry. And a third chance for our respective disciplines to be conjoined. Trevor's new show is up, at the Tibor [de Nagy] gallery (haven't seen it yet, Joe too) and, post-opening, just a few days, he's zapped out three black-and-white drawings and the color cover, all top-notch Trev. The book'll be a beauty to eye and fondle.

Title, also hard for my memory to wrap itself around naturally, makes me think: *AGENDA MELT*. Simultaneity. Larry was sitting at my work/dining table, & we both hit the same poem title. *SIBLING RIVALRY* (longest poem) scrapped. Contents are a mix, two-thirds

---

16   *Agenda Melt,* Kenward's collaboration with English artist Trevor Winkfield (Adventures in Poetry Press, 2004). Larry Fagin was publisher.

poems, one-third show lyrics, plus-as lead-in to the lyrics, *Joe Babe*, a monologue from a scrapped version of a musical, *Postcards on Parade*, that surfaced—and swiftly vanished at the York.

Proofed copy ready for pick-up by Larry: 5 PM. I'm hopeless at hyphens. Chip to the rescue! As he's making lunch or supper, I query him. He knows the rules, from his three years in Journalism School. A table near the kitchen is always the best place to work with words on paper, final stage, away from the computer. Coffee, snacks, wine after close-off, reward. Sleep. Primary TV. Oy, Dean.[17] Sad, you blew it . . .

After a bit of back-and-forth vision conflict, the printer (a most dedicated and easy to work with Trueblue Lady) has set the lyrics differently from the poems—following my line-by-line design. The poems are simpler, flush left. The song lyrics skitter about more, lines centered. But the Miami poem skitters. Some poems have no & need no punctuation. Need to check that. The works look tiptop on the page, and I'm starting to like the poems-as-poems, whatever that means. Seeing them on a page gives them independence from me, so I can accept them on their own, without worrying about their welfare, or if they warrant a second glance, an umpty-umpth rewrite, a speed pill, or should hit the cutting-room floor. Printed classily, they salute me from their new station in life—self-sustaining survivors. Out of the house. On the page. Closure. Me: move on.

Work work work. I've found the Loosha Letters you sent me—wanted to cannibalize two for the book, especially the description of the *Lizzie* set. But no dice. Bad squeeze. So I'll send them back, I know right where they are. They vanished for awhile. Thanks for entrusting them to me, despite my vagaries as File Clark, as the Brits say.

Keeping cheerful these days, as my writings seem to attract people I trust, think highly of and enjoy being with—and they're being very sweet to me. One day, Ron came over to exercise my swollen, aged bod. Very gentle touch. On a mat. Stretches. He really wants me to shape up, take care of myself, not be so fat and physically lazy. I'm starting to get the message. Take care of myself. Take care of myself. Take care of

---

17   Former Vermont governor Howard Dean, 2004 presidential candidate.

myself. Makes me want to rush out for breakfast at the Den, waffles, live it up. Extra butter.

Say hi to the HOLLYWOOD sign from me. TV works. Computer works. Hot water again. Blue sky outside. Freezing cold. And I get to stay in, and ponder the pros and cons of waffles.

Love,

Kenward

MARINA DEL REY, CA

JANUARY 29, 2004

Dear Kenward,

Well, I was going along, minding my own business, watching the ducks and gulls, the construction guys at the skeleton of a new house, all over-achievers except for one who spends a great deal of time working on his tan, has a really good tan. The house is now getting a second story, has become a house. It happened overnight, just like you. I thought you were dozing away on chaise longue in Coconut Grove, yawning, eating tapioca and mangos then wham bam thank you ma'am these action-packed letters start overflowing with lyrics and phone calls and editings, cuts and new sequences, stars being born.

Wow, a revue AND a book. I am Totally confused even though I feel I know Jimbo and Trevor by now. Had I known the book was going to be with Trevor? Or even that it was such an imminent reality? Is the revue called Lingoland? (I think better than Lingo Land, no?) What is the title of the book? Please don't toss out the minimalisma and charisma, mooning/deKooning piece. I've been singing it to sort of a Chattanooga choochoo tune.

My email not working right for weeks. Hate to take it in . . . last time it was several weeks before I got computer back. My television broke down, the dish receiver part did, for three days. Missed Golden Globes, New Hampshire, etc. Or rather I Didn't miss them at all, and when I turned on the TV yesterday everything was the SAME. Bomb in Israel, truck blown up in Iraq, Weapons of Mass Destruction, Michael, Martha. Kerry, so well brought up. Can't believe how quickly everybody turned on Dean.[18] Rightly or wrongly, so much depends upon image. They don't want to let it go either, only mean thing going on right now.

I'm learning only now to closely read your letters, not just enjoy them. The paragraph about the printing of the poems is wonderful, a prose poem itself.

"Some poems have no and need no punctuation. Need to check that. The works look tiptop on the page, and I'm starting to like the poems as poems, whatever that means. Seeing them on a page gives them independence from me, so I can accept them on their own, without worrying about their welfare, or if they warrant a second glance, an umpty-umpth rewrite, a speed pill, or should hit the cutting room floor. Printed classily, they salute me from their new station in life, self-sustaining survivors. Out of the house. On the page. Closure. Me: move on." Great to copy this to see how the punctuation adds to the cadence and elegance. This is a beautifully written description about the making of a poem.

Your letters make me so happy. Nice to hear your acceptance of the love shown to you, the awareness that your friends truly do want you to stay well. You have always been a loving person, Kenward, but I hear your heart opening still wider . . . Dare I use the corny word: spiritual? Well, whatever it is, a radiance, is what I have been yattering on about for several months now, a new jubilant quality, showing in your work.

God, all I do for lord's sake is say corny things. Best thing I can say about ME is . . . Sorry . . . this is actually funny. I can't think of a best thing! In third grade Sister Cecilia wrote on my report card "Lucia has a pleasant disposition." Well, that will simply have to do.

Do take care of yourself. I HAVE been good. Feel good. Do my yoga and deep breathing, eat well. Back is still terrible but I'm not weak or shaky anymore. Do you and Patti walk in the city?

Now that I said that, I find myself weak and shaky! Time for dinner.

---

18   Michael Jackson, Martha Stewart, Senator John Kerry, Governor Howard Dean.

Oh no. The Debates? Rebecca West's "The Fountain Overflows."[19] If Joe didn't like her, he would have I think.

> *All my love,*
> *Loosha*

MARINA DEL REY, CA

FEBRUARY 1, 2004

Dear Kenward,

I am very happy that you plan to get your letters together. Great news. I think once you see 10 or 11 in sequence, or not, for that matter, even just collected . . . you will realize that they will make a solid and wonderful book.

I'm very excited about this. Don't forget about it! Put LETTERS on list of important projects. My student friends here have gone off to schools . . . if any show up I'll put them to work sorting letters on this end, especially ones with collages etc on them. Don't know how they got so disordered. 1000's of them![20] I'll start serious organizing . . . especially of the ones with drawings and collages.

Now that I realize that you Will listen to me I will keep bothering you.

Wonderful to get still another letter from you written with energy and flair. You are on a roll: the tone, tempo playful and sexy. The revue . . . Agenda Melt?[21] will be great. Of course you'll be in it. Keep up the workouts with Ron.

Thanks for the Trevor page. Combination of you two is so good: elegant crisp witty.

Glad you had good meeting with Oz-woggly. I'm relieved that it is over . . . Chip becomes a total irrational wreck when Oz is around. Convinced that you hate him, etc. Jealousy is so terrible. I remember

---

19   Rebecca West, *The Fountain Overflows* (Viking Press, 1956).

20   Referring to organizing their letters into a publishable correspondence, the work done to create this book.

21   Lucia is mixing up the two titles. Kenward was currently working on a musical revue, *LingoLand*, and a book collaboration with Trevor Winkfield called *Agenda Melt*.

Mr. Oz as such a mild-mannered chap, certainly not capable of inciting such passions![22]

Oh I wish I had more people and gossip in my life. Dan tells me the scoop on his dates with women from the internet matchmaking place. Not much scoop.

I am absolutely miserable. Broken lower tooth. Two more days to go without taking blood thinning medicine . . . so surgeon can yank it out without me bleeding non-stop. Can't remember if we were writing that time when I got nosebleed and was finally hospitalized, transfusions etc. So I'm nervous as well as wishing I could eat a steak or an apple. Ensure at room temperature, taken with a straw.

Everything is so relative. What a silly sentence . . . sounds like the caption for a family reunion! I've had so much yoghurt and cream of wheat that last night acorn squash seemed the most delicious food I had ever eaten.

Watched full moon set this morning over dark, rain slick city. Today is clear with gathering clouds. The workmen are hammering away on the new house. Yesterday they spent hours covering it with blue tarpaulins to protect it from coming rainstorm. This morning there were blue tarps scattered for blocks around, rained all night long.

Dan is here, hooray, will send this with him.

>   Love,
>   Lucia

NEW YORK, NY

FEBRUARY 9, 2004

Dear Loosha—

Breakfast table gab with Madame Zapata, broken Anglo-Espagnol. Chipster (Ron's renaming) heated up a tasty egg-white quiche, sped off, bundled up. More gab with Madame Zapata re her dynasty. She

---

22   When Lucia asked me to consider moving to New York to be his assistant, part of the reason was because previous helpers had taken advantage of him and she trusted me. I saw Mr. Oz taking advantage. Mr. Oz saw me as standing in his way.

hails from the Dominican Republic, three kids. Her oldest daughter is turning thirty, three kids too. Her sister has eight, much to her disapproval.

Chatted with Chipster about Jimbo's set for the revue. Jimbo's gone off to Coconut Grove, Miami enclave where I stay, on occasion. Boring "money" theatre job: directing, scene design. Yesterday, Jimbo began designing the revue's set, at table, where lots keeps happening, besides eating, lately. Back & forth interchange helped him. His final sketch is a wow. The show title arches between two latticework towers you can see through, front-porch style. Background between them: part of an amusement park—roller-coaster, Ferris wheel. He wants to implant words on the stage itself, and in the sky—a curvaceous surf, waves of words—show and book names, fragments of poems and lyrics.

A fine meeting, though we were both a bit dawg-tired—end of day energy diminution. Chipster sat at table too, found a photo-book by an artist friend,[23] with words implanted behind & below the Human Subject. Very helpful. He also e-mailed the script from my computer to Jimbo's computer, painstakingly laborious, in clumps of pages—unflappable good humor—a tech feat way beyond me. His boyfriend is somewhere in Canada, touring, touring, which doesn't turn him mean and grumpy. He's a prince.

New revue spoken material added to the pot includes four letters to you, which Jimbo just loved. They'll need "tweaking"—(his word for revising) for clarity. Not all of all of them, and I may invent fake letters—as needed—as spoken bridges between songs. So, your Letter Campaign is bearing juicy fruit. But if the fruit taste is off-putting to you, privacy invasion, please just say halt! Plus scenes from a play, *City Junket*, which correspond to "skits" in traditional revues formatted thus: song, skit, song, song, skit etc.

Today, free!!! A date with Trainer Ron [Padgett] tomorrow: One leg went bum, but today it's fine. He's so responsible and focused! He knows my body weak points—the exact placement of a shoulder muscle that was frozen, is thawing, gingerly, thanks to his ministrations.

---

23   Bill Hayward, *Bad Behavior* (Rizzoli Press, 2000).

He's so pleased by my progress. I can stand longer, repeat movements faster. A generous-hearted & strict body mentor. On the case.

My dithering about displaying my Seventy Something Self come April to paying customers, with expectations that need to be gratified fully, continues unabated. Jimbo's designed a niche, left side of the set—my purported desk—where (my idea) I can tap away at a laptop, and read my letters to you.[24]

But I'll still need to join the cast, terror terror, in song, and move about the stage, ambulatory as all get-out. Get Out! Get Out! Get the Hook!

But my comfort zone is starting to widen, inch by inch. I think I can swing singing *They*[25]—and maybe one or two or three more songs, two per act.

So I needs must invent a persona for myself that isn't fake or cutesy-wootsy, so I won't feel obligated to be "myself"—which is impossible. I've semiinvented a "myself" for gigs, minimal performance, relying on my voice to deal as honestly as it can with songs. I've tried, on occasion, to "perform"—and I go fake, badly show-offy. It's a sticky wicket—to stabilize my nonperformance so it carries over the footlights. One entitlement is a body mike. That'll help a lot, though it'll involve, technically, working out a balance with the cast of four, who have no need to be miked.

Waiting for Jimbo yesterday (he's always late, always apologizes profusely) I began reading Bill Berkson's new book—his art criticism. Amazing, such beautiful prose. His style Daddies are John Ashbery, Frank O'Hara, and Edwin Denby (on dance). Trevor Winkfield came over, one day, his show uptown about to close, and complained about feedback, perhaps because his show has been reviewed most favorably in the *NY Times, NY Observer*, and a third rag. Largish flocks of viewers. He can't stand it, justifiably, when viewers come up to him, at the

---

24 This was the format of the eventual *LingoLand* musical revue. Kenward sat at a desk onstage, from which he sung and spoke, and four dancer/actors performed the action around him.

25 Elmslie, "They," song lyrics published in *Routine Disruptions: Selected Poems & Lyrics* (Coffee House Press, 1998).

gallery, and mouth a generic pleasantry, and then ask him how his show is doing—i.e. sales.

He recalled, enviously, attending a book-in-hand production of *The Grass Harp*,[26] ages ago, at the York, and how, when Jimbo (pre-curtain speech) mentioned me & motioned for me to take a bow, the applause meter shot up. I'd forgotten that—this show has its loyal fans, who pay attention to lyrics, as well as music—so different from almost all opera-goers.

Continuing the Complaint Roundelay, I bitched to Chipster about theatre critics, how flatly they write. Except for George Jean Nathan, ages ago, and one Brit, name escapes me, died young from drink, wrote brilliantly for the *New Yorker*.[27]

Soon, the "blues" of *Agenda Melt* (book) will wing back from Italia, Fate Accompli. Hope your mouf (Firbankian spelling) is pain-free, and the blue tarps continue to offer you inspirational daily round eye candy . . .

Love,
Kenward

MARINA DEL REY, CA
FEBRUARY 13, 2004

Dear Kenward,

Terrific cascade of letters from you. Like a *Seagull* set . . . your kitchen table, with Jimbo and Madame Zapata and Chipster. Lovely description of final sketch . . . curvaceous surf, waves of words. Lattise work towers.

Just after dusk I can see the ferris wheel on the Santa Monica pier.

4 pm. The young Mexican workers quit work on the roof of the [neighbor's] house. So young, perhaps brothers, they sparred and horsed around on the grass of the house next door, laughing, teasing in Spanish. My door was open . . . sweet to hear their voices, hoarse, just

---

26   *The Grass Harp*, York Theatre production, January 17–19, 2003.

27   George Jean Nathan, American theatre critic and magazine editor, 1882–1958. Kenneth Tynan, English theatre critic, 1927–1980.

8PM, Wednesday April 28th, 2004

75th Birthday Bash
for
Kenward Elmslie

POETRY SONGFEST
COLLABORATIONS
VISUALS   VIDEOS

The Poetry Project
St. Mark's Church
131 East 10th Street, NYC

Dear Sooha,
Spring is here...
Why don't I feel even
Spring is here.... amtn,
Love,
/Kenward

Postcard invitation to 75th birthday party from Kenward.

changing from boy to man. The boss called down to them, laughing, from the new house. He and electricians? few other more serious men still working. The rhythm they all move with shows what a good comradery they have. I think they are proud of the house. Hell, I'm proud of the house!

I'm proud of the [*LingoLand*] revue in the same way. Feeling a part of watching it grow. Delighted that letters to me will be in it. Of course I have no reservations at all . . . Aw Contrayer! as my mother would say. I feel like a muse. Loosha the Moosh.

My worry would be performing every single night in a row. Certainly don't worry about you getting "cutesy-wootsey" or fake. Your entire Being prevents this. I can see how you might feel it or feel fake and show-offy, but by the time you feel this you have prevented being that way. You are so emotionally honest, so open a person, falsity can't exist with you.

What does this mean? "The "blues" of Agenda Melt" will wing back from Italia."[28] Hmm . . . what did I miss?

I spent two Naropa afternoons in the tent . . . Green green grass. Anne [Waldman]'s bracelets clanking. Art Lectures by Bill Berkson. Terrific. Included poets of the time as well of course. He was still healthy. So quietly elegant and sharp. Hate to think of him ill, diminished in any way.

My favorite critic, these days, is Hilton Als,[29] whose writing I first read in *Granta*. Often in *New Yorker* now. He is gay and black, especially good at writing about actresses. Has style, feels the works. [. . .]

I'm seriously thinking about trip to NY. Will see Dr in two weeks. See what he says . . . about Prednisone . . . Dan thinks it is great idea. If I'm in pain go to bed, he says, I'd at least see you guys for lord's sake. I would love to see the revue. Meet the Padgetts. Etc.

Glorious sunset!

Much love,

Loosha

[The following letters recount Kenward's 75th birthday dinner and a celebration of his life in music and letters at the Poetry Project, with presentations by John Ashbery, Ron Padgett, Anne Waldman, Bill Bamberger, Anselm Berrigan, and Mary Kite; musical tributes by Broadway singers and Steven Taylor; I read Kenward's "Vermont Letter to Loosha."]

---

28   *Agenda Melt* was printed in Italy.
29   Hilton Als, American writer and theatre and art critic, b. 1960.

Dear Loosha—

Double Birthday 75th ovah! Up till all hours, but 7:30 AM, sunny
out, dawn earlier every day, time to get cracking. I had a fine time both
occasions. The Bash at the Poetry Project was well attended, couple of
hundred souls in the pews. Mr. Oz arranged everything poifect, the
dinner beforehand, private dining room, oldie Eyetalian fave of Joe and
me, Beatrice Inn, us 14 got along fine, my date being Brenda Lewis, the
first *Lizzie Borden*, cracking along spiritedly in her Early Eighties, good
hair, good cheek-bones, esprit seemingly boundless, clarity of memory
recall amazing: gutsy, smart, and sharp-eyed, but lots of judicious heart.
Whisked with Brenda, to the Church, in a limo, on the way picked up
Jean Boulte[30] at home, so frail, one-eyed now. On the way, Brenda
remembered Brazil, opera house stint, before Jean was even born: dicta-
tor in power, a longie classic that started at 9, broke for dinner. She had
to wake up for the last scene, in which she re-emerged: 2 AM. She sang
Carmen (one of her favorite roles).

She found *Lizzie Borden* harrowing (NYC Opera). Marital break-up
while she was studying the role, and study it she did, micro-managing
her interpretation, complex ambivalences, familial love-hate needle in
constant movement. I was shy and sidelined back then, bossy composer, must have been more assertive second time around. Plus website
interview, enabled my diva innards to speak to her diva innards, so she
had a face she could have some spunky interchanges with.

A highpoint of the Bash was Chip. I rewrote the letter (read on)
to you for him to read,[31] which followed his new love sonnet. The
Poetry Segment had its dips into dullness, but Chip came through with
stunning grace. Good presence, enunciation, naturalness, no trace of
podium stiffness or compensatory self-importance. The other comer

---

30 Brazilian artist who lived in Kenward's townhouse.
31 At Kenward's 75th birthday celebration at the Poetry Project, Kenward
asked me to read his "Vermont Letter to Loosha," (296), an edited version of a
July 11, 1999, letter he'd written Lucia that also was included in the script of his
revue, *LingoLand*.

was Bill Bamberger, in the first part (Collaboration) who hadn't realized he was on the participants' list: heart-felt improv, how he loved my work passionately, met me, tough, as he was scared me-as-person would intrude and disrupt his caring deeply about me-as-wordsmith. He urged the audience, in no uncertain terms, to go to my words, and track the heart in them. So felt, his words, but no trace of gush. Steely certainty.

Ron was terrif, elegant cogency about Collaboration with artists, and a most moving Joe-and-me sum-up. Anselm Berrigan,[32] a total prince, read from *Bare Bones*: strong presence. Anne Waldman, one more time, read from *City Junket*, the Steel Genius speech, and sang *The Woolworth Song* (first tune, way way back, I ever thought up for my words, walking along the beach at Westhampton, where I liked to sing away, my voice bombarded by ocean noise). Mary Kite & livewire Karen Koch (Kenneth widow) turned into mumblers, but Anne, a showgirl from way back, did fine. And the great John Ashbery stumbled up to the podium to read a bit from *The Orchid Stories*.[33] Hard to hear, breath problem, but one section that repeated the word "beets" he sailed through with savvy comic aplomb.

Very short intermission. Then The Songs. [. . .]

Steven Taylor and I did fine, blink-and-you'll-miss-it poem-song I made up ages ago, *And I Was There*. And then the four singers plus Steven and I (lined up) tackled Claibe's march, *Yellow Drum* from *The Grass Harp*.

And we were home free. Parish Hall: eats & vino. Nobody watched the video of *The Seagull* by Bill Weir Jr.

Lotsa Weirs turned up—and didn't roast me as they were supposed to. I'd bumped Fambly Speechifying to the Parish Hall eats-and-drinks aftermath, with the proviso there'd be two roasts . . . Gordon Weir, diabetes doc, did mention me taking him to see a French Navy aircraft carrier, and surmising my unexpected interest in warships was incited by a chance

---

32   Anselm Berrigan, American poet, b. 1972. Former director of the Poetry Project, son of poets Alice Notley and Ted Berrigan.

33   Elmslie, *The Orchid Stories* (Doubleday, 1973). Kenward's only novel.

to ogle cute French sailors . . . on the mark, and got a laff. Chester Weir, dreamboat youth, fresh Graduate Architect, a bit gushy . . . but there were young folks there, so they could tune in to his looking up to a role model roadster, I mean oldster. He has a girlfriend, lives on a houseboat he designed, in Seattle . . . and that's where he's headed.

Time for breakfast. Sugar sky-high, too much fridge birthday cake post-Bash. Ron let me off this morning (got to bed two-ish, nice aftermath chat at table, wee hours, with Chipster and his sweet paramour Colin) so—no crunches, etc.

Mr Oz sure has proved his caring-for-me, this trip. So much arranging, which, granted, is what he does in real-life, but, still. I'll take him someplace very nice for dinner tonight, and try to limit my caloric intake. Chipster and he are getting on easier now, actually starting to like each other, to forget about me as bringer-together, plus Carer Protectiveness threatened—as well they should . . .

Time for a sensible breakfast (garlic & jalapeno toast & coffee). Loved our phone chat . . . I'll call you soon, soon as I settle into 75th-dom flatlander (pre-Vermont) status.

Love,
Kenward

MARINA DEL REY, CA
MAY 5, 2004

Dearest Kenward,

Joyful, wonderful letter.

But first: Eerie to read the letter from Vermont,[34] like rereading a classic story. The shape is perfect. So much in this beautiful piece from the visual images, the bats and the pine path, to the live living people to the terrific observations on motivation, words, and all with a flow and a tempo that makes everything you write seem like music, I am so honored to have received so many of these letters.

And the last one! Wow. What a night. I loved it that you wrote it at 7:30 AM, "Time to get cracking," after huge festivity, late night, days of

---

34   See figure 17. Original letter was July 11, 1999.

carryings on. Thanks for all the details and people, from Brenda Lewis (super) to Chester dreamboat youth, a bit gushy.

Glad it was such a successful event, that everything was top-notch and well-executed. Jenny Dorn told me all about it! Described the whole program for me . . . everybody is raving about it in Boulder! It makes me so happy to think of your good friends, like the Padgetts, how deeply felt the evening's tributes to you. Wonderful birthday, dear friend. As I said in last letter, after seeing your new book . . . feel this next year will be stellar, by starlight. Lord, have to stop gushing!

I had email from Chip too, telling me how great the evening was. He was modest about his part in it, was simply thrilled to be there and to read his poem, your letter. His knowing you makes me very happy too.

Glad that the two boys are making friends, for lord's sakes. I think Chip worries that you will replace him with Oz any minute.[35]

[. . .]

I'm fine. Enjoying spring birds. We're having heat wave . . . 90's, low 100's. Breeze from the bay keeps it pleasant, wafts spring blossom scents, songs from convertible radios. Dan will be in Honduras for two weeks, scuba diving.

Will send this off, to send kisses, abrazos and congratulations for the celebration.

All my love,
loosha

MARINA DEL REY, CA
MAY 24, 2004

Dear Kenward,

Sending this to Calais. Haven't heard, but seems like it's about that time. Summer here. I heard it this morning. Last December, when I

---

35   In the summer of 2005, Kenward called me from Vermont and told me not to let Mr. Oz into his New York house and to change the locks on the front door.

moved in, I could see down into yards, windows, and alleys for blocks and blocks, on three sides. Spring was lovely because every day something new bloomed somewhere and people came out more so got to know who lived where. Suddenly trees and bushes have grown in and I look down on greenery. Leafy trees and bushes cover my view into houses and yards, give a soft and billowy quality to the neighborhood, soften it not just visually. The foliage muffles sounds, barking, radios, hammering. Because all the nearby sounds are hidden so the freeway and the ocean are loud. I have really liked seeing this change of seasons. Surely there is no real autumn?

Have had monster red tape week, working on Medicare pharmacy card, senior discount, senior housing etc. There are many offices, like CIA, FBI, Homeland Security overlap and underlap, nobody knows right place, and none seem to be the right place. Now the phones don't ask you to dial one for bananas, two for cherries, etc. They tell you to SPEAK your choice slowly. I got such stage fright that I forfeited my turn, had to keep phoning again ARRG.

I'm mad at Dan. He treats me like an idiot. Well, no he doesn't but he gets really impatient. I do act balmy. I am easily intimidated by Agencies and authority of any kind. (him!)

It will all be fine. I do know this. I had a big terror when I faced the fact that the grant money will end in December. Total panic. Have pulled myself together. What I'm feeling now is gratitude for huge blessing. I don't know how I could have gone through illness without that help. I know you say you weren't involved in it. Well, thank you and whoever was, with all my heart.

All will be fine once I get medicare/medicaid figured out. Things like $ for prescriptions settled. It is better really that I have LESS $, since most of it goes to medical bills. The other chunk goes for rent, but am also applying for Section Eight, which will help me there.

I have plenty of time to see about kinds of places available, etc. Dan wants to buy a trailer and I pay the lot fee. I loved my trailer in Colorado, am not sure why I react to living in one here. It seems that LA is so sleazy and I don't think there will be deer and hares running around.

Well, we'll see. Dan says I'm GOING to like it. That's when I got mad at him. He is in Las Vegas, phoned to say hello.

Thought of you when I read about an Elaine Stritch special on May 29.

Look forward to moving in letter. I miss emails from Chip. Still have troubles with my emails, mine to him returned, so please send my fondest hellos.

> *All my love,*
> *LOOSHA*

[During this summer period, there are gaps in the letter exchange. Kenward was in Vermont, with both Mr. Oz and Jimmy Tampubolon, and wasn't faithfully responding to Lucia's letters like before. Lucia had inquired about the expiration of her Z Press grant and feared the mention of money had distanced him. She continues writing him of her outings around Venice Beach and her family and visitors. Kenward finally replies, wondering what to do with Prince Tampubolon, and reports of work on his book of poems, Agenda Melt.*]*

MARINA DEL REY, CA
JUNE 16, 2004

Dear Kenward,

It is childish of me not to be able to write a letter to you without one of yours to spark or inspire me. I miss hearing from you. I'll write this though as maybe you miss hearing from me. I remember why it is hard . . . you are the one of us with news.

I do have news in that my dear nieces were here. Monica had H, that German husband with her, but he is witty and nicer now. Andrea has a two-year-old, the most charming and lovable child ever. They were not here that long but we ate everywhere delicious, drove all around sight-seeing, talking with people. The two women are still gorgeous, attract crowds. Husband had work here, doing sound on a Mexican film, the three of us girls talked for hours and hours. (Jonas and I would nap and they would go on talking, laughing, eating take-out Chinese, watching videos, using us as pillows.) We walked on the pier in the morning before coffee and newspapers like in Mexico.

I do believe the happiest time of my life was that year or so with Molly[36] in Mexico. We all grew so close, truly did live each day at a time. I loved the hugging and kissing from everyone, grandmas, aunts, uncles, cousins . . . sincerely affectionate. It was nice for me that all these people who loved me had never known me when I drank, with my own sons, with whom I'm equally close, I can never let go of feelings of remorse, how I could have been a better mother to them.

Oh, now for sure. Mark is homeless, has decided to live on the beach. Sleeps in an alley off of Windward Way. He claims that he loves this life. Maybe I told you this already. He is writing a book about homeless people. I pray that he can stay sober enough to do it. He's a good writer, it could be great.

The Mexicans were here during Reagan week,[37] thank heavens. Kept me in touch with reality . . . reminded me of Iran-Contra, etc. Los Angeles was besieged, like mecca during Ramadan. Hordes of mourners bumpertobumper on the freeways, flags flying. I don't understand it. How can people adore him so much? They want to put him on the 10 dollar bill? I detest the media. Turns out G.E. owns 80% of NBC, stand to earn 8 million rebuilding Iraq. Another reason to skew the news . . . I don't trust any of it now.

The prison scandal disappeared soon enough . . . then Bush elects as JUDGE one of the men who Authorized it. Tom Brokaw[38] let slip that there are efforts afoot in the senate to make a bill allowing people to run for president who have not been born in USA. Thank God I won't be here when Schwarzenegger[39] becomes president.

Time off to watch painful Laker-Piston game. Baseball is ruined . . . it truly used to be the one true American institution left, money has ruined that completely. Basketball still ok . . . except my team is losing. Oh, Kenward, life is so harsh!

---

36   Lucia's sister, Molly Brown.
37   Memorials for former president Ronald Reagan, who died June 5, 2004.
38   Tom Brokaw, American journalist and author, b. 1940.
39   Arnold Schwarzenegger, Austrian-American actor turned politician, then governor of California, b. 1947.

VERMONT LETTER TO LOOSHA

Dear Loosha,

It's midnight. Insomnia time. Stars are out. Absolutely still. There's a tiny dead bat on the front porch. Invaded the downstairs a few nights ago, swooping its way around and around, much to the delight of my cats. Repeated lunges, as it nestled high up on a wall. Mystery demise. Found it on the bedroom floor, scooped it up, still quivering, plunked it on the porch, hoping it'd fly away.

Patty Padgett, my daily walk walker, is away in the big city, so Ron volunteered to take her place. Down the dirt road, over a mowed field, past apple trees to a path that leads to the field uphill where Joe's Stone is.

Halfway up -- veer to the right, shady pine-needle-soft path, freshly smoothed by the Mad Mower, Harold Camp, "prostrate" cancer survivor.

Vermont weather has returned, cool nights, dry air days, blue skies, zephyrs -- all the perks that got lost in the shuffle of Jakarta-intense mugginess and an exhausting heat wave, last week and the week before that. A twin-trunked fallen pine blocked the needle-soft path, removed by Ron, who sawed its trunk into rough-hewn seats, by the side of the path, low one for Patty, higher one for long-legged me. Ron and I sat a bit, indulged in poetry biz talk. Some show-biz problems of mine got aired.

Oh, dear. Shop-talk. Claibe Richardson, the composer of *The Grass Harp*, objected to a few words that will be performed next October in San Fran, in a new, final version by a tiny tiny company that calls itself, endearingly, Forty Second Street Moon Theatre.

"Vermont Letter to Loosha" was an edited version of a July 11, 1999, letter from Kenward that he revised to be read in "performance."

Claibe objected to *lounge lizard, halfway house, cutesy-wootsy* and the motivation of a new song for Judge Cool. I never figure out a character's motivation ahead of time. To justify my words to Outsiders, I make it up, the motivation, afterwards. It's a safety net, to placate the director and the performers. But something in me regards this as downright foolish.

This is the dark side of writing words for musical theatre. Justifying *everything*. I'm an unashamed word hedonist. I love a phrase, a rhyme. They come to me -- given words. I stick 'em in. I run with them. No sweat. And then I needs must fabricate the *why*. Mucho sweat. Weird.

To complete the Walk Loop. After a level pine-needle stretch, the path meanders down onto a cleared area, where, in winter, snow-mobiles turn in, gouging the soil. Then Ron and I headed back onto the road, actually dubbed Elmslie Road on county maps. Uphill to The Padgett Manse. Then, solo, pant-pant, steep stretch to Home. Named Poets Corner, by me. Takes forty minutes. Still not sleepy. Love, Kenward.

Lakers lost. Detroit Pistons US Champions. They were great. 9 pm. I'm fast asleep.

Let me know how things are going in Calais. Are you and Chip getting along ok? He's sounding jealous of Mr. Oz again. Are you and Patti walking? How is your health? What are you reading? Watching on the Tele?

> *All my love,*
> *Loosha*

CALAIS, VT

JUNE 25, 2004

Dear Loosha—

I've moved from my outbuilding workspace into the house—what was Joe's Studio, which overlooks the Big Pond, from high up. Slate sky today. Waterfall greatly reduced to a near trickle.

In half-an-hour, appointment with Ron: treadmill dread to overcome.

Mr. Indonesia showed up, out of the blue a few days ago: Jimmy Tampubolon—in Sulawesi, the spice isle he hails from, he was technically, thanks to the Dutch, co-opting landowners, a bona fide Prince, whose aunt & uncle, also titled, lived in a mountainside hut, looking down on "their" fiefdom. Villagers brought them food offerings, so they never starved, and, due to their feudal position, they escaped all stoop labor. Thanks to the Dutch, in Jakarta, they'd led a posh, westernized life: cushy gov't position, deluxe perks, golf club afternoons. Lost, via Independence—they were downgraded as collaborator-exploiters.

Jimmy has perfect white hair, a buffoon body, a melon face. Gleaming teeth. I forbade him to visit, but he didn't get the e-mail.[40] Take each jolt one-at-a-time mode right now. He relishes being helpful, so that's why I'm at a big desk, big cat Rilke stretched out against the windows, fax & copy machine at the ready to Rilke's left. I pulled myself

---

40   Tampubolon would appear like this, unexpected and with his suitcases at Kenward's front door. Later he'll show up at Lucia's in California.

together, typed up my Summer Sked, which I need to start dealing with as daily round reality. Typing up future duties can be a marvelous denial mechanism. Finito! That's done! So the actual work skitters away— plotted on paper is enough.

Two gigs I should start preparing for.

1) Milwaukee.[41]

2) Robert Wilson Land,[42] Bridgehampton, L.I. Coach theatre students + a solo show I'll entitle *Agenda Melt*. Incredible letter about it, the book, from Bill Bamberger. Not disappointed by its catch-up catch-all thrown togetherness. Just the opposite.

Made up two occasional B-Day poems. [For] Chip. And Ron. Keep waiting to feel "settled in" versus temporary alighting, twittery bird on jiggly branch.

Ron, it came out, work-out post-treadmill confidence, very sensitive to beloved friends in aged disrepair, plus losses via death. Relieved Bill Berkson's new lung, just implanted, is working 100%. Ron reports Bill is his old, jaunty, cheery teasy self. Guess that's why Ron's taken me on, as trainer, so I'll last longer, despite my penchant for heedless self-indulgence at table. He massages me as my reward! Non-kinky homo-eroticism: his focused hands lead him into a trance state, shared by me, some days.

Well, I don't know what to do about Jimmy. He wangled a tourist plus work visa, good for years and years. Rooting through old photos with me, he came upon one he took: my step-ma & half-sis ages ago, Palm Beach. Prince Tampubolon drove me about the Fla East Coast. I had it in my head I should become a Fla resident, avoid NY & NYC taxes and city winters. I was trying to emulate my father's fiscal shrewdness: self-exile in a balmy, barmy tax haven. He became a Bahamas yachtsman, a non-resident alien, and avoided any income tax anywhere, much to my sister Cynthia's fury. She believed in Good Citizenship.

---

41   Kenward's reading at Woodland Pattern Book Center, a nonprofit organization in Milwaukee, WI, founded 1979.

42   The Watermill Center for the arts and humanities in Water Mill, NY, founded by Robert Wilson in 1992.

Marched for abortion in D.C. etc. Anti-Nam. From Vassar to Social Worker.

Conversations with Jimmy are in Pidgin Anglois that, occasionally, takes off refreshingly. He's very smart about machines that intimidate & infuriate me. Faxes etc. So, now, everything works. Time for Ron. Workout. He's down with a summer cold, which he's given to Pat. Dinner invite downhill with Jimmy, which they shouldn't do, postponed.

Another day, another dolor.

Typed up my summer sked, showed it to Jimmy. He'll stay on in Vermont till my chores heat up—ten days more? Week of July 12th: Jimbo [Morgan] and Janet [Watson] (choreographer) come up to "talk through" *LibrettoLand*, the York revue. The flyer announcing it & the York Season is tacked up—"real life."

Jimmy'll head back to Jakarta: no room at Inn. Tears, clutched at me. Ron very severe, how he was bad for me: manservant. Preying on my frailties. Sample: Jimmy crouches down to tie my sneaker laces, no sense of demeanment. Natural! Partly I'm White Boss, partly agism: Indonesian deep-blood culture: Respect & Preserve The Old. Fascination/aversion—my Old School Tie embarrassment at odd proximity flares up without warning. [. . .]

I should write down his ups and downs, keep them straight in my noggin. Confessed he's sad how I've grown old, legs curved & bent now.

Love,
Kenward

MARINA DEL REY, CA
JULY 3, 2004

Dear Kenward,

Your letter made me so sad. You don't seem to be in at Calais but displaced, homeless. I usually hear you relax into the countryside and into your place very physically.

You are so kind . . . would never admit to yourself what an imposition Jimmy has been and how his visit has affected your rhythm and peace of mind. I think this has been very hard on you, hope he has moved on by now. Thank heavens for Ron and Patti, who will ever love and protect you.

Congratulations on your physical progresses. The diet part is terrible. Oh, it's so hard. I'm fine until 7 pm, then it is a Ben and Jerry or a brownie and a glass of milk . . . What no sweets in the house? Peanut butter and jelly will have to do.

I'm working hard on transfer to life after the Z poet Grant.[43] Starting to save money for tax payments next year. Have been interviewing counselors for medicaid card-pharmacy payments . . . I hope, and senior living. Counselor said I would need to allocate $350 for rent, which would mean group home for seniors.

I wish I were living with the group of you all in Calais! Feeling blue about this group home idea. Used to visit patients in group homes, didn't seem so bad. I've lived alone for so long don't know how living with One other will go, much less Several. The word itself . . . GROUP . . . crowded and imposing. Well, we'll see, I have started calling already, will get something lined up. So far no vacancies.

So I am blue. Helene Dorn's[44] death has been hard. So many of us, close friends from that time, have gone this past year or two.

Youth is ok too tho. Have never been "into" tennis, but was busy with apartment searching when the Wimbledons games were on, watched the Russian girl play Serena Williams.[45] It was so beautiful, the fine game, her grace, joy. I felt grateful to be witness to that youthful triumph.

A lovely detail of the game . . . the Sound. Serena's raw gasps, loud groans, [Maria's] chortles, childish laughs. Quite lovely.

---

43   Referring to a five-year Z Press Foundation grant that is nearing the end of its fifth year.
44   Helene Dorn, American artist, 1927–2004. Ed Dorn's first wife, friend of Lucia's. Helene Dorn's letters with writer Hettie Jones were collected and published, as were their husbands' letters, Ed Dorn and LeRoi Jones (Amiri Baraka).
45   Maria Sharapova defeated the two-time defending champion Serena Williams in the 2004 Wimbledon championships.

I hope you and I cheer up. I wish I could spend a few lazy afternoons with you.
> *All my love,*
> *LOOSHA*

*[In the gap between these letters, Kenward's friend Jimmy had flown to
California and arrived with his luggage at Lucia's studio apartment.
He told her Kenward had sent him there to take care of her. Lucia was
frantically calling me on the phone in New York, asking me how to reach
Kenward in Vermont. This next letter warns of Jimmy's impending arrival,
and Kenward explains the proposal—if Jimmy would be of help. He then
writes a second letter the same day, and by the end of that letter, Jimmy
has phoned him and explained that Lucia did not want or have space for a
live-in helper.]*

> CALAIS, VT
> JULY 6, 2004

Dearest Loosha—

Prince Tampubolon knows your Marina Del Rey whereabouts.
He's just taken off, and will phone you, when he arrives in La-La-
Land, soon. He has a Work Permit, so he hopes to find a position,
via an L.A. Indonesian agent, with an elderly individual who needs a
live-in helper.

So I thought of you. IF you think he'd be at all serviceable and
compatible, let me know. He's good-hearted, reliable, respects The Old,
likes to laugh, has a benign mischievous streak, is transfixed by the lure
of domestic order, drives capably, and is computer-savvy. So, if you're
up for it, meeting him, he'll come by, and if you wish, once you've
had a look-see, step by step, trial basis, he'll be at your service, when
needed, and will find a residence of his own. Please let me send him
his wages—whatever they come to. The feudal aspect of this wouldn't
bother him, if it doesn't trouble you, and, my opinion, it shouldn't. It
would ease my worriment side to think of you, looked after by a trustworthy Sumatra Prince.

Should Jimmy be a wild card bad idea, he can proceed on to his

mysterioso Indonesian agent. Or divide up his time, between you &
the agent's client.

Trainer Ron is irked at me, as my eyes are rheumy from allergy,
and I grope my way around, sheathed by milky, Celtic twilight visuals. I had recourse to drops Jimmy brought with him, inscrutable info
in Indonesian, which worked for a few days. I rallied for a 4th of July
feast, helped a lot by Jimmy—KFC, extra-crisp. Vermont smoked
ham. Fresh peas, perfect. Shelling peas at table wafts me into nirvana.
KFC Mashed Potatoes. Three kinds of salad. Richissimo choc cake.
Cherries. Grapes. Sparklers were sparkled on the lawn afterwards,
brought by Son Wayne & his Irish colleen, Shuvaughn.[46] A sweet
occasion.

Hope you had a riotous 4th—

Love,

Kenward

PS I tried returning your phone call today[47] . . . only have disconnected numbers. So I'm contacting Chipster.

CALAIS, VT

JULY 6, 2004

Dearest Loosha—

A quiet sunny slightly humid morning. Pond lilies to gaze down
at, from my desk. I face the pond through eight oblong windows. I'm
dressed for a workout with Ron at 10 AM, usual time, but maybe he's
seeing Patty off, choo-choo, NYC dentistry trip she dreads. 4 PM? I
keep mixing times up something awful, lately.

Housekeeper has appeared: house muss serious—from Jimmy
visit. Last night, Ron & Pat picked me up, drove to a Culinary Institute restaurant in downtown blink-and-you'll miss-it Montpelier.
Fancy meal. Ron restrained himself as I gobbled a creme brulée.

---

46   Wayne and Siobhán Padgett.

47   Lucia was calling Kenward and me furiously about Jimmy Tampubolon,
who showed up at Lucia's apartment with his suitcases and said Kenward had sent
him to live with and take care of her.

Kap-aCheena (never know how to spell it Italiano) not as foamy as Ron's: his triumphant specialty, guaranteed climax to dinner down-hill.

Chatted a bit about Andy Warhol,[48] occasioned by a letter I must answer, from the Keeper of his Videos, at the Whitney Museum. I lived, back then, in my own rented house, on a block-long side street, at 28 1/2 Cornelia Street, a few doors down from where the great W.H. Auden once lived. Three floors, narrow house. The middle floor room good-sized, smallish bedroom third floor, adjacent to a cubbyhole of a writing room. I was "seeing" Andy then, at the Factory, a loft where the action surrounding him transpired—and a few times where he lived—a possessions jumble, cartons piled up.

He made a video of me, came down to Cornelia St with his machine—and, as this was back in the days of scabrous real-life per-forming, Chelsea girls style, drag queens and nudity, I thought I had to do something a tad shocking, to warrant his attention as filmer. So I languished, torso naked, on my third-floor bed, with my whippet, Whippoorwill, starved the day before. I plastered my then spindly torso with gobbets of raw hamburger, and that was my idea of kinky visual content to keep Andy's video machine whirling. I once saw the result. Quite gorgeous. He left the dog-fest portion as negative, black-and-white, so Whippoorwill became a graceful ghost dog, whitish, surrounded by black, feasting, with swan-like neck grace, on body meat blobs.

I must have seen Andy's film, somewhere, somehow, as this section struck me as worth the time and trouble. Patty and Ron have met the curator, very nice they agree, so I'll make a date to see the film & meet her.

I have it down in my 2004 Standard Diary that James Morgan, York maestro, and his choreographer, Janet Watson, are supposed to visit, this week, to chat in depth about the revue, still entitled LingoLand. Saturday: Jet Blue to NYC—teaching stint & gig in Bridgehampton, L.I., at the Robert Wilson Emporium.

---

48   Andy Warhol, American artist and filmmaker, 1928–1987. Friend of Kenward's.

[. . .]

Glad our disconnectedness has tapered off!

Sorry I thought for a moment Prince Jimmy might be of help to you. Dumb. He just phoned. Needs money to get wherever he's going. Scenario: mail check to Chipster, attention Jimmy, & hope he makes it home, wherever home is for an Ex-Prince.

Love,
Kenward

MARINA DEL REY, CA

JULY 16, 2004

Dearest Kenward,

So sweet your letter of introduction to Prince Tampoubolon. Amazing. My response to his arrival would have been totally different. What really makes me sad is that I would have been much more gracious and welcoming. I sent him off with dispatch to his Samoan agent.

Timing all wrong, in every way. I was in shower when he rang downstairs. I beeped him into the front hall, had hoped to get dressed before he got upstairs but he came quickly and right on in, filling one end of the room with his bags. I was too embarrassed to ask him to go outside while I got clothes, so I just put my pajamas back on and came out of the bathroom. (My hair soaking wet.) Then it was Hello Hello, and very pleasant. He really is charming. He is a prince of a fellow!

But first thing he said was that you had sent him to me, he would be my live-in helper who would do whatever I needed. I hadn't had coffee yet, said Let me first make coffee and toast and we'll talk. But he wanted to make it, no all HE wanted was some warm water. He was aching to make things comfortable for me, I was aching for my little morning routine and/or to let mother/hostess come thru . . . coffee and scones, whatever.

As I live my days I am continually gasping for air and/or quietly groaning because of back pain. This goes on, as they say in one of most annoying new catch phrases: 24/7. He kept jumping up and coming over to do something "Let me help you!" And he was upset because I was making the coffee. Everything he did was good and kind. I swear he was driving me nuts. I WANT TO MAKE THE COFFEE. Gasp gasp groan. Oh, Lucia, Are you all right? Let me help you sit down.

I was going to say I batted him away . . . I didn't, just in my mind

He looked around and realized there were no other rooms. Reading your letter I see that you must have said to him that he would live elsewhere and check with me. Alas I think you told him so many nice things about me he was ready to stay with me. But he did notice that I live in one room. Kitchen, bed, table, bookcases, tiny love seat and a TV set fill the room. I wouldn't really have that much for him to do, actually. It's so hard to say. Everything exhausts me but when I break it down, yes I can do my laundry, drive to post office. I don't know what I am going to do when I get sicker, older, when my back really goes . . . I could use 24-hour care Now except I can't stand having anybody There that much. Oh . . . I'm going to be one of those old ladies that bite, I can tell.

Anyway, I am so sorry I was not more welcoming to your friend.

I'm very ashamed too about bothering you with any money question. Can't imagine why $ was brought up at all . . . I had been reassured by the New York person. I thought it had stopped coming in April.

I think I'm having mini-breakdowns here.

Can you imagine how grateful I am to you, for everything, for each letter that is totally distinct from the one before. I often feel so discouraged and lonely, fed up . . . I am immensely grateful for continuity of our friendship, the brilliance of your letters is the lagniappe . . . (hope I use that properly.) Your letters sustain me.

This previous paragraph is so awkward because I kept cutting out sentimental passages and putting in new ones. I give up . . . can't remember what the lagniappe was all about.

And their timing . . . fantastic . . . the way they go from a lazy afternoon to that wild Warhol movie of you and Whippoorwill! I love Joe's painting, paintings? of Whippoorwill, would be great to see him in this context!

> *Love,*
> *Loosha*

[In the following letters, Kenward has returned to New York City during the Republican National Convention, which Lucia also writes about watching on television. He describes the chaos and traffic trying to get uptown for LingoLand *auditions, then relays the audition and production details.]*

Dear Loosha,

Safe. Home. 5:30 AM, rainy out. The nightly protect Bush umbrella of helicopters quiescent. First night, extreme Amazon-muggy heat & placement disorientation. Yesterday, Mr. Oz fetched me, limo, to go to the auditions for *LingoLand* cast, uptown at the York Theatre. Traffic bulloxed up by the Republican Convention, abandoned limo, took the subway: much faster, a miraculously direct route, with the longest escalator in the world rising effortlessly back to street level.

10 AM to 6 PM sat in the York Theatre. Lunch break in a backroom. A steady stream of performers. Fell asleep at one point, ten demerits—sleep deprivation. They looked so fresh and pretty, the girls, except for one homely lady, worn comedic face with an upended clown nose. I kept being fixated obsessively by her twin face holes: huge black nostrils accentuated by stage lighting.

Ritual: the performer enters, gets introduced to the accompanist, stage-right, and to a clump of watchers seated down front. Jimbo does the introductions:

#1 the musical director, oldie baldy (Jack Lee[49])

#2 York casting director

#3 blonde lady, production assistant, very nice, Katherine Puma

#4 Mr. Oz

#5 me, word author

Performer passes 10" by 12" photo out, pro autobio on its back, confers with accompanist at the grand piano. Jack Lee has a set routine

---

49   Jack Lee, American musical director, 1929–2016.

to test the performer's resilience and readiness to obey & fill specific esthetic needs.

Almost all sing in a hard-pressed ta-da style, to make a good impression pronto. Jack stops the auditionee fast, asks him/her not to move, or gesture—or performance-sing. Let the song do the work. Lean on the piano. In time, a conversation with friends out-front. Sometimes an amazing and immediate outreach of talent emerged, buried under angst-to-please-and-nab-job stress. [. . .]

9:40 AM

Sitting alone in an empty theatre, second row. Love this special solitude, always have, goes way back to The Sixties, when operas I'd written the words for began to be performed. Production gang gathers. Jack Lee, musical director, Row A. Showbiz Gab. [. . .]

Janet Watson, choreographer, is sitting behind me. She hails from Tulsa. Kevin Wallace, genial, unflappable rehearsal pianist, jokes about turning into his mother, who made banana bread. Which he brings, passes out. "Our" Mom. What I love about theatre is the instant, unearned Family I'm part of productions bring me.

Chitchat about how *The Little Foxes* by Lillian Hellman was turned into an opera, *Regina*, by Marc Blitzstein. Brenda Lewis (*Lizzie Borden*) took over the title part. Jack Lee: "She offended me, too broad—a bump and a grind . . ."

Matthew arrives. Conductor. Mr. Oz goes to the lit up grand onstage, noodles gently. Katherine Puma arrives. Audition scheduler. Blonde, performer, nice smile. During a break, Jack teases me—he loves teasing me—someone nameless in the gang finds me sexy.

Response pantomime: I turn around—is there a second Kenward in the house, an imposter, sexy version of me? Miss Puma? Is she the culprit? We keep exchanging "looks." I'm drawn to her, though not "that" way. She's late, flustered. Wasn't let off the bus. Midtown Bush security. Hatred of Republicans vented: unanimous.

[. . .]

I'll keep you posted, what happens next. So lucky, my bod is pain free. Subject to exhaustion, though. Mr. Oz had to help me walk home after eats, after eight-hour rehearsal. Had to crawl up the stairs to my

3rd Floor bed. Must treadmill tomorrow with Chipster as Substitute Trainer, appointed by Ron to keep me crunching.

Love,
Kenward

MARINA DEL REY, CA
SEPTEMBER 4, 2004

Dear Kenward,

Chip said that you were writing a letter to me. Hooray! I have missed hearing from you. Don't know if you received my letters, sent to Vermont.

So is summer over? I got no sense of Calais this year, has your stay there ended? Have many questions, about your revue etc., but will wait and see what your letter brings. I hope your silence is because you are busy with revue, writing poems and songs, not because you are cross with me, and especially not because you are exhausted or unwell.

I hope you have been taking care of yourself. Eating well, exercising, resting. In e-mail Chip mentioned that he was going to steam a salmon so sounds like diet is ok. Where is Guru Ron? Do you walk in New York? Lord, your city looked terrible, terrifying last week; you must be glad that it is over.

The convention was painful to watch. I'm afraid it looks like Bush will be reelected. Lies, lies.

I've been mad at the TV for weeks now. First it was the Olympics, which are always great in a way. I used to love the march at the opening, of all of the countries in the world. Now it is simply sad. The events nice to watch really, the dedication and focus of the athletes. Rowing, men's diving are so elegant. But this year was so distracting. Why have they added those stripper-like codas to the gymnastic events? How could they keep showing over and over the near porn volleyball finales?

What I don't understand is how a country so lacking in sensuality and physical grace can be so obsessed with sex? Seems like they would have caught some of the actual elegance of sex somewhere. Bikini beach dancers were gross.

So then we got the REPUBLICAN NATIONAL CONVENTION.

PORNOGRAPHIC IN a different way, but definitely something pruriently sexual and leering about those macho republican fools. Plath's "Every woman loves a fascist"[50] applies to these smirking strutting guys, like Schwarzenegger. Oh, they are all liars, power mad and ugly sadists.

So you would think I'd be relieved to get to the Hurricane. This is infuriating because the media is so disappointed. They are apologetic for the fact that Frances went down from Class 5 to Class 3. It's still a mess, but not mess enough. I don't think anybody even died.

I remember this syndrome actually, from working in Emergency Room. We really cheered up when there was a tragic accident, a crazed gunman.

How did I get so carried away? Sorry. I'll stop here, go watch TV!

Dear Kenward, if you didn't write to me . . . please do. Your letters cheer me more than anything else does.

> *All my love,*
> *LOOSHA*

NEW YORK, NY

SEPTEMBER 10, 2004

Dear Loosha—

I do believe Friday has rolled around, as Chipster gave me a reminder last night—Apex Pest Control get check $125 plus tax—I squashed a waterbug, which I thought was a roach—great sport for the kitties, mysterious lunges and pounces. Basement overrun.

Delicious home-cooked-by-Chip supper, Mr Oz & I—(Chip went off to dine with Colin). To bed, early. Scribbled a letter to you on a legal pad, sitting at table at the York.

Dear Loosha

11:25 RAIN INTERMITTENT . . . REHEARSAL OF *LOVE-WISE*. JACK LEE PLUNKS OUT THE MELODY ON A PIANO (ITS BASE NEEDS TUNING BAD) ONE FINGER STYLE.

Tender longings fill me every time I take your hand.

JACK LEE: "TIME" HAS TOO MUCH *E* IN IT. DON'T

---

50 "Every woman adores a Fascist" is a line from "Daddy," by Sylvia Plath, American poet and writer, 1932–1963.

BRIGHTEN OR DARKEN *Tender longings.* CUT OFF *hand* RIGHT
ON THE HEAD OF THE THIRD BEAT. WE'RE AFTER PURITY.
THAT "NATURAL" IS QUESTIONABLE. *Tender* DOESN'T
MOVE. DON'T STOP. IT'S A CONTINUAL FLOW OF TONE.
YOU'RE THE PEDAL TONE. POUR TONE.

Face-wise attractive—

"tr" AS QUICKLY AS YOU CAN MAKE IT. [. . .] DON'T STOP
TO FINISH *"wise."*

Guy #1 comes over, touches me. I'm developing a mild sublimation-
type crush on him. Tall and well-built, sort of homely crinkly ski-jump
nosed face. Touching is part of theatre folk conversation: unabashed
intimacy. I love it! Writers don't ever touch while conversing—just
hello and bye-bye contact. Guy # 1 used the Joe Babe Monologue at an
audition—he'd asked me if he could keep his audition copy. He didn't
get the part. Too "good-looking"—the part is a Loser. Back to: this con-
tented feeling.

[. . .]

Assignment for today. Confer with Jimbo. Songs that were written
to be solos (and have proved themselves as such) must remain solos. So
obvious. Must control my fury at this time-wasting stupidity. Ghosts of
Postcards on Parade debacle hover. Terrible director. And I lost my way
as reviser of my words, trying to please, problemsolve. Mr. Oz comes by
to pick me up in a car, so I'll ask his advice how best to confront Jimbo
with the obvious: the "numbers" must be done as written, or, whatever
isn't right for the cast (gifted bunch)—cut it immediately.

End of account. Hope this on-going account doesn't get wearisome:
theatre can be so dumb-dumb. And such a treat, when it works.

Love,

Kenward

MARINA DEL REY, CA

SEPTEMBER 23, 2004

Dear Kenward,

I'd worry about you . . . stress and too much work . . . but your writing is terrific. The section of your letter beginning with

"Tender longings fill me every time I take your hand,"
Jack Lee: Time has too much E in it. Don't brighten or darken.
all the way to
"sounded like something's gone wrong with the air conditioning
ducts,"
terrific. Jack Lee and Guy #1, dialogue. Love it.

Ridiculous and so WRONG breaking up the lyrics. Especially *Take me Away, Roy Rogers*, which should be you only, with others perhaps in the chorus. *Miss Got Rocks* should be only one woman. I don't understand WHY they wanted to double up and to mete out the lines in such a way. Yes, totally dumb. As my grandson Truman would say, "You got that right." I hope you got all those things settled. What a terrible feeling it must be . . . to see your work jostled and scattered and "disrespected" in such a way.

When (dear) poet Peter Davison,[51] my editor, and others at the Atlantic Monthly Press so wanted, "suggested," insisted on changes in my novel . . . more sex, etc., I felt vulnerable, helpless FURIOUS because obviously they didn't GET IT, or they would leave it. I simply stopped writing the novel. (Part of it later became that long love story set in Chile, "Andado.")

I wrote an entire new novel instead: THE PEACEABLE KINGDOM about El Paso during World War 2. Grandparents, Uncle John, Mama . . . alcohol, incest, violence. Loneliness. Nobody was writing such raw material then . . . maybe *God's Little Acre?*[52] . . . so I shocked and disappointed *The Atlantic*. I destroyed both of these manuscripts. This long digression started to be simple sympathy for you. It is such a fine line . . . to change things enough to please the editors or producers without compromising your, er, soul? Heart? Self is enough I guess.

Nevertheless, Kenward, I think this production will end up being wonderful. When is it scheduled? Glad you have Mr. Oz and Chip

---

51   Peter Davison, American poet, essayist, publisher, 1928–2004.

52   Erskine Caldwell, *God's Little Acre* (Viking, 1933).

to help you. I'd love to write a Wildean play, Chekhovian actually
. . . "The Seagull on Greenwich" . . . The famous poet with his two
assistants who outdo each other, scheme and plot to win his favor,
discredit and disqualify the other. Seconal in a glass of wine, oh oh
the UPS guy drinks it, exploding packages. A houseboy that looks like
Guy #1.

Actually it sounds like all goes well between them. Chip still so
grateful and happy to be there. I wish I were there and well enough to
be one of your assistants.

Back pain has been really bad, also arthritis in hands and knees. Got
injections in my hands yesterday, huge relief. But my overall health is
GOOD. I'm slowly losing weight, feel healthy and alert. Lungs great. I
get off my air hose for a few hours a day.

Started to say that I looked good too, forgetting my new haircut.
My doctor asked why I didn't get up and leave my salon. I was simply too fascinated. It turned out that Tiffany has Lupus, was heavily
drugged and is nearly blind now after oxycontin so long. Well, it was
scary. I have a shaggy look that was in during the punk and grunge
era.

An ex-student took me to a special showing at the Screen Actors
Guild. Movie "Around The Bend," which will be out in next few
months, in time, I hope, to get Oscars. Christopher Walken, Michael
Caine, a young actor and a boy . . . four generations. Painful, powerful,
funny. Small audience, mostly young actors, writers.

Divine to be in that responsive audience . . . nothing was missed.
Everybody reacted to good lines, strong moments. People applauded,
cried, laughed loudly. It was an affectionate shared experience . . . especially when Christopher Walken spoke afterward and answered questions. He was brilliant. Lovely experience.

Sorry for too long a letter. I loved your last one. You sound frenzied
but Good. Sharp, crisp language.

> *Your truest fan—*
> *With all my love—*
> *Loosha*

Dear Kenward,

Week now of foggy days, cool, dark. Reminds me of ocean trips between New York and Valparaiso. 32 days at sea, time to really feel that you were at sea, on a voyage, down the continent, through the canal, through the seasons, from winter to summer. Stretches of rain and fog quite lovely, the ocean churning and navy blue, decks deserted, even the big hall deserted except for a few groups playing bridge or canasta, some chess players. Americans at the bar. The ship would roll and buckle; spray splattered the windows. Years later, when I read *The Magic Mountain*, I was reminded of this room, its art deco elegance, the echo when the door banged, the friendships that grew up there isolated from the world.

Passengers were from all over the world. The children always ended up speaking an entirely different language. These were working ships, half cargo, half passenger. Wm R. Grace.[53] They also shipped ores for my father's Co., American Smelter. I Remember Peter Grace and Mr. Murphy, Simon? (one of the) Guggenheims. We always sat at the Captain's table. My father and I did. My sister ate at first sitting (I sat with her). My mother stayed in bed. She did like the ships though, played poker and bridge for hours. One night in fact she disappeared, had ended up below deck, drinking and playing poker with sailors. Bad scene with my father. She did this again, on trip alone, years later, lost all of her money. My father made her turn around the day the ship docked, fly back to Chile, accompanied by Mr. Murphy.

Wish I were sipping consommé on deck, a blanket against crisp wind.

Recovering from serious bout with the flu. Very sick. I got scared, felt very alone and helpless. *Ensure* drinks and apples were all that I could eat, if not keep down, for days. Dan was on heavy schedule, still

---

53   William Russell Grace, Irish-American politician, mayor of New York City, and founder of W. R. Grace and Company, 1832–1904.

is, so even though he called (and would have come if I needed him)
I didn't see him or anyone. Sorry to go on about my health troubles.
Hope you'll sympathize. How are all your aches and pains? Are you getting enough rest? Sticking to meals cooked by Chip? Does Ron still give
you massages?

You never answer my questions. Still have no idea when the revue
is due. Still worry that you are cross with me? Hope not, and that this
is simply "age appropriate" paranoia. My dear doctor reassures me
about everything this way . . . hearing loss, anxiety, memory black-
outs, insomnia, paranoia, depression. These are all age appropriate.
Great idea! He doesn't just blame age for these troubles, but makes it
sound like you are supposed to have them. Suicidal? How appropriate!

Saw a lovely movie on HBO channel: Almodóvar's *HABLE CON
ELLA—TALK TO HER*. I think you would like it.[54]

Debates[55] tomorrow. Hope Kerry does as well as first time. I'm still
appropriately terrified about elections, war, the future of our country.
We were lucky, weren't we, to have known a much sweeter time. Seems
like my sons were just beginning to grow up when wham bam it was
wars and assassinations. Dan says that we had the holocaust and seg-
regation, McCarthyism, the bomb, many other ills. Not the pervasive
cynicism, the sneer that colors everything now, it seems, says she with
A.A. negativity. I'm sorry! I'll stop now.

Hope all is going really well.

I love you,
LOOSHA

*[In the following letter, Kenward writes to Lucia about finding himself in
the pages of poet James Schuyler's book of selected letters, as well as in Ron
Padgett's new biography of Joe Brainard.]*

---

54 Pedro Almodóvar, *Hable con ella,* El Deseo S.A., 2002.
55 October 8, 2004, U.S. presidential debate between John Kerry and
George W. Bush.

NEW YORK, NY

OCTOBER 10, 2004

Dear Loosha—

Turn for the worse, rumor—hope your pain has gone away, has the good sense to leave you in peace.

It's a windy mild gray Sunday, and I get to stay in, the whole day, ahh. No callers, brief chat with Chipster, who keeps rallying as carer, with total grace of being. Rilke, fat cat, began not eating or peeing. Chipster to the rescue: trip to vet, pills, recalled same genetic blowout happened back aways to Satie, the skinny 'lil bro who is wilier at enticing human cuddling. Rilke's back, keeping to himself today. Pill regimen. No crunch-crunch food allowed.

I've been on a Blast from the Past reading binge. First Ron Padgett's *Joe*, then Jimmy Schuyler's letters,[56] edited & benoted painstakingly by William Corbett of Boston, neighborly Vermont summerer. I'll send them your way. I think both immersions would intrigue & move you. Too close for me to circumscribe them via a period feel. Perplexing how much time has already elapsed, so they're closer, counting up the decades, seems like, to E.M Forster's remembrances, or [Christopher] Isherwood, or goners like Scott Fitzgerald, than to anyone who can pass him/herself off as Boy 2004 or Madam Now.

I got off easy in both books. Ron tactfully left out my abandonment of Joe, to run off to a Pacific isle with a Naropa kiddo who looked a bit like a young Brainard—that isn't even touched on—no sweaty exposé. Pat Padgett pipes up, here and there, on its pages, concerned that Joe isn't "faithful."

A bunch of Jimmy's letters spring from staying in Vermont—such a blessing to read his daily round accounts, particularly one hilarious autumn weekend that was a total disaster—the cast of characters included DD Ryan III,[57] an NYC fashion world icon with an unre-

---

56   Kenward must have an advanced readers copy of the forthcoming *The Letters of James Schuyler to Frank O'Hara*, edited by William Corbett, to be published by Turtle Point Press in 2006.

57   D. D. Ryan, former editor for *Harper's Bazaar* magazine, 1928–2007.

quited passion for Bill Berkson, and her two English schoolboycute Newporty snob sons, plus Jimmy and me. Super-fastidious, DD was appalled at all the dead flies on the window ledges, the filthy kitchen, windows coated with dust, cans and bottles that hadn't been disturbed, not for decades, on grimy shelves above the stove, . . . a vacuum was bought, horrible new house sound, but her homemaker culture shock, close call, didn't flare into out-and-out hysteria.

Jimmy wrote me a lot from his safe-house in Southampton.[58] Schizoid that he was, his on-looker self maintained its probity, off and on, increasingly squelched and dampened by hopelessly futile love objects, shadowy fantasy figures that loom voraciously into his fragile daily round. Such a cautionary tale for me, who've been there myself, the futile love object route, more often than I care to admit.

I don't miss the hurly-burly of the daily trek uptown to partake of the *LingoLand* workshop at the York. January, I'll need all my inner fortitude to face rehearsals, the real thing. And then real audiences.

Time to forage for supper & then work on my gig. Next weekend, I head for Milwaukee, to a performance space I've been to before: Woodland Pattern. The couple who run it, with scant help, are angels. Time to get my act together. But—grub first.

Mucho Love,
Kenward

[In this final letter Lucia wrote to Kenward, she updates him on her memoir progress, recalls a Schuyler reading she attended and reading Schuyler's diaries. She reports on her sons, her return to Proust. Seeing the white space at the end of the page after printing it, she fills the rest with handwriting, presented in italics.]

MARINA DEL REY, CA
OCTOBER 17, 2004

Dearest Kenward,

Glad to hear you so sharp, witty . . . "together." You sound confident

58   Referring to Schuyler's mental breakdowns and hospitalizations.

and angst-free about the Revue. It's going to be terrific. You know this, I think. Good that you trust your cast, that it will be fun for with everyone.

Sunday here for me, after stormy night. Gorgeous clear day. No callers for me. Last one was the chap who took me to Walken movie. Dan stops by a few times a week. I'm no good at making friends. I'm Friendly though, I think. I mean if anybody stopped by.

That movie "Round the Bend" is getting terrible reviews, alas. I loved it, especially Christopher Walken.

Sorry about Rilke. Was this an infection or something permanent? Nothing worse than a sick cat. Dogs are just sick and are bad patients. Cats seem to think it is a humiliation.

Spent an hour looking for Schuyler's journals, diaries. Have his collected poems but must have accidentally sold the journal when I got rid of so many books. I loved it and really would like to read his letters. Especially if you are in the book.

He read in San Francisco . . . in the '80s, early nineties? My friend Steve [Emerson] said I had to go to the Art Institute to hear him, was appalled that I had never read his work. (Steve is the friend, tall-distinguished fellow, who so loves your work, finally met you on your last trip.) So I didn't know what to expect. The auditorium was packed. This was not the usual people making the poetry scene. Many older handsome men and women, serious looking. Can't explain what made the audience different from usual audiences. The intensity of their expectation? And when he read, their complete attention? Anyway, the dude had some serious fans.

It was a fantastic reading. A reciting really as he seemed to know the poems by heart, speaking softly, shyly. Never looking up. Sometimes it seemed he wanted to smile, or even laugh. He didn't but we all did. Of course I got his poems the next day.

I really would like both books. I am so happy that you had Joe and James Schuyler as lovers. What perfect combinations.

I wish I had been a gay man and one of your lovers. Does this make me a fag hag? What IS a fag hag?

Kenward . . . this prose of yours, these worlds you experienced are crying to be published, DD Ryan!!!! Did you make that up?

I still have about ten Trollopes but regret selling many others, like *Can You Forgive Her?*, which is where we meet Lady Glencora. I'm reading [Proust's] *Swann's Way* now, in dear friend Lydia Davis' splendid translations. "On the Pleasure of Hating," wonderful essay. I am in love with [William] Hazlitt . . . seriously.

Oh, Kenward . . . here is another letter where I haven't talked about Mark. He sleeps now under a concrete stairwell behind a furniture store in San Diego. It stormed and stormed last night, was so cold. He has been staying sober and on anti-psychotic meds, has 22 days. If he stays sober and checks in every day for next two months, he can get into a house, supervised for alcoholics with psych problems. His brothers and I know that if any of us take him in he ends up resenting it, getting off meds, drinking, violent, etc. He and I talk on the phone several times a week. Sweet talks.

He is the Fool in the Tarot deck. If he stays sober and writes his homeless book, finishes it, it will be a fine book. He gets a (large it seems) monthly check. If he gets settled he could write, take classes, etc. I am constantly worried about him. I think I have let go of guilt, all my fault, just feel fear for him.

Whew. Needed to tell you this, it is so much on my mind.

I forgot the good news. I'm writing again . . . got my poor folks out of Chiapas, any day now they'll be out of Mexico! Feels good . . .[59]

Phone sex!!? How does one get into the business? I have the breathing down for sure . . .

Hope Woodland Pattern is fun. Tell them about Naropa and Pacific Isle.

[printed letter ends here, with handwritten addition below]

Impotence: Nature's way of saying "no hard feelings"

---

59   Working on her memoir, *Welcome Home.*

Young blonde woman was walking on the riverbank . . . across the water she saw another woman . . . she called out to her.

"Hallo! How do I get to the other side of the river?" the woman said.

"You are on the other side."

Sorry. Hated to see that white space of paper.

> *All my love dear—*
> *Have a good trip—*
> *L.A. Loosha*

Afterword

Lucia Berlin passed away in her California home on her sixty-eighth birthday, November 12, 2004. On December 11, a funeral service was held in Boulder, Colorado. Kenward and I flew from New York to find, upon arrival, that one of Kenward's cats had curled up inside his checked luggage. Satie the cat, miraculously safe and sound, helped distract us from our grief, though many tears were shared as Lucia's friends and family stood together in the cold, light rain at Green Mountain Cemetery.

Before we departed for the University of Colorado Library for a reception and memorial reading, Lucia's sons approached me with a brown paper grocery bag; it was full of some of the most visual and decorative of Kenward's collaged letters to Lucia. I returned those letters to Kenward and they are now among his other papers in his archives at UCSD. That afternoon in the CU library, Lucia's sons, her friends, and former students honored her life with our words and songs. Kenward was last to pay her tribute, and he sung a cappella a lyric he wrote for his play *City Junket*, Lucia's favorite of his songs: "Who'll Prop Me Up in the Rain?"

I continued to work as Kenward's assistant for seven more years, seeing him through additional book publications and theatrical productions. His musical revue *LingoLand* opened at the York Theatre in January 2005 and included several "letters to Loosha."

In 2015, Farrar, Straus and Giroux published a collection of Lucia's selected stories. *A Manual for Cleaning Women* became an international bestseller, winning wide critical acclaim. It was named best book of the year by the *El País* newspaper in Madrid and was in the top ten on annual lists by the *New York Times*, *Los Angeles Times*, and others.

When I hear people say what a shame it is that Lucia's talents weren't as widely celebrated in her lifetime, I think of what she wrote to Kenward on July 31, 1999: "Whereas I couldn't care less about recognition or fame, I do want to be immortal!"

Kenward Elmslie passed away in his New York City home on June 29, 2022. He was ninety-three years old. As the news of his death was shared among friends, along with photos and recordings of his songs and poems, I was reminded of my own years with Kenward, especially carrying a newly printed letter for Lucia to be mailed at the post office, or delivering to Kenward a letter that had arrived from Lucia. I am eternally grateful for the lives and works of these two beloved friends and outstanding writers. For me, and for many of us fans and readers, they will forever remain immortal.

"WHO'LL PROP ME UP IN THE RAIN"

Used to be
When it poured down cats and dawgs,
I'd go prop up apple branches, and talk purty to the hawgs.
    Laughing at the thunder,
    Watching lightning streak,
    Naked as a jaybird,
    I'd plunge into the creek.
    What I want to know is:
    When my high times wane,
      Who'll prop me up in the rain?

    Used to be
I'd find skulls with giant jaws.
I'd find porcypines of bone, and old turkey buzzard claws.
    Prowling in the backwoods,
    Through a dark ravine,
    Naked as a jaybird,
    Back when I was green.
    What I want to know is:
    When I'm dead and gone,
      Who'll prop me up in the dawn?

    Some bumbling bird,
    Who'll pick me up,
    Turn me round, peck a bit,
    Stare a while and start to smile
      At my remains.

    What I want to know is:
    When my high times wane,

Who'll prop me up in the rain?

All I want to know is:
When the good times end,
Who'll say, come on in, my friend.[60]

---

60   Elmslie, "Who'll Prop Me Up in the Rain," song lyrics published in *Routine Disruptions: Selected Poems & Lyrics.* Reprinted with permission from Coffee House Press.

Bibliography

Selected Works by Lucia Berlin

Berlin, Lucia. *Angel's Laundromat.* Turtle Island, 1981.
———. "B. F. and Me." *Sniper Logic* #9, 2001.
———. "Del Gozo Al Pozo." *Sniper Logic* #4, 1996.
———. *Evening in Paradise.* Farrar, Straus and Giroux, 2018.
———. "Evening in Paradise." *Sniper Logic* #5, 1997.
———. *Homesick: New and Selected Stories.* Black Sparrow Press, 1990.
———. "Mama." *New American Writing* no. 13, 1999.
———. *A Manual for Cleaning Women.* Farrar, Straus and Giroux, 2015.
———. *Safe and Sound.* Poltroon Press, 1988.
———. *So Long: Stories 1987–1992.* Black Sparrow Press, 1993.
———. *Welcome Home: A Memoir with Selected Photographs and Letters.* Farrar, Straus and Giroux, 2018.
———. "Welcome Home." memoir excerpt, *Square One* no. 1, 2003.
———. "Welcome Home, Part II." memoir excerpt, *Square One* no. 3, 2005.
———. *Where I Live Now.* Black Sparrow Press, 1999.
Berlin, Lucia, and Margaret Weir, Bill Weir, and Sophie Constantinou. "Pen Pals." Video interview, 2002, for Kenward's website. Citizen Film production 2016, vimeo.com/136148720.

Selected Works by Kenward Elmslie

Elmslie, Kenward. *Album.* Kulchur Press, 1969.
———. *Bare Bones.* Bamberger Books, 1995.
———. *Blast from the Past: Stories, Poems, Song Lyrics, Remembrances.* Skanky Possum Press, 2000.
———. *City Junket.* Adventures in Poetry Press, 1972; republished Bamberger Books, 1987.
———. "Elegy for Loosha." *Square One* no. 3, 2005.
———. *Moving Right Along.* Z Press, 1980.
———. *Nite Soil* (postcards). Granary Books, 2000.

————. *The Orchid Stories*. Doubleday, 1973.

————. Pavilions, Tibor de Nagy Gallery, 1961.

————. *Routine Disruptions: Selected Poems & Lyrics*. Coffee House Press, 1998.

————. "Sibling Rivalry." *New American Writing*, 2003; *Best American Poetry 2004*.

————. *Sung Sex*. Kulchur Press, 1989.

Elmslie, Kenward, and Joe Brainard. *The Champ*. Black Sparrow Press, 1968.

————. *Power Plant Sestina*. *Paris Review*. 1967.

Elmslie, Kenward, and Mary Kite. *Spilled Beans: A Conversation*. Skanky Possum Press, 2001.

Elmslie, Kenward, and Trevor Winkfield. *Agenda Melt*. Adventures in Poetry Press, 2004.

————. *Cyberspace*. Granary Books, 2000.

————. *Snippets*. Tibor de Nagy Editions, 2002.

Selected musicals and operas with book, lyrics, librettos by Kenward Elmslie

Elmslie, Kenward, and Jack Beeson. *Lizzie Borden*. Boosey and Hawkes, 1965.

Elmslie, Kenward, and Thomas Pasatieri. *The Seagull (An Opera Libretto . . . Based on the Play by Anton Chekhov)*. Belwin-Mills, 1974.

————. *Washington Square*. Belwin-Mills, 1976.

————. *Three Sisters*. Theodore Presser, 1986.

Elmslie, Kenward, and Claibe Richardson. *The Grass Harp*. Thackery Falls Music, 1971.

————. *Lola*. Painted Smiles Records, 1985.

Elmslie, Kenward, and Ned Rorem. *Miss Julie*. Boosey and Hawkes, 1968.

Elmslie, Kenward, and Steven Taylor. *Postcards on Parade*. Bamberger Books, 1993.

Elmslie, Kenward, et al. *LingoLand, a Musical Revue by Kenward Elmslie*. Jay Records, 2006. With music by Claibe Richardson, Jack Beeson, Marvin Fischer, Andrew Gerle, Doug Katsoros, Thomas Pasatieri, Ned Rorem, Steven Taylor.

Works Referenced

Arenas, Reinaldo. *The Palace of the White Skunks*. Viking, 1991.

————. *Before Night Falls*. Viking, 1993.

Ashbery, John. *Rivers and Mountains*. Holt, Rinehart and Winston, 1966.

Arshile: A Magazine of the Arts, literary journal founded in 1993 by poet Mark Salerno.

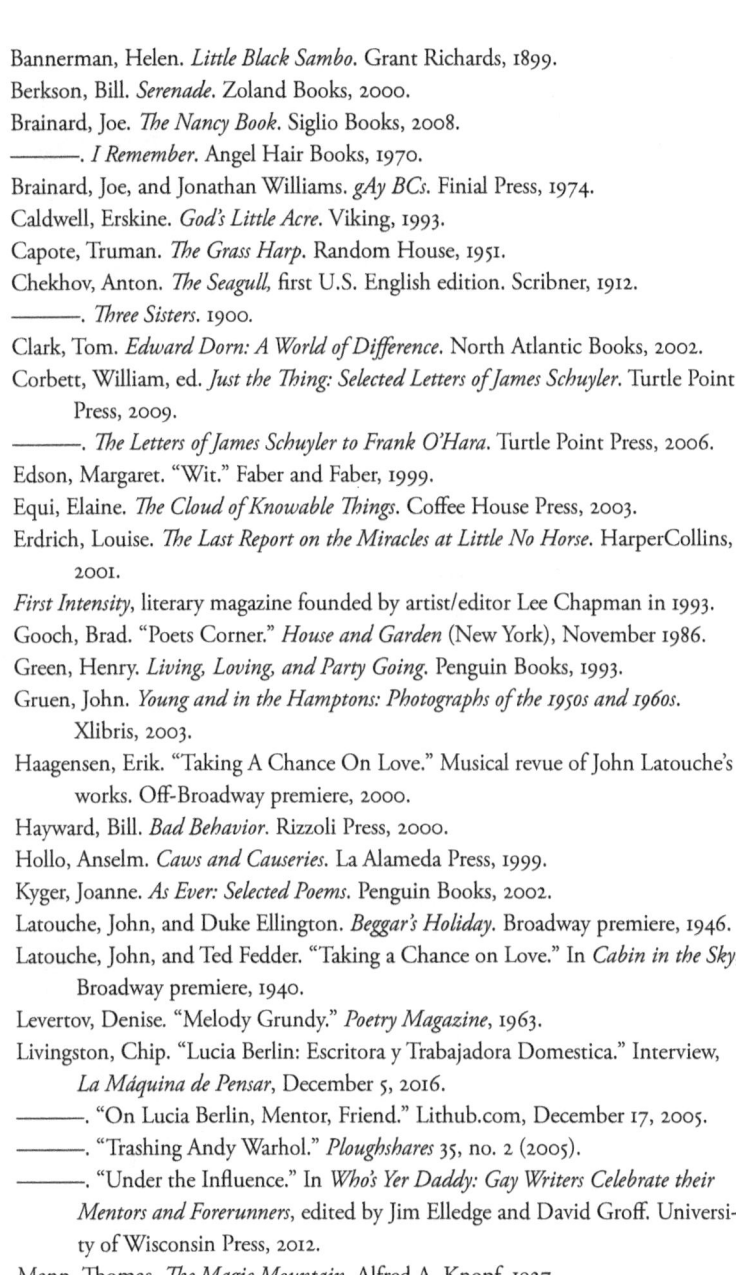

Bannerman, Helen. *Little Black Sambo*. Grant Richards, 1899.

Berkson, Bill. *Serenade*. Zoland Books, 2000.

Brainard, Joe. *The Nancy Book*. Siglio Books, 2008.

———. *I Remember*. Angel Hair Books, 1970.

Brainard, Joe, and Jonathan Williams. *gAy BCs*. Finial Press, 1974.

Caldwell, Erskine. *God's Little Acre*. Viking, 1993.

Capote, Truman. *The Grass Harp*. Random House, 1951.

Chekhov, Anton. *The Seagull,* first U.S. English edition. Scribner, 1912.

———. *Three Sisters*. 1900.

Clark, Tom. *Edward Dorn: A World of Difference*. North Atlantic Books, 2002.

Corbett, William, ed. *Just the Thing: Selected Letters of James Schuyler*. Turtle Point Press, 2009.

———. *The Letters of James Schuyler to Frank O'Hara*. Turtle Point Press, 2006.

Edson, Margaret. "Wit." Faber and Faber, 1999.

Equi, Elaine. *The Cloud of Knowable Things*. Coffee House Press, 2003.

Erdrich, Louise. *The Last Report on the Miracles at Little No Horse*. HarperCollins, 2001.

First Intensity, literary magazine founded by artist/editor Lee Chapman in 1993.

Gooch, Brad. "Poets Corner." *House and Garden* (New York), November 1986.

Green, Henry. *Living, Loving, and Party Going*. Penguin Books, 1993.

Gruen, John. *Young and in the Hamptons: Photographs of the 1950s and 1960s*. Xlibris, 2003.

Haagensen, Erik. "Taking A Chance On Love." Musical revue of John Latouche's works. Off-Broadway premiere, 2000.

Hayward, Bill. *Bad Behavior*. Rizzoli Press, 2000.

Hollo, Anselm. *Caws and Causeries*. La Alameda Press, 1999.

Kyger, Joanne. *As Ever: Selected Poems*. Penguin Books, 2002.

Latouche, John, and Duke Ellington. *Beggar's Holiday*. Broadway premiere, 1946.

Latouche, John, and Ted Fedder. "Taking a Chance on Love." In *Cabin in the Sky*, Broadway premiere, 1940.

Levertov, Denise. "Melody Grundy." *Poetry Magazine*, 1963.

Livingston, Chip. "Lucia Berlin: Escritora y Trabajadora Domestica." Interview, *La Máquina de Pensar*, December 5, 2016.

———. "On Lucia Berlin, Mentor, Friend." Lithub.com, December 17, 2005.

———. "Trashing Andy Warhol." *Ploughshares* 35, no. 2 (2005).

———. "Under the Influence." In *Who's Yer Daddy: Gay Writers Celebrate their Mentors and Forerunners*, edited by Jim Elledge and David Groff. University of Wisconsin Press, 2012.

Mann, Thomas. *The Magic Mountain*. Alfred A. Knopf, 1927.

O'Hara, Frank. "The General Returns From One Place to Another (A Play)." *Art and Literature*, 1965.

Padgett, Ron. *Joe: A Memoir of Joe Brainard*. Coffee House Press, 2004.

———. *Oklahoma Tough: My Father, King of the Tulsa Bootleggers*. University of Oklahoma Press, 2003.

———. *You Never Know*. Coffee House Press, 2002.

Pisano, Claudia Moreno, ed. *Amiri Baraka and Edward Dorn: The Collected Letters*. University of New Mexico Press, 2013.

Proust, Marcel. *Swann's Way*. Translated by Lydia Davis. Viking, 2003.

Publisher's Weekly. March 1, 1999, review of Lucia's collection, *Where I Live Now*.

Rain Taxi, a Minneapolis-based book review and literary organization founded in 1996.

Smith, Dale. *American Rambler*. Thorpe Springs, 2000.

Spoerri, Daniel. *An Anecdoted Topography of Chance*. Something Else Press, 1966.

Stadler, Matthew. *The Sex Offender*. HarperCollins, 1994.

Thackeray, William Makepeace. *The History of Henry Esmond*. Smith, Elder & Co., 1852.

Vidal, Gore. *The City and the Pillar*. Dutton, 1948.

Waugh, Evelyn. *A Handful of Dust*. Chapman and Hall, 1934.

West, Rebecca. *The Fountain Overflows*. Viking, 1956.

Index